THE UNOFFICIAL COMPLETE ENCYCLOPEDIA OF
Formula One

THE UNOFFICIAL COMPLETE ENCYCLOPEDIA OF

Formula One

MARK HUGHES

FOREWORD BY JENSON BUTTON

LORENZ BOOKS

Contents

This edition is published by Lorenz Books

Lorenz Books is an imprint of
Anness Publishing Ltd, Hermes House
88–89 Blackfriars Road, London SE1 8HA
tel. 020 7401 2077; fax 020 7633 9499
www.lorenzbooks.com; info@anness.com

© Anness Publishing Ltd 2003, 2006

UK agent: The Manning Partnership Ltd
6 The Old Dairy Melcombe Road, Bath BA2 3LR
tel. 01225 478 444 fax 01225 478 440
sales@manning-partnership.co.uk

UK distributor: Grantham Book Services Ltd
Isaac Newton Way, Alma Park Industrial Estate
Grantham, Lincs NG31 9SD
tel. 01476 541080; fax 01476 541061
orders@gbs.tbs-ltd.co.uk

North American agent/distributor: National
Book Network 4501 Forbes Boulevard
Suite 200, Lanham, MD 20706
tel. 301 459 3366; fax 301 429 5746
www.nbnbooks.com

Australian agent/distributor: Pan Macmillan
Australia, Level 18 St Martins Tower
31 Market St, Sydney, NSW 2000
tel. 1300 135 113; fax 1300 135 103
customer.service@macmillan.com.au

New Zealand agent/distributor:
David Bateman Ltd, 30 Tarndale Grove
Off Bush Road, Albany, Auckland
tel. (09) 415 7664; fax (09) 415 8892

Publisher: Joanna Lorenz
Editorial Director: Helen Sudell
Editors: Sarah Ainley and Jay Thundercliffe
Text Editor: David Malsher
Editorial Reader: Jay Thundercliffe
Design: Michael Morey
Photography: Sutton Motorsport Images
Indexer: Helen Snaith
Production Controllers: Pedro Nelson
and Ben Worley

1 3 5 7 9 10 8 6 4 2

Foreword

"I've known Mark since I first came to Formula One in 2000. He's charted the various highs and lows of my career in the pages of *Autosport* with a lot of insight. Here he gives the full story of Grand Prix racing right from the very start up to the present day. There's technical stuff as well as sporting. It's a good read, and hopefully in some future edition it will tell the story of my first Grand Prix victory."

Jenson Button

▼ The BAR-Honda 007 of Jenson Button during qualifying for the Italian Grand Prix in 2005. He started the race from third on the grid, with team-mate Takuma Sato in fourth.

▲ Jenson Button on qualifying day for the 2005 Belgian Grand Prix.

▶ Jenson Button during a pit stop at Canada in 2005.

Introduction

It was man's very nature that made motor racing so inevitable. Clever enough to have devised the car, he is intrinsically competitive enough to have then made racing cars a mere formality. The ultimate form of the discipline came to be called Grand Prix racing in 1906, just 11 years into the sport's history, and Formula One Grands Prix are still the pinnacle of the sport today. What also remains, unaltered through over a century, is the essence of the sport. The qualities it demands of drivers, who face the ultimate stakes, and technicians, who experience the most intense of challenges, make it arguably the most majestic of all sporting endeavours.

▼ Fernando Alonso in his Renault R25. during qualifying for the Brazilian Grand Prix, 2005.

▼ Juan Pablo Montoya in the McLaren-Mercedes MP4-20 at the 2005 Turkish Grand Prix.

Though latterly it has become more overtly commercial than in the past, that is simply a reflection of the world in which the sport exists, just as the cars have mirrored the level of technological sophistication of the modern industrial world. It shouldn't be forgotten that motorsport was conceived as much with business in mind – by a group of pioneer car manufacturers – as it was for sport. Formula One owes its existence to business, and always has, but the superficial trappings melt away to nothing in the intensity of battle, once the start flag has dropped or the lights have gone out. Between that moment and the chequered flag, the sport exists in its purest form.

▼ Jenson Button overtakes David Coulthard during the inaugural Turkish Grand Prix in 2005.

▼ Ferrari's Michael Schumacher during the controversial US Grand Prix – his only victory in 2005.

◄ The Renault R25s of Alonso and Fisichella tackle the nouvelle chicane at the Monaco Grand Prix, 2005.

The History of Formula One

The thread of the sport's lineage is long and sometimes complex. But it is very clearly a thread, a brilliantly vivid one in which heroes have been made, celebrated and – over the decades – largely forgotten. The nature of the sport gives it a here and now intensity, and leaves the past in black and white dusty memory. But revisiting the deeds of the drivers, the manufacturers, engineers and designers can bring their achievements back to life, and lend them their true perspective. Here, we look at the men, the cars and the races that made their mark on history, stretching from the first true motor race in 1895 right up to the present day.

◄ Ayrton Senna's last race.
Senna's Williams FW16 follows the
safety car at Imola, 1 May 1994.

The Seeds are Sown

Motor racing is very nearly as old as the motor car itself. Karl Benz and Gottlieb Daimler are widely credited with the invention of the car – each had their first petrol-fired prototypes running in 1885 – and within a decade the first significant motor race took place.

In the early years cars did not race round and round, but from place to place. The organizers did not charge an admission fee to watch, and the cars were not recognizably different from those driven as a means of transport. But the sport's essence, to get from the start to the finish against both the clock and each other, was exactly as it has been ever since.

The First Race

Although the car was born in Germany, France can be said to have invented motorsport. The first true race was a contest from Paris to Bordeaux and back, a distance of just over 1190 kilometres (740 miles) on public highways. Twenty-seven vehicles congregated at Porte Maillot in the early hours of 11 June 1895 and, one by one, were sent on their way. Only those in the car – of whom there had to be at least two – were allowed to work on the car during the race, using only those tools carried with them.

The event was devised by a group of pioneer manufacturers with the

▲ Emile Levassor's Panhard-Levassor car in the 1894 Paris–Rouen reliability trial that led to the 1895 race.

idea of publicizing the practicality and speed of the motor car. The winner, Emile Levassor, was a partner in the firm of Panhard et Levassor, an old French engineering company that had recently embraced car manufacture. Levassor's drive was heroic. He had

planned to change over with his relief driver some time before Bordeaux but, finding him asleep at around 3am, decided to continue. In fact, he drove the entire event, and the relief driver became simply a passenger. As he passed each time control still in command of the race, news of Levassor's epic solo performance spread like wildfire and when he arrived back in Paris in the afternoon of 13 June,

▲ Chevalier René de Knyff seated on the Panhard-Levassor car that won the first Paris–Bordeaux race in 1898.

◄ Degrais competing in the Paris–Madrid race of 1903.

▼ Callan is pictured here in his Wolseley motor during the Circuit des Ardennes race, Belgium, 1903.

thousands were there to greet him. With an average speed of just under 24km/h (15mph), he was five hours ahead of the next man. The new sport had its first hero.

The heat of competition fed a technology drive that advanced the car at breakneck speed – to the great benefit of the customers. Pneumatic tyres and the steering wheel were just two of the more obvious advances the sport generated in its early years. By 1901, racing machines were capable of up to 120km/h (80mph). Meanwhile, sales of the motor car soared: France produced 13,000 of them in 1903.

The First Tragedy

The sport's honeymoon period came to an abrupt end later that same year. Millions of spectators lined the route of the Paris–Madrid race in May 1903 to watch in awe the cars that were, by now, powered by monstrous engines of up to 14 litres. It was a tragedy waiting to unfold. Competitors Marcel Renault, Lorraine Barrow, Philip Stead

and two riding mechanics were all killed in various brutal accidents along the route. But the biggest, most unacceptable tragedy occurred in the town of Chatellerault, when a child walked into the road and a soldier ran to pull him clear. Tourand's car hit them, killing both, before veering into the crowd, killing one spectator and injuring many more.

As cars and distraught competitors rested overnight in Bordeaux, the French government stepped in and stopped the race. The silent cars were pulled to a train by horse and transported back to Paris. City-to-city racing was over.

▼ Fernand Gabriel wins the 1903 Paris–Bordeaux race in a Mors that produced 70hp. It marked the end of city-to-city racing.

From Cities to Circuits

T he tragedy of the 1903 Paris–Madrid race came close to killing the sport for ever. It was only granted a reprieve by a saner approach. No longer would races run through major towns with big population centres; they would instead utilize the roads of sparsely populated rural areas. More critically, no longer would the races run from place to place, but instead around roads comprising circuits, thus making the routes easier to police.

The New Era of Circuit Racing

The first major event of the new format had been the 1902 Circuit des Ardennes in Belgium, ironically the race that immediately preceded the 1903 Paris–Madrid. The race comprised six laps of an 80-kilometre (50-mile) circuit of public roads through the countryside, and was won by Englishman Charles Jarrott in his French Panhard.

The success of the event and the end of city-to-city racing meant that the Circuit des Ardennes became the blueprint for the new era of the sport. One of the first post-tragedy races run to this new format was the Gordon

Bennett Cup, held in pre-republic Ireland in 1903.

Gordon Bennett was a millionaire newspaper magnate and a vital early supporter of motor racing. As well as helping to fund the first races and

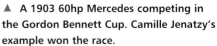

▲ A 1903 60hp Mercedes competing in the Gordon Bennett Cup. Camille Jenatzy's example won the race.

giving them the lifeblood of publicity through one of his publications, the *Paris Herald*, he also devised the competition that made the sport truly international, and that bore his name.

The Gordon Bennett series was first held in 1900. Countries could enter up to three cars each in the race. From 1903 each country was identified by the colours of its cars. The winning nation would host the following year's event. France dominated initially but, in winning the 1902 event for Britain (by virtue of being the only finisher), Selwyn Francis Edge ensured that the Royal Automobile Club had to have an Act of Parliament passed to host the 1903 race in Ireland; racing on the public highway had always been forbidden by British law.

Camille Jenatzy won the race for Mercedes, and thereby took the event to Germany for 1904. The French industry didn't take kindly to being beaten in

◄ Christian Lautenschlager was first to the finish in a Mercedes in the 1908 French Grand Prix at Dieppe.

what it saw as its own specialist field, and after winning the event in 1904 and being the winning host in 1905, the French declined to stage the event the following year. The Automobile Club de France had instead devised another competition in which no restrictions would be put on the number of entrants a country could provide. The name of this competition was the "Grand Prix". Its lineage continues to this day.

The First Grand Prix

Held at Le Mans in 1906, the inaugural Grand Prix was won by the Renault of Ferenc Szisz, a Hungarian who had previously been Louis Renault's riding mechanic in the city-to-city races. The event was a great success and other countries copied its format, though it would be many years before the term "Grand Prix" was applied to races outside of France. For now, the USA came the closest, with its American "Grand Prize".

For the 1908 event, the Paris-based international governing body of the sport formulated regulations to ensure uniformity from country to country. Motor racing flourished, even surviving a mass pull-out by manufacturers concerned at spiralling costs and the first downturn of sales. As early pioneers such as Panhard and Mors faded, Mercedes remained very much

a central force and was joined by Fiat and Peugeot.

By 1914, on the eve of World War I, the French Grand Prix attracted 13 manufacturers and 33 cars. The race saw an epic fight between the twin-cam 16-valve Peugeot of Georges Boillot and the might of the Mercedes team. Christian Lautenschlager's Mercedes won after Boillot retired on the last lap. The engine of Lautenschlager's car was based on that which would soon be put to use in fighter planes.

▲ Vincenzo Lancia in his Fiat at the very first Grand Prix, held near Le Mans, France, in 1906.

▼ (left) The front cover of the French periodical La Vie au Grand Air shows Hungarian driver Ferenc Szisz at the wheel. He was the winner of the first recognized Grand Prix held near Le Mans in 1906.

▼ (right) Ferenc Szisz in his Renault at Le Mans, 1906. Szisz and the French manufacturer won the race that year.

Boom Between Wars

The armistice period that followed World War I accelerated the pace of technology, and lessons learned there were soon applied in motorsport. Advances made in metallurgy and in understanding the combustion process more fully meant that engine efficiency rocketed. The 1921 Fiat's 8-cylinder motor became the blueprint for racing engines for decades to come.

Grand Prix Racing Spreads

In 1922, the new Monza track near Milan hosted the Italian Grand Prix. This was a purpose-built race circuit – it was the first time a major European race hadn't been held on public roads – and it enabled Grand Prix race promoters to charge spectators an entrance fee for the first time. Soon afterwards, other tracks were built in a similar vein, such as Montlhéry on the outskirts of Paris, and Sitges just south of Barcelona.

Most of the races continued to be run on public roads however, and in order to stop speeds escalating out of control, a 2-litre formula was imposed for 1922. This signalled a parting of the ways between European and American

▲ Rudolf Caracciola in his Mercedes-Benz on his way to winning the 1937 Swiss Grand Prix. German cars now dominated racing.

▼ Luigi Fagioli (Mercedes) passing Soffietti (Maserati) at the 1935 Monaco Grand Prix.

▼ Independent team owners came to the fore from the mid-1920s to early 1930s.

racing which, until this time, had overlapped. The American Duesenberg team had won the 1921 French Grand Prix, while European cars had dominated for a time at the Indianapolis 500. American racing was chiefly conducted on closed tracks, not public roads, and with its wide open spaces, the American car industry was producing passenger cars with ever-bigger engines: the new European 2-litre formula was an irrelevance there.

The Pioneering Teams

Such was Fiat's dominance during the early 1920s that rival manufacturers had to resort to poaching technical staff from Fiat in order to compete. It was in this way that Alfa Romeo and Sunbeam became serious Grand Prix forces, with the former team being advised by one of its drivers, Enzo Ferrari. Sunbeam became the first British constructor to win a Grand Prix, when Henry Segrave triumphed in France in 1923.

The economic downturn of the late 1920s saw manufacturers pull out of the sport and, for a time, wealthy independent team owners formed its backbone, with specialist car companies such as Bugatti and Maserati providing the hardware. It was during this time that Tazio Nuvolari graduated to the sport from motorcycle racing, and created such a sensation that he is still often cited as the greatest driver who ever lived.

Hitler came to power in Germany early in 1933, and he immediately identified Grand Prix racing as a powerful tool in propagating the image of Aryan superiority. Backed by Nazi subsidies, Mercedes-Benz and Auto Union entered the competition with revolutionary new models in 1934 that rendered the various Italian and French machinery completely obsolete. Their independent suspensions allowed huge horsepower gains to be utilized and, before long, speeds of up to 320km/h (200mph) were being reached. The German domination continued until the cessation of Grand Prix racing on 1 September 1939, the day that Britain declared war on Nazi Germany.

◄ *(left to right)* Manfred von Brauchitsch, Christian Kautz, Tazio Nuvolari and Hermann Muller at the Donington Grand Prix, Donington Park, England, in 1938.

▼ Tazio Nuvolari, Auto Union, during the 1938 Italian Grand Prix.

Post-war Recovery

During the period of German domination before the outbreak of World War II, several constructors had turned instead to voiturette (small car) racing. With Germany in no position to partake in international motorsport in the early post-war years, pre-war voiturette Alfa Romeos, Maseratis and ERAs formed the basis of an early revival of the sport.

The Birth of Formula One
The reconstituted governing body arranged a loose calendar of "premier" Grands Prix for 1947, and for the following year it announced a new Grand Prix formula: Formula One. Sensibly, it catered for existing machinery and was therefore largely based on the pre-war voiturette formula, which allowed for supercharged engines of 1.5 litres. As a means of bolstering the grids, Formula One also catered for unsupercharged engines of up to 4.5 litres, in order to encourage the entry of the sportscar-derived racers that had performed a similar makeweight class in the immediate pre-war period.

With their Italian factories in ruins, wheeling out their pre-war cars and winning some Grands Prix was a vital tonic for Alfa Romeo, which was the dominant racing force in these early post-war years. Ironically the car – dubbed the "Alfetta" – had been created under the guidance of Enzo Ferrari, who had now ceased to be Alfa's racing manager and had instead

▲ Froilán González wins his own and Ferrari's first Championship-status Grand Prix at Silverstone in 1951, defeating the previously all-conquering Alfa Romeos.

become a constructor in his own right. Alfa's financial plight precluded it from taking part during 1949 and, in their absence, the Ferrari marque racked up its first Grand Prix victories.

▲ The Argentinian Juan Manuel Fangio, five times World Champion.

◄ Juan Manuel Fangio in his Alfa Romeo 158 during the 1950 International Trophy at Silverstone.

▼ Juan Manuel Fangio in his Alfa Romeo 158 Alfetta during the Belgian Grand Prix, at Spa-Francorchamps in 1950.

▲ Giuseppe Farina pictured at home, shortly after winning the first Drivers' World Championship in 1950. He won the British, Swiss and Italian Grands Prix.

The World Championships

Alfa was tempted into a return in 1950 by the inauguration of a World Championship. In a move designed to regain the sport its pre-war following by popularizing its appeal, the contest would find a "World Champion" driver. Points were awarded based on the results of six nominated Grands Prix. The first race of the World Championship was held round the perimeter track of a disused British wartime airfield called Silverstone. Actually, all of the Grands Prix were held on European soil, but the "world" title was justified by the inclusion of results from the American Indianapolis 500 race. This anomaly continued for much of the decade until genuine Grands Prix outside Europe began to appear on the calendar.

Alfa Romeo won every Grand Prix in 1950, and the title contest was fought out between their drivers Giuseppe Farina and Juan Manuel Fangio. The former just got the verdict on account of a better reliability record, though it was the Argentinian Fangio who set the pace. Fangio went on to his first world title in 1951, but from mid-season of that year, his supercharged Alfa Romeo was pushed hard by a new challenger – the unsupercharged V12 Ferrari.

Technology 1951

Ferrari 375

After trying – but failing – to beat Alfa Romeo with a similar 1.5-litre supercharged car in 1950, Enzo Ferrari and his designer Aurelio Lampredi re-assessed. They had noted that the pre-war 4.5-litre unsupercharged Talbots could occasionally push the much more powerful Alfas uncomfortably close over a race distance by virtue of using less fuel and therefore making fewer refuelling stops. The rationale behind the 375 of 1951 was of a 4.5-litre car more modern than the Talbots that would retain an economy advantage over the Alfas but close the power deficit. Its V12 engine produced around 330bhp at a time when the Alfas were giving over 400bhp, but critically it consumed fuel at around 7.2km/g (4.5mpg) rather than the 2.9km/g (1.8mpg) of its rival, which had such high supercharger boost pressure that fuel was needed for cooling as well as combustion. The turning point came at Silverstone in 1951, when José Froilán González was able to run his 375 wheel-to-wheel with Fangio's Alfa, and then pull clear when the supercharged car had to make its inevitable early pit stop. Enzo Ferrari was famously quoted as saying he felt as if he had killed his mother, given his former close links with Alfa.

▼ José Froilán González on his way to the first Championship-status Grand Prix win for Ferrari at Silverstone in 1951.

Ferrari Maintain Italy's Lead

Ferrari's speed in the second half of 1951 put Alfa Romeo on the defensive. As the newer design was honed into an ever-faster machine, the development potential of the Alfetta – which had debuted in 1937 – hit a brick wall. Having retained the championship by the skin of their teeth, and without the finances to design and build a new model, Alfa made an honourable withdrawal at the end of the year.

Switch to Formula Two

The departure of Alfa Romeo left Formula One with a problem: Ferrari now had no worthwhile competition. Maserati was operating on a hand-to-mouth basis, building and selling outclassed cars while making plans for the future. There was the almost mythical BRM, an exciting idea borne of British post-war optimism and

▲ Ascari in the Ferrari 375 at the 1951 German Grand Prix. This marked his first Championship-status victory.

▼ Belgian Grand Prix 1952: Alberto Ascari in his Ferrari. The Italian won every Grand Prix he contested for a dominant season.

Shapers

Enzo Ferrari

The founder of the most revered of all racing teams described the essence of his ability as "a flair for the agitation of men". Ruthless and autocratic, he was also shrewd and single-minded, traits that were evident from his days as racing manager for Alfa Romeo in the 1920s, right up to his death in 1988. He was a moderately successful driver in the early 1920s, but his real value to Alfa came as an organizer; it was he who succeeded in poaching key technical staff from Fiat, for instance. His links with Alfa were finally severed in the late 1930s, and in 1948 the first Grand Prix car bearing the name of "Ferrari" appeared on the track.

His relationships with his drivers and other key personnel were often stormy as the success of his race team overrode any human considerations, though for certain rare men – Peter Collins in the 1950s and Gilles Villeneuve in the 1980s being the most notable – he made exceptions.

financed by that country's industry. The power potential of its supercharged V16 engine was said to be fantastic, but no-one knew for sure because it never hung together long enough to find out. It was a frail hope on which to rest a World Championship contest.

Race promoters, fearing no-one would come to watch a Ferrari demonstration, switched their main races to Formula Two, a junior category for 2-litre unsupercharged cars. The governing body followed suit and announced that the 1952 and 1953 World Championships would be for Formula Two cars. Ironically, Ferrari dominated anyway, with its lead driver Alberto Ascari achieving a sequence of successes that has yet to be equalled. He won six of the seven Grands Prix comprising the 1952 season, followed by a further five in 1953, and in the course of his run he established a record of nine consecutive victories that still stands today.

Ascari's luck ran out in the final race of 1953, at Monza, where he lost a thrilling battle to chief rival Fangio, who was driving the ever-improving Formula Two Maserati. Ascari and Fangio, the two fastest drivers in the world at the time, shared the front row of the grid, but the latter made a poor start as Ascari surged into the lead ahead of his Ferrari team-mate, Farina. Fangio's friend and Maserati team-mate Onofré Marimon then slipstreamed past both Ferraris to lead as Fangio made up the lost ground and made it a four-car slipstreaming battle. Time after time, the positions changed between the four until, at half-distance, Marimon was forced to pit with a radiator leak. He rejoined a lap down but, crucially, still with the leaders on the road.

Into the last corner of the last lap, Farina made a desperate bid for victory, and leader Ascari spun trying to avoid contact as Farina ran wide. The spinning Ascari was hit by Marimon, allowing Fangio to nip through for his first victory since breaking his neck at this same track the year before.

▶ **Alberto Ascari and Ferrari took their second World Championship title in 1953.**

▲ Ascari leads Fangio, Farina and Marimon in the battle of the 1953 Italian Grand Prix.

◀ Ascari takes the plaudits again in 1953. His sequence of nine consecutive wins is an impressive record that has not yet been broken.

The Brief Return of the Factories

Motor racing had been invented by the big European customer-car producers, and largely dominated by them until the advent of World War II. Thereafter, with their factories in ruins, they had little choice but to stay out of it, Alfa Romeo's flurry with their pre-war cars notwithstanding.

The Specialists

In their place, the sport came to be dominated by specialist race car constructors, such as Ferrari, Maserati and Gordini, who built cars for sale to race entrants and ran their own teams of "works" machines. The specialist constructors existed on revenue from the sale of their machines, from start and finish money from race organizers, and from trade deals with suppliers who could then advertise their part in the ensuing success.

But in 1954, with the post-war recovery process now well established, the factories began to return. First Mercedes-Benz, then Lancia announced Grand Prix programmes and the fact that they had respectively signed Fangio and Ascari, the top two Grand Prix drivers, signalled the seriousness of their intent.

▲ Lancia's D50 was an even more advanced design than the rival Mercedes.

The Return to Formula One

With such an undertaking of support, the governing body felt confident in the reintroduction of Formula One as the basis for the World Championship. This time the formula stipulated engines of no more than 2.5 litres unsupercharged. Ferrari and Maserati came up with new

▼ Mercedes-Benz W196 *Stromlinienwagen* exiting Champel Curve at Silverstone in 1954. The streamlined body of the car did not suit the airfield circuit.

machines, but when Mercedes unveiled the W196 racer, the different scale of their resources became very clear.

Fangio gave the car a win first time out, in the 1954 French Grand Prix, with his team-mate Karl Kling close behind, and the rest nowhere. For the remainder of the season, the Mercedes would be beaten only twice, and Fangio duly delivered the Championship – something he repeated for the company after an even more dominant performance in 1955, this time backed up by the highly promising young British driver, Stirling Moss, who took his first victory that year at Aintree.

▼ Stirling Moss in his Maserati 250F at the 1954 British Grand Prix. He retired from second place with only ten laps to go.

The Factories Withdraw Again

The introduction of the Lancia D50 had been delayed until the end of 1954, but it set pole position by a full second in its debut race, and looked set to give Ascari victory before breaking down. In concept it was arguably even more advanced than the Mercedes, but the financial problems of the parent company meant its potential was ultimately untapped. Ascari's death while testing a Ferrari sports racer in May gave Lancia the justification it needed to withdraw from the sport at the end of 1955.

Mercedes withdrew too, for reasons even more catastrophic. In by far the biggest tragedy the sport has ever suffered, over 80 spectators were killed in the 1955 Le Mans 24 Hours sportscar race, when a Mercedes was launched into the crowd after hitting another car. The fall-out affected all of motor racing and several Grands Prix were immediately cancelled. Mercedes suddenly found its participation in the sport changed from a public relations benefit to a liability, and it pulled out at the end of that year, not to return for a very, very long time. All of which, of course, left Formula One back in the hands of the specialists, with significant long-term consequences.

Technology 1955

Mercedes W196

Innovation and attention to detail was everywhere on this landmark racer. Its eight cylinders were fed by inlet and outlet valves that were not closed by conventional springs but by "desmodronic" actuation, whereby they were directly mechanically controlled for more accuracy and reliability. Its chassis was not the conventional metal ladder frame with bolstering tubing. Instead, the tubing was arranged in such a way that its geometry formed a load-bearing structure and the heavy ladder frame was dispensed with; this was termed "spaceframe" construction. Its brake drums were initially mounted inboard

▲ The two Mercedes-Benz W196, driven by Juan Mauel Fangio and Karl Kling, receive attention behind the pits. Fangio has his back to the camera, on the left.

rather than within the wheels, thus reducing the unsprung mass of the car, to the benefit of road-holding. But the most visually dramatic feature was its all-enveloping bodywork that made traditional open-wheelers look previous-generation. Ironically, this induced a handling imbalance and the car more usually ran in more conventional open-wheel form.

▼ The enclosed-wheel "streamliner" bodywork was only used occasionally.

The Unstoppable Fangio

▼ Five times Formula One World title holder Juan Manuel Fangio driving through Becketts in the Ferrari D50.

The specialist constructors were quick to take advantage of the factory withdrawals. Enzo Ferrari's shrewdness was never more apparent than when he contrived to get paid for taking over the assets of the Lancia Grand Prix project – including the D50 cars, which were a big advance over the existing Ferraris. Fangio was signed up to drive them and he duly delivered the 1956 Championship, his fourth and Ferrari's third.

Fangio and Ferrari

But it was a far from smooth road to glory for both parties. Enzo Ferrari and Fangio failed to hit it off, and there was a lot of tension and mutual distrust in the team. As they arrived at Monza for the final round of the title contest, Fangio's biggest threat was his own team-mate, Peter Collins, the young British driver, who was a particular favourite of the boss.

Fangio was in the leading group, a couple of places ahead of Collins, when he suffered a steering-arm breakage on lap 18 and pulled into the pits to retire the car. At that time, teams were allowed to use more than one driver in a single car and have them share the

points. When the third Ferrari driver, Luigi Musso, pitted to refuel, he was asked if he would hand his car over to Fangio. He refused.

This meant that Collins, now in third place, stood poised to win the title. But when he came in for a tyre stop on the 35th lap and saw Fangio standing

watching, he immediately jumped out and offered his car to him. Fangio took it and with it finished second – enough to clinch him the title. It was a supreme act of sportsmanship from Collins. Asked why he had done it, he simply replied, "Because Fangio deserved it." Fangio was indebted.

▲ Fangio (2) behind the lead car, in action for Maserati.

◄ Juan Manuel Fangio takes the winner's garland after winning the 1956 German Grand Prix.

Maserati and "That" Race

Fangio was approaching 47 years old as the 1957 season began. He had originally planned to retire at the end of 1955, but an economic crisis in his home country of Argentina had persuaded him to continue. But any thoughts that his competitive spirit was waning were utterly demolished in 1957. Neither he nor Ferrari had any interest in continuing their partnership, and he switched instead to Maserati, who had continually refined and developed their 250F model over the last three years until it was a beautifully responsive and balanced machine, just the sort of car in which Fangio could display his genius.

At the German Grand Prix, Fangio clinched that year's Championship – his fifth – with his final Grand Prix victory. It was also his greatest. Around the mountainous 14-mile Nürburgring

◀ Juan Manuel Fangio in his Maserati at Monza in 1957.

▼ Mike Hawthorn and Peter Collins lead Fangio's Maserati at the German Grand Prix of 1957.

circuit, he overcame a mid-race delay in the pits to claw back a 51-second deficit, a task that had looked impossible. He broke and re-broke the lap record on each subsequent lap, leaving it at 9 minutes 17.4 seconds, over 8 seconds faster than his own pole

position time. The Ferrari drivers were unable to respond, and he passed them both on the last lap. Fangio later recalled that on that day he had driven at a level he had never reached before, and did not wish to reach again. Many regard it as the greatest race ever driven.

The British Challenge

Britain had enjoyed its moments of Grand Prix glory, but never for any great duration. Sunbeam had won races in the 1920s in partnership with Henry Segrave before becoming financially strapped. In the late 1930s, rising British star Richard Seaman displayed such immense promise that he was employed by the Nazi-backed Mercedes team and actually won the 1938 German Grand Prix. He suffered a fatal accident while leading the 1939 Belgian Grand Prix.

The New British Breed
What occurred in the 1950s was quite different; it was a movement, and for the first time it became conceivable that the centre of motor racing might move away from France and Italy, its twin homes for half a century.

British law had never allowed the road racing seen in those countries, and consequently British motorsport initially took a different direction, being centred around the specially-built enclosed circuit of Brooklands. This was in

essence an oval shape: no corners, just flat-out running around a dramatic, banked track. The demands of this sort of racing were rather different to those of traditional road circuit-based Grands Prix. But World War II rendered Brooklands unusable as a race track as

▲ Tony Brooks *(left)* and Stirling Moss after winning the 1957 British Grand Prix. Moss took over Brooks' car after his own suffered problems.

▼ Harry Schell drives his Vanwall at Castle Combe in 1955.

▼ Brooklands hosted the British Grand Prix in 1926 and 1927 but more usually held domestic events around its speed bowl.

much of it was demolished to make room for expanded aircraft-manufacturing facilities.

What the war gave British motor racing in place of Brooklands were dozens of redundant wartime airfields. These made ideal race venues, and the tracks more nearly reproduced the demands of continental road racing. Concurrent with this, the country's governing body, the RAC, approved a new low-cost, entry-level class of racing, Formula 500 (later renamed Formula Three). This catered for motorcycle-engined cars of 500cc and attracted an entirely new breed of driver to British sport. No longer was it exclusively an idle pastime of wealthy men; it attracted ambitious young

talent who wished to become professionals. Stirling Moss and Peter Collins were the outstanding graduate drivers of this formula. Among their rivals were three men later to have a huge influence on Grand Prix racing outside of the cars: John Cooper, Ken Tyrrell and Bernie Ecclestone. The 750 Motor Club, another post-war British attempt at low-cost motorsport, was meanwhile proving incredibly fertile ground for engineering talent, with Colin Chapman as its vanguard.

Vandervell and British Success

Concurrent with these movements was another British initiative, but a private one: that of the industrialist Tony Vandervell. He had become a very wealthy man as the boss of Vandervell Bearings, whose patented "thinwall bearing" was behind major efficiency gains in aircraft and car engines. With the aim of one day having his own

Grand Prix team, he initially bought customer Formula One race cars from Enzo Ferrari. Called the "Thinwall Specials", these modified Ferraris were the precursors to the Vanwall, which first appeared in 1955. Using his industry contacts to the full, Vandervell

commissioned de Havilland aircraft aerodynamicist Frank Costin to design a highly advanced body, while the engine was a scaled-up version of that used in Norton motorcycle racers. By 1957, it was the fastest car in Formula One, and Stirling Moss and Tony Brooks took it to a shared victory in the British Grand Prix of that year. It was the first wave of British success, and was soon to be followed up in devastating fashion as the young racing community that had built up around Formula 500 transformed itself from a movement to a revolution. In the space of a couple of seasons, the whole fabric of Formula One had changed fundamentally.

▲ (left) British driver Stirling Moss in his Vanwall at Aintree for the 1957 British and European Grand Prix, where he lapped at 144.5km/h (89.85mph).

◄ The young Stirling Moss with his 500cc Formula Three car.

Walls Come Tumbling Down

"Suddenly, there were green cars all around me. I wasn't part of that world. I drove red cars. It was time to leave." The words are those of Juan Manuel Fangio, who retired part-way through the 1958 season after a record five world titles, four of them in the Italian colours of red. British racing green had reached a landmark in the 1957 Italian Grand Prix, where the race organizers had to change the grid formation to 4-3-4 from the usual 3-2-3, in order to get an Italian car onto the front row. The fastest three qualifiers were Vanwalls.

British Racing Green

For 1958, a new world title was initiated – for constructors. This ran alongside the Drivers' Championship. Vanwall won it, but their success was spread between Moss and Brooks, who were therefore pipped to the Drivers' Championship by Ferrari's Mike Hawthorn (and even he was British). Ferrari effectively had only one driver in the championship fight after the

▲ A relaxed Mike Hawthorn in the pits during practice for the British Grand Prix at Silverstone in 1956. Driving the BRM P25, Hawthorn was an early leader in the race, but he soon retired.

death in the German Grand Prix of Peter Collins.

But for all the glory days enjoyed by the streamlined, thoroughbred Vanwalls, the year's most significant victory went to a tiny, runtish-looking jumped-up Formula Two car, also British. Called a Cooper, it won the opening race of the season in Argentina. Driven in this race by Moss, it signalled the arrival into the rarefied Grand Prix ranks of the Formula 500 movement.

Because the cars of Formula 500 had used motorcycle engines with chain-drives, the logical place to put the engine had been between the driver and the driven rear wheels. This brought further, unforeseen, advantages. The pre-war Auto Unions had been "mid-engined" too, but they were monster cars whose size disguised the superiority of the layout, and thus left it unexploited until the Coopers – father and son, Charles and John – came along.

The Coopers Pave the Way

Because Formula One had been the preserve of small specialist teams since the pull-out of Mercedes and Lancia, the engineering was not progressive. As specialists rooted in the fabric of Grand Prix racing, Ferrari and Maserati had neither the resources nor the breadth of vision to fundamentally re-evaluate; they simply honed and refined. Vanwall, another specialist, had been created in the image of Ferrari. But Cooper came from leftfield, from different roots entirely, and they were not constrained by any convention other than those established in a very young junior formula.

It soon became clear that the funny little car with its engine in the "wrong" place – which had precipitated jeers of derision when it first turned up at practice in Argentina 1958 – had made instant dinosaurs of thoroughbreds. The DNA of the Grand Prix car had just been altered.

◄ Mike Hawthorn laps Giulio Cabianca on the start/finish straight of Monza in 1958. Hawthorn finished second.

▲ The supremely gifted Stirling Moss, who, along with Tony Brooks, helped British Formula One racing take on the Italians.

▲ Moss winning the 1957 Pescara Grand Prix in his Vanwall, one of the three victories they took that year.

▼ Tony Brooks, for Vanwall, wins the Belgian Grand Prix at the Spa-Francorchamps circuit in 1958.

Front Engine's Last Goodbyes

There was to be no stopping Cooper in 1959. The car with which Moss had won the Argentinian Grand Prix in 1958 had not been a proper Grand Prix machine, merely a Formula Two car with a slightly enlarged engine.

The "Garagistes"

Encouraged by this success, the Coopers set about building a proper Formula One car. But though its lines were sleeker, and its engine more powerful, it was built very much to the formula of their breakthrough Argentina car. Not only did it retain the mid-engined layout, but it utilized parts from wherever they could be found, and adapted them as required: a gearbox based on that of a road-going Citroën, key suspension parts borrowed from the Volkswagen Beetle, and steering components from a Triumph. The engine was bought in from Coventry Climax, who had developed it out of what was originally a fire-pump motor.

If Ferrari and Maserati, who always

▲ Tony Brooks won the 1959 French Grand Prix in his Ferrari Dino 246 V6, but by then he was fighting against the tide of Coopers.

made their own engines and components, had been previously considered racing "specialists" to distinguish them from the big car-producing factories, this took the concept several stages further. Cooper simply designed and assembled their cars and used a network of specialized sub-contractors to provide necessary hardware. Enzo Ferrari contemptuously described them as "garagistes". He also famously said his cars would never have mid-mounted engines as "the horse should pull the cart, not push it".

Here to Stay

▼ Jack Brabham's Cooper on the Oporto circuit of the Portuguese Grand Prix in 1960.

Technology 1959

Cooper T51

A centralization of the car's masses was the critical advantage endowed by the mid-engined layout. In much the same way that a door with heavy weights bolted to the middle would be easier to move than one with the weights bolted to the outer edge, the mid-engined car was able to change direction quicker and with less momentum. In scientific terms, it had a lower "polar moment of inertia" than a traditional front-engined car.

The benefits of the layout multiplied. Because the front of the car didn't have to accommodate the engine, it could have a lower frontal area, making it quicker down the straight and more economical. Because no propshaft was needed to carry drive from a front engine to rear wheels, the car could be lower, giving benefits on the straights and in the corners. No propshaft and a lower

body meant it could be smaller and lighter, and therefore quicker to accelerate, brake and manoeuvre. The 1959 Cooper weighed in at 460kg, a massive 20 per cent lighter than the rival Ferrari 246. Even with 60 brake horsepower less, the Cooper had it covered. The weight and aerodynamic benefits meant less fuel was needed,

▲ Masten Gregory driving a Formula One Cooper T51 at Aintree in 1959.

furthering its weight advantage at the start. The lower weight also made it gentler on its tyres, which would thereby retain their grip for longer. The advantages for car and driver just kept snowballing.

The network of racing specialists that had formed in Britain around Cooper and the Formula 500 movement was soon servicing other constructors. A whole community of geographically close teams formed in the south of England, knowledge between them spread fast, and soon these "garagistes" were dominating the Grand Prix grids. That community has formed the mainstay of Formula One ever since.

Ferrari's beautiful front-engined dinosaurs fought valiantly against an irresistible tide in 1959, and their driver Tony Brooks was unlucky to miss out

▲ Jack Brabham, driving for Cooper, was the 1959 World Champion.

▶ Tony Brooks' front-engined Ferrari (24) fights it out with Jack Brabham's rear-engined Cooper (8) in the 1959 French Grand Prix.

Rear-engine Revolution Completed

With a further development of their mid-engined wondercar, Cooper steamrollered their way to the 1960 World Championship – again with Jack Brabham as their driver – in a yet more convincing demonstration of the layout's superiority.

Ferrari Converts

As Ferrari continued to campaign hopelessly outdated front-engined machines, they were left outclassed, and even Enzo Ferrari was forced to eat his words about the horse pushing the cart. At the Monaco Grand Prix, his team debuted a prototype that had been crudely converted to the mid-engined layout. The lessons learned from this were applied as the team effectively wrote off the 1960 season to prepare for 1961, when a new 1.5-litre (unsupercharged) formula was due to replace the 2.5-litre one that had run since 1954.

Cooper and Lotus

The closest rival to Cooper in 1960 was another British constructor, Lotus. Using the same bought-in Coventry Climax engines as Cooper, and relying on the same network of specialist

▲ Jack Brabham, winner of the British Grand Prix, 1960, in the Cooper T53, on his way to a second successive world title. This confirmed front-engined cars were dead.

sub-contractors, Lotus built their first mid-engined car for the 1960 season. Team boss Colin Chapman had a reputation as a brilliantly original thinker from his days in the 750 Motor Club in Britain. It was partly his pride in this reputation that had prevented him

▼ Jack Brabham, winner of the Portuguese Grand Prix, 1960, in the Cooper T53. Brabham benefited from the absence for much of that season of Stirling Moss.

from copying the Cooper mid-engined formula earlier; Lotus had struggled with front-engined Formula One cars in 1958 and 1959.

With his Lotus 18, Chapman combined the Cooper's layout with a much more scientific approach.

▲ After giving Cooper its first Grand Prix victory in Argentina in 1958, Moss continued to rack up wins for the marque in 1959.

The spaceframe chassis had a more sophisticated geometry, and the suspension was designed to give the tyres an easier time. His obsession with weight reduction was reflected in a kerb weight of just 390kg, still the lightest winning Grand Prix car of all time. As part of the 1961 regulations, the sport's governing body stipulated a minimum weight of 450kg, fearing that cars such as the Lotus were frail. Regulation minimum weights have been a feature of Formula One ever since.

Maybe the fear was justified. Stirling Moss gave the Lotus its first victory at Monaco in 1960, but two races later broke his back when practising for the Belgian Grand Prix. He was thrown out of the car after crashing because a rear wheel had fallen off due to hub failure. It put Moss out for most of the year, and gave Brabham and Cooper their relatively easy runs to the Drivers' and Constructors' Championships.

▼ Winner Jack Brabham in the Cooper T53 at the British Grand Prix, Silverstone, 1960.

Shapers

John Cooper

▼ John Cooper in 1968.

John Cooper and his father Charles founded Cooper Cars in the late 1940s to produce machines for the new British Formula 500 series. Charles had been an amateur racer at Brooklands pre-war, and John was a fairly successful competitor in the new formula, though he soon hung up his helmet to concentrate on the business, which was run from a garage in Surbiton, near London. Coopers became the dominant machines in the low-cost junior series and drivers such as Stirling Moss, Peter Collins, Ken Tyrrell and Bernie Ecclestone all cut their teeth in them.

Easy-going and friendly, John formed a stark contrast to the short-tempered Charles, and the two rowed frequently. Nonetheless, it was John who had the vision and who took the technical concept of the Formula 500 cars and applied it to bigger, faster machinery, until even Formula One surrendered to his funny little cars. His trademark victory somersault at the trackside became very familiar in 1959 and 1960. He later lent his name to the Mini Cooper and stayed in Formula One until 1968, thereafter concentrating on his garage business. He died in 2001.

Ferrari Bite Two Bullets

errari came back with a vengeance in 1961. Preparation was the key to their success. The British constructors had opposed the formula change to 1.5 litres. The governing body had made the change to combat escalating speeds, but the British teams believed it would leave them without suitable engines, thereby effectively handing the competitive advantage to Ferrari, who made their own engines. This became a self-fulfilling prophecy as the British teams failed to make adequate provisions for the formula change, while Ferrari concentrated on readying their new engine and cars.

Ferrari Returns

The subsequent Ferrari 156 was the team's first effort at a proper mid-engined car, and even though its chassis was not as advanced as those already produced by Lotus or even Cooper, its engine was considerably more powerful than the 1.5-litre version

▲ Phil Hill's Ferrari finished third in the Monaco Grand Prix, Monte Carlo, 1961. It was the start of his title campaign.

of the Coventry Climax the British teams relied upon. It recalled another of Enzo Ferrari's famous maxims: that he built engines with wheels on.

Only one thing kept the Ferraris from completely annihilating the opposition: the genius of Stirling Moss. In the privately-owned Lotus of his entrant Rob Walker, Moss twice beat the Ferraris – at Monaco and Germany. But in championship terms, the contest was between Ferrari drivers Phil Hill and Wolfgang von Trips. Hill won, becoming America's first World Champion after von Trips crashed to his death at Monza in the penultimate round of the championship. Fourteen spectators died with him.

By the end of the year, Coventry Climax had produced a new V8 1.5-litre engine that for 1962 gave Lotus power

▼ Winner Phil Hill in the Ferrari 156 leads team-mate Wolfgang von Trips at the 1961 Belgian Grand Prix. They led a Ferrari 1-2-3-4.

parity with Ferrari, enabling their superior chassis technology to give them the winning edge once more.

BRM Triumphant

Stirling Moss had received career-ending injuries at the beginning of the season, and it was Lotus' works driver Jim Clark who assumed his mantle as the accepted number one. Yet it was Graham Hill and BRM who won the 1962 world crown on account of a better reliability record than the Lotus.

It was the culmination of over a decade's effort from BRM, a team

originally set up as a trust funded by contributions from British industry. By this time, however, it was privately owned and rather better organized. The P57 with which Hill won the title was powered by BRM's very own V8 engine. It was this that transformed the fortunes of the team, turning it from a laughing stock to a world beater. Hill's determination played a key part in driving the team forward.

◄ Graham Hill, here wearing a cap featuring the same London Rowing Club colours as his helmet, won the 1962 title.

Technology 1962

Lotus 25

Lotus redefined Formula One technology with the monocoque construction of their 25 model. Instead of a spaceframe of metal tubing clothed with panels, the aluminium shell was load-bearing and tubing was discarded. The monocoque was stiffer and lighter than the spaceframe, and enabled the suspension to work more effectively. It was also far safer in the event of a serious impact. The technique had long been used in aircraft, but this was its first Formula One application. The entire design of the car was

tailored to the compact dimensions of lead driver Jim Clark, with a cockpit just wide enough to accommodate him and no wider. He was also reclined to an almost horizontal driving position of 35 degrees. It all resulted in an impressive cross-sectional frontal area of just 0.37sq m (3.98sq ft), which compared to 0.54sq m (5.81sq ft) for the rival Ferrari car of 1962.

◄ The gearbox and exhaust end of the revolutionary Lotus 25, the pacesetter of Formula One from 1962–65.

◄ The 25 unclothed, showing just how tightly it was tailored around Jim Clark's dimensions. Chapman confers.

▲ Jim Clark giving the thumbs-up after taking his Lotus 25 to victory in the 1963 Dutch Grand Prix, on his way to the title.

Clark Becomes the Master

The combination of the Lotus 25 and Jim Clark could not be denied indefinitely, and in 1963 they stormed to victory in seven of the World Drivers' Championship's ten rounds. Frequently their level of performance reduced the rest to bit-players: in the Dutch Grand Prix, Clark lapped the field; in France he led from start to finish, despite a couple of broken valve springs. If he failed to win, it was usually because something in the car broke.

Clark and Chapman
Scotsman Clark had formed a symbiotic relationship with Lotus boss, Colin Chapman. Here was the greatest driver of his era working in harmony with the greatest designer. Few doubted that all records would succumb to the pairing.

It did not always go to plan, however. In 1964, some of the unreliability bugs returned and John Surtees was waiting to pounce. The

▲ Jim Clark (*left*) and Colin Chapman, arguably the greatest pairing of driver and designer ever seen in Formula One.

▼ Jim Clark takes victory in the 1965 French Grand Prix at Clermont Ferrand in his Lotus 33, an update of the 25 model.

Shapers

Colin Chapman

Widely cited as the greatest Formula One designer of all time, Colin Chapman's Lotus cars repeatedly took Formula One technology down new roads, leaving the rest to follow in the dust trails of his fertile mind.

He set himself up as a secondhand car trader while studying engineering at London University, and later designed, and competed in, a trials car based on a pre-war Austin 7, dubbed a "Lotus". While training as a pilot in the Royal Airforce, Chapman built a circuit racer for 750 Motor Club events. So successful was he with it that he took orders for replicas; Lotus, the cutting edge of Britain's Formula One invasion, was born.

The success of the business meant that Chapman had to withdraw from racing cars himself, though his driving

talents were considerable. He was even given a drive in the 1956 French Grand Prix by Vanwall, and was quick in practice but a non-starter in the race after damaging his car.

Colin Chapman died from a heart attack in 1982, aged 54. Everyone who worked with him attests to his enormous charm, yet for each of these stories there's another telling of a hard, and ruthless edge. In business, as in car design, he would always search for the loophole, and this trait left his memory tarnished by his involvement in the DeLorean Motor Company scandal of the early 1980s.

◄ **Chapman, here sitting in the Lotus 25, frequently took technology from elsewhere and applied it to Formula One.**

---

former motorcycle champion had begun his Formula One career at Lotus but was now at Ferrari, where he helped hone a new V8 machine, and clinched the title in the final round after Clark's oil pipe came adrift. Surtees remains the only man to have won world titles on two wheels and four.

Clark and Lotus re-established themselves in 1965, the final year of the 1.5-litre formula. They won six of the nine races they contested on their way to both the Drivers' and the Constructors' titles, missing one round in order to compete in the Indianapolis 500 in America. They won that too!

▼ *(left)* **John Surtees, 1964 World Champion for Ferrari. Surtees was already a multiple world title winner on motorbikes when he began his Formula One career.**

▼ *(right)* **Surtees' 1964 season came alive with victory in that year's German Grand Prix around the 14 mile Nürburgring.**

Return to Power

Formula One cars were given their power back in 1966, with the inauguration of a new 3-litre formula. The 1.5-litre regulations had run their allotted time, and there was a hope from the governing body of tempting the American car manufacturers into the sport, to make it appeal more genuinely to a global audience.

Factories Stay Away

Already a Japanese company, Honda, had entered Formula One and had won the final race of the old formula, at Mexico in 1965. Those who controlled the sport hoped this might herald the return of full factory participation in Grand Prix racing. But it was not to be. Whilst Honda produced some

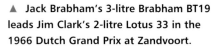
▲ Jack Brabham's 3-litre Brabham BT19 leads Jim Clark's 2-litre Lotus 33 in the 1966 Dutch Grand Prix at Zandvoort.

▲ Denny Hulme, 1967 World Champion, driving for Brabham. A solitary figure, he retired from Formula One in 1974.

◄ Race winner Jack Brabham leads the Coopers of John Surtees and Jochen Rindt in the 1966 German Grand Prix.

▼ Hulme leads Clark and Brabham on the first lap of the 1966 Dutch Grand Prix. Clark led, but later suffered a car problem.

▼ Jim Clark, Lotus 49, won first time out with the brand new Ford DFV engine, at the Dutch Grand Prix, Zandvoort, 1967.

exceptionally powerful engines, their chassis technology was a long way behind the established top teams, and their success was very sporadic.

The "garagiste" era initiated by Cooper in the late 1950s had made Formula One such a specialized exercise, far removed from road-car production, that a factory could no longer expect to come in and immediately dominate. Although Cooper themselves were, by now, a spent force, their influence was everywhere – in the format of the teams doing the winning and in the offshoots created directly from Cooper.

The Cooper Legacy

Jack Brabham, Cooper's former lead driver, won the world title for a third time in 1966, this time driving a Brabham car. He was not the only ex-Cooper driver to incorporate the lessons learned there and set up on his own either: Bruce McLaren had done the same thing and would win McLaren its first Grand Prix in 1968.

But a major manufacturer, Ford, did become involved. The European off-shoot of the American car giant funded the development of a new Formula One engine from Cosworth of Britain, the DFV. Labelled as a Ford, this motor would fill the role of providing off-the-shelf Formula One horsepower previously taken by Coventry Climax. It debuted in the Lotus 49 of 1967, and instantly proved the class of its field, but early unreliability let the title slip to the Brabham of Denny Hulme.

Technology 1967

Cosworth DFV

Keith Duckworth, in partnership with Mike Costin, formed Cosworth Engineering in 1958. The company made its name with some devastatingly successful racing engines in the junior formulae, often based on Ford production units.

Helped by a £100,000 investment from Ford, Duckworth designed the V8-cylinder DFV (double-four-valve). It was probably the first Formula One engine designed with the dimensions of the car specifically in mind, and not only was it decently powerful, with an initial 405bhp, but it was also small, relatively light and could be packaged very efficiently. It was also made sufficiently stiff that it could be mounted in such a way that it formed

part of the car's rigidity. This helped the suspension to do its job.

It won first time out, with Jim Clark in the 1967 Dutch Grand Prix, and won for the final time in 1983, in narrow valve-angle DFY form, in the back of Michele Alboreto's Tyrrell at Detroit. It took over the role of the standard Formula One engine and totalled 155 Grand Prix wins to become the most successful of all time. It was one of the most important parts of the matrix of specialist suppliers that allowed the British race car community to thrive and dominate Grand Prix racing.

◀ Keith Duckworth, designer of the revolutionary Cosworth DFV engine, looking at his handiwork, 1967.

Making a Lethal Game Safer

T he long-overdue safety movement in Formula One truly began one wet afternoon in June 1966, when Jackie Stewart suffered a terrifying accident in the first lap of the Belgian Grand Prix, from which he was fortunate to emerge with his life.

Stewart's Great Escape

The Spa-Francorchamps circuit, nestled in a forested Ardennes valley, always featured changeable weather and though the track was dry as the race began, when the leaders first arrived at Malmédy some miles down the road, they were confronted with a sudden downpour. Eight drivers spun, some of them many times. Among them was Stewart, whose BRM overturned in a ditch after striking a stone wall. Trapped inside and with petrol from the tanks leaking down onto him, Stewart was convinced the car's hot exhausts were about to trigger a fire.

With no marshals at the scene, he was rescued by fellow drivers Graham Hill and Bob Bondurant, who had to borrow a spanner from a spectator in order to remove the steering wheel to facilitate Stewart's exit from the car. It then took 20 minutes for an ambulance

to arrive. As an illustration of how little forethought was being given to driver safety, it was horrific.

Stewart's Crusade

From that moment and for the rest of his career, Stewart fought tirelessly for improved safety standards, and was highly unpopular with race organizers, circuit owners – and even some fellow drivers – for doing so.

▲ **A cigarette-wielding fire marshal douses the Cooper T86B of Brian Redman, following a high speed accident at Spa in 1968.**

▼ **(left) The Spa track of the mid-1960s shows the lethal proximity of houses and solid objects.**

▼ **(right) Richie Ginther's 1961 Ferrari 156 with roll-over bar; but Ginther still wears just a T-shirt instead of fireproof overalls.**

The wearing of helmets had only been compulsory since the beginning of 1952, and since then there had been very little safety progress. Seatbelts had not had universal take-up as many drivers feared being trapped by them in a burning car. The wearing of fireproof overalls only came into vogue in the late 1960s, around the time that the first full-face helmets began to appear – though many drivers still opted for open-facers in the following years, showing how difficult change was.

Standards began to improve in car construction. The 1969 regulations stipulated compulsory on-board fire extinguisher systems and sealed rubber bag fuel cells within the tanks. These were the first safety regulations since the introduction of cockpit roll-over bars in 1961.

But the biggest struggle was with circuit owners. It came down to a Stewart-led drivers union – the Grand Prix Drivers' Association (GPDA) – to act militantly and demand changes. Trees were felled from trackside locations, Armco barriers were erected, barbed-wire fencing cleared, marshal training improved, and circuit medical facilities upgraded. Eventually, medical helicopters would be present every time the cars ran, ready to ferry injured drivers to hospital. In time, some venues – notably the public road circuit of Spa-Francorchamps where Stewart had crashed in 1966 – were deemed too dangerous and fell from the calendar.

The changes helped, but the sport remained lethally dangerous. In the 1960s, 12 drivers and 16 spectators were killed in Formula One events. Several more Grand Prix drivers died competing outside of Formula One, notably the great Jim Clark, who

was killed in a Formula Two race at Hockenheim shortly after breaking Fangio's all-time record of Grand Prix victories. He had racked up win number 25 in South Africa on New Year's Day 1968. Even the world's greatest driver could become a victim.

◄ Monaco had one of the worst safety records in Formula One during the 1960s. Lorenzo Bandini died here in 1967, the flames from his car fanned by a helicopter taking film footage.

▼ (left) There was scant protection for the spectators, let alone the drivers. Sixteen spectators were killed during Formula One races of the 1960s.

▼ (right) Lotus mechanics look on at the remains of the Lotus 49B of Jackie Oliver, after he crashed in practice in France in 1968 as a result of aerodynamic turbulence.

Money Talks

Commercial sponsorship hit Formula One in 1968, when Imperial Tobacco plastered their Gold Leaf brand livery over the Team Lotus cars. Until this time, such a practice had been restricted to American national racing, while Formula One teams had plugged only trade backers, with small stickers for tyre, fuel, oil or brake brands in exchange for a free supply of their wares. The Lotus deal took things onto a different scale entirely.

Advertising Enters Formula One

The competitive push of the teams, notably Lotus' Colin Chapman, had led them to pressure the governing body to relax restrictions on commercial advertising on the cars in order to give them bigger budgets for development and design. This duly happened at the end of 1967, and Lotus were the first to take advantage. National racing colours – something first established in the 1900 Gordon Bennett competitions – soon became a thing of the past. Ferrari were an exception, though team boss Enzo Ferrari was able to show disdain for the new trend only because his team had been acquired by motor giant Fiat in 1969, giving financial security but retaining Enzo's autonomy. He was now able to get back to full strength.

▶ Winner Graham Hill clutching his Monaco trophy, 1968. The victory put him into a firm lead of the championship.

▲ Race winner Graham Hill in the Lotus 49B made it four wins around the Principality. Monaco Grand Prix, 1968.

Life After Clark

Lotus bounced back from the death of Clark, largely thanks to the grit and determination of Graham Hill. With team boss Colin Chapman devastated, Hill took the initiative and in winning the very next Grand Prix following Clark's death, helped the team recompose itself. That was in Spain and in winning the following event in Monaco too, Hill put himself and Lotus in command. Nonetheless, to win the fight they had to fend off two very serious challenges: Jackie Stewart in

▼ By winning the 1968 Spanish Grand Prix immediately after the death of team-mate Jim Clark, Graham Hill helped Lotus recover.

the new Matra and reigning champ Denny Hulme in the McLaren. All three contenders were powered by the Ford Cosworth DFV engine.

Stewart's French-built and designed Matra was run by his former Formula Three entrant, Ken Tyrrell, as the pair re-established their partnership to form what would become one of the sport's golden liaisons. Their first victory came in Holland that year but their greatest was at the Nürburgring in a wet and foggy German Grand Prix. Stewart won by over four minutes in one of the greatest performances ever seen around the formidable 14-mile circuit. Hulme won the next two events, with Stewart again on top in the penultimate race. Going into the final round, in Mexico, it was a three-way title shoot-out between Hill, Stewart and Hulme.

Hulme was an early retirement as the race developed into a thrilling dice at the front between Hill and Stewart, with the pair passing and re-passing. Eventually, falling fuel pressure began to lose Stewart power, enabling Hill, Lotus and Gold Leaf to win the race and the Championship. Hill's grit had got the job done once again.

▲ Bruce McLaren (McLaren-Cosworth M7A) finished in sixth place at the USA Grand Prix, Watkins Glen, in 1968.

▲ Bruce McLaren (McLaren M7A) leads Jackie Oliver (Lotus 49B) at the Mexican Grand Prix, Mexico City in 1968. McLaren finished second and Oliver third.

▼ Johnny Servoz-Gavin (Matra MS10) crashed out on lap 71 of the Canadian Grand Prix, Mont-Tremblant, in 1968.

Downforce: The Genie Escapes

At the 1968 Monaco Grand Prix, the Lotus 49 appeared in revised "B" trim. On either side of the nose were two small wings, while the rear bodywork featured an upsweep designed to provide similar download at the rear. The concept of downforce had arrived in Formula One, heralding a completely different scale of performance. It has been with the sport ever since. By the next race, at Spa, Ferrari and Brabham appeared with devices that took the principle a step further, featuring full-width rear wings, separate from the body, mounted direct to the gearbox. Chris Amon took pole position in the Ferrari by the huge margin of 3.7 seconds.

Aerodynamic Technology
The principle essentially involved taking an aerofoil shape, as used for aircraft wings, and turning it upside down so that it provided downforce instead of lift. If air is forced to travel a longer distance over a lower surface than an upper one, it creates a pressure that will force the car to the ground, through the medium of the tyres. In this way, braking and cornering capacity is increased hugely.

Mounting the wings higher up on the car got them out of the disturbed

▲ Jochen Rindt's Brabham BT26 in the 1968 Canadian Grand Prix shows the ugly and dangerous heights wings had reached.

▼ Chris Amon drives the Ferrari 312 to second place in the British Grand Prix at Brands Hatch in 1968.

▼ Graham Hill climbs from his wrecked Lotus after an accident caused by wing failure. He was saved by the retaining barrier.

airflow created by the car itself, and within just a few races, almost all the cars were running front and rear wings mounted on hugely high stalks, feeding the loads directly into the suspension. Teams also began to experiment with wings that could be retracted on the straights to overcome the straightline speed penalty of their drag. It all made for a bizarre spectacle – and a highly dangerous one.

Wings of Unreason

At the Spanish Grand Prix of 1969, Graham Hill crested a rise in his Lotus, and his rear wing snapped off its mounts. Suddenly shorn of its downforce, the car became airborne and crashed heavily. As Hill was making his way back to the pits to get the team to warn his team-mate Jochen Rindt, the sister car suffered exactly the same failure over the same crest, and cannoned off Hill's abandoned wreck. Rindt was trapped in the car but fortunately had suffered only a broken nose. It was a miraculous escape for both drivers, not to mention the spectators. The governing body decided

it had to act, and at the next Grand Prix it banned wings outright. After a subsequent meeting with constructors, a compromise was reached; wings were allowed once more, but no longer could they be either movable or mounted to the suspension. Less effective fixed wings mounted only to the bodywork were allowed, with dimensions and height drastically reduced.

Amid all the controversy, Jackie Stewart and his Ken Tyrrell-run Matra-Ford glided from one immaculate victory to another on the way to their first World Championship. Jochen Rindt was the only one to consistently challenge them, but his Lotus lacked reliability. The Ford Cosworth DFV engine took victory in every single race with Matra, Lotus, Brabham and McLaren cars.

▲ Remarkably Jochen Rindt escaped from this wing failure-induced accident with just a broken nose. It led to wing restrictions.

▲ The remains of Hill's Lotus 49B after his 1969 Spanish Grand Prix accident. He broke a leg in the US Grand Prix later that year.

▲ Jackie Stewart, in car, and Ken Tyrrell pose for some publicity shots for a brand of whiskey at the Canadian Grand Prix, 1969.

The Stewart Years

Jochen Rindt and Jackie Stewart were widely acknowledged as the world's two best drivers as the new decade began. But their competitive circumstances were about to change. Matra, now backed by Chrysler France, could not be seen running Ford engines and so the arrangement with Stewart and Tyrrell came to an end. While making plans to have his own machine built for the following year, Tyrrell purchased a car from a manufacturer new to Formula One, March, for the 1970 season. Unfortunately it wasn't up to the task of sustaining a championship challenge.

◀ Jackie Stewart (left) with Jochen Rindt at the British Grand Prix, Brands Hatch in 1970. Rindt was later made Posthumous World Champion of 1970.

▼ Rindt, in the Lotus 72C, wins his fourth Grand Prix in a row at Hockenheim, Germany, in 1970.

A Brutal Season

Jochen Rindt, by contrast, found himself behind the wheel of a new Lotus, the 72, that moved the technical goalposts of Formula One and gave him a real advantage. After a stunning win at Monaco in the old 49 model – where he pressured race leader Jack Brabham into running wide and hitting the barriers on the last lap – Rindt took up residence in the 72 and reeled off four successive victories. Although he was not to know it, these effectively secured him the World Championship crown. Rindt was killed practising for the Italian Grand Prix, through a suspected wheel hub failure. In the remaining four races, no-one overhauled his points score and he became the sport's only posthumous World Champion.

It had been a particularly brutal season, with Piers Courage and Bruce McLaren also killed. With his friends being slain around him, Stewart worked harder than ever on his safety campaign. But he still found time to dominate the 1971 season in his new Tyrrell-Ford, with which he won six races.

The five he didn't win were split between his own team-mate François Cevert, the Ferraris of Mario Andretti and Jacky Ickx, and the Yardley Cosmetics-sponsored BRMs of Jo Siffert and Peter Gethin. The latter triumphed in Italy, where his race average of 241km/h (151mph) is still the fastest recorded in a Grand Prix. Thereafter chicanes were installed in the super-fast Monza track for reasons of safety.

▼ Winner Peter Gethin (BRM, *right*), Ronnie Peterson (March) and François Cevert (Tyrrell) at the Italian Grand Prix, 1971.

Technology 1970

Lotus 72

While the advent of wings in 1968 made Formula One cars substantially faster round a circuit on account of their vastly improved braking and cornering capabilities, the aerodynamic drag they created actually made the cars slower on the straights than before. The 1970 Lotus 72 – conceived by Colin Chapman, translated into reality by Maurice Phillippe – brilliantly resolved the conflicting requirements of downforce and straightline speed.

Its wedge shape made the cigar-like structures of before obsolete. This, combined with the re-siting of the radiators from the front to the side of the car, lowered the frontal area while the wedge bodywork itself helped create downforce. This enabled smaller wings to be fitted for equivalent downforce; powered by the same Ford Cosworth DFV engine, the 72's terminal speed was 14km/h (9mph) higher than the 49's, its predecessor. Other novelties included inboard brakes front and rear to lower the car's unsprung mass, and rising-rate suspension to resolve the requirements that the very different aerodynamic loadings of high- and low-speed corners placed upon it.

▲ The launch of the Lotus 72 in 1970. The radical car took a few races to be fully sorted but it was devastating thereafter. It was still winning in 1974.

New Eras Beckon

The seeds that eventually flowered to make Grand Prix racing one of the biggest sports in the world were planted some time in 1971. Jack Brabham had retired from racing at the end of 1970 and, at the age of 44, he sold up and went back home to Australia. Initially his designer Ron Tauranac took over the reins of the Brabham team, but later in 1971 Bernie Ecclestone – the late Jochen Rindt's manager – also bought into it.

Big Business

It gave the Brabham team a new lease of life, but very few at the time realized the enormous implications for the future of Formula One. Ecclestone's ownership of a team made him party to business dealings with the race organizers, whom he felt were exploiting the teams. As an incredibly astute businessman, he banded the teams together and negotiated on their behalf. The much-improved deal he secured them was just the start. He also had the vision to see the true business

▲ **Bernie Ecclestone (***left***, with Brabham designer Gordon Murray) brought a new era to Brabham – and to all of Formula One.**

▼ **Emerson Fittipaldi winning the 1972 British Grand Prix at Brands Hatch, on his way to becoming the youngest champ.**

potential of Formula One to international sponsors, and so set about securing worldwide television coverage.

Fittipaldi and Lotus

On the track, Emerson Fittipaldi became the youngest-ever World Champion when he clinched the 1972 title at the age of 25 years, eight months and 29 days. The livery of his Lotus 72 had been changed from Gold Leaf to the black and gold colours of John Player Special cigarettes in one of the sport's most distinctive branding exercises. Treadless, "slick" tyres, introduced to Formula One in 1971 but originating from drag-racing, were the norm now, giving a greater surface area of rubber, and therefore more dry-track grip. The combination of downforce and slicks saw cornering forces rise to 2g.

Fittipaldi's Championship campaign had been eased somewhat by Jackie Stewart suffering a stomach ulcer, but for 1973 the Scot came bouncing back to take his third title. At Monaco he scored his 26th Grand Prix win,

breaking the record held by his friend, the late Jim Clark, and at the German Grand Prix he took his 27th and final race victory. At the end of the season, 34-year-old Stewart retired. But at Watkins Glen in the United States, the death of his team-mate François Cevert in practice for what was going to be Stewart's final race, had illustrated that the Stewart-initiated safety campaign had to continue.

▲ *(left)* **François Cevert in 1973. The Frenchman perished at the end of the season, on the verge of great success.**

▲ *(right)* **Emerson Fittipaldi (Lotus) leads winner Jean-Pierre Beltoise (BRM) at Monaco in 1972. It was to be BRM's last victory.**

Shapers

Bernie Ecclestone

The Mr Big of modern Formula One started out as just another Formula 500 racer in the early 1950s, combining this with his business of selling second-hand cars and motorcycles in south London. Ecclestone wasn't a bad driver, but his real talent lay in the world of business. He cut his links with the sport after the fatal accident of his close friend Stuart Lewis-Evans in the 1958 Moroccan Grand Prix, and made his fortune in property dealing.

He returned as the business manager of Austrian driver Jochen Rindt in the late 1960s. Rindt was killed at Monza in 1970, but Ecclestone this time stayed around and bought into the Brabham team, following the retirement of its founder Jack Brabham. From that time

onward, Ecclestone almost single-handedly transformed Formula One into a big business and, eventually, one of the biggest sporting series in the world. In the process, he made most of the team owners extremely wealthy, and himself even more so.

Along the way, Ecclestone's Brabham team gave Nelson Piquet world titles in 1981 and 1983, though Ecclestone sold the team in 1987. As head of the Formula One Constructors' Association (FOCA), he continues to wield enormous – some would say ultimate – power in the sport.

◄ **Bernie Ecclestone, Brabham owner, at the South African Grand Prix in 1972. Big changes were coming.**

The Ferrari Renaissance

Ferrari were badly in the doldrums by the end of 1973. They had just suffered an appalling season in which they never came close to winning a race, and they hadn't been World Champions since John Surtees' triumph of 1964. The top British teams with their "garagiste" kit-cars, using bought-in components, had basically run rings around the Italian thoroughbreds, with their exclusive self-made engines, for the best part of a decade. It was time for a reorganization.

Ferrari Revamps

Enzo Ferrari took the bull by the horns. He made wholesale changes to his technical team, and recruited a new driver line up. A brilliant young lawyer with close family ties to Fiat's Agnelli family, Luca di Montezemolo, was put in charge of the day-to-day running of the team, while Mauro Forghieri was made head of Formula One development. He toiled away to produce the 1974 312B3 model. Distribution of masses

▲ *(left)* Ferrari designer Mauro Forghieri and Niki Lauda in 1974, the two driving forces behind Ferrari's success.

▼ The new Ferrari 312T of Clay Regazzoni *(left)* alongside the previous 312B3 model in the pits at the South African Grand Prix, Kyalami, in 1975.

was his theme. The powerful flat-12 engine – used since 1970 – already brought the centre of gravity down low. Forghieri now set about centring the masses of the car as much as possible too, to make it more manoeuvrable. To this end the cockpit and fuel cells were moved forward within the wheelbase.

Concurrently, Ferrari signed a promising young Austrian driver, Niki Lauda. His technical feedback and appetite for endless hours of pounding round Ferrari's new Fiorano test track pleased Forghieri immensely. Together, they made the 312B3 1974's fastest car – as Lauda's nine pole positions testified. Some impetuosity on Lauda's part, and the occasional glitch from the car, handed the title to Emerson Fittipaldi and McLaren. But for 1975 there would be no such weaknesses as Lauda and Ferrari annihilated the opposition with the new 312T model. After a gap of 11 years, Ferrari were once again on top of the world.

► Winner Emerson Fittipaldi, in the McLaren M23, at the Canadian Grand Prix, Mosport Park, in 1974.

▼ (right) Winner Emerson Fittipaldi, in the McLaren M23, leads second-placed Niki Lauda at the Belgian Grand Prix at Nivelles, in 1974.

▼ (left) Emerson Fittipaldi, the 1974 World Champion, driving for McLaren.

Technology 1975

Ferrari 312T

The 312T was the car that broke a seven-year Championship-winning streak for Ford Cosworth DFV-powered machines. It was the masterpiece of Ferrari's chief designer Mauro Forghieri.

At the car's heart was Forghieri's flat-12 cylinder engine, which had first appeared in 1970. With the cylinders arranged in two horizontally-opposed lines of six, it had a lower centre of gravity than the vee-cylinder formation of the DFV, which benefited handling. With 12 smaller cylinders, it also had a greater combustion chamber area, lower inertia and fewer heat losses, allowing it to rev higher and produce more power. But 12 cylinders also meant it was heavier and thirstier. With 495bhp, it had around 35bhp more power than a DFV of the time, but was 25kg heavier and had to carry an extra 20kg of fuel at the start of a race.

The innovation of the Ferrari 312T was Forghieri's transverse gearbox. This further centralized the masses of the car, and enabled its handling to be more responsive. Forghieri also opted for the maximum width allowed by the regulations which meant more frontal area but brought a twofold advantage: firstly,

▼ Clay Regazzoni won twice in the 312T in 1975 and 1976, as support to team leader Niki Lauda.

The Greatest Story Ever Told

After a fiery mid-season accident, Niki Lauda came back from the dead to fight for the 1976 World Championship, a contest that went down to a dramatic final round in the rain and mist of Japan, overlooked by the menacing Mount Fuji. Lauda's rival was an English former public schoolboy, James Hunt, who could have arrived straight out of a comic-strip. Dashing, blond and caring little for convention, his beautiful model wife had left him for film star Richard Burton earlier that season. It all made for the most fantastic story, one that transcended the sport and brought Formula One unprecedented public attention throughout the world.

Lauda vs Hunt
Lauda began the season as he had ended 1975, by winning in dominant fashion. By the time of the German Grand Prix in August he looked comfortably on his way to a second successive title, despite the often brilliant showings of Hunt in the Marlboro-McLaren. But then Lauda crashed, his Ferrari caught fire and he

◀ **James Hunt at the South African Grand Prix in 1976, where he took his second successive pole position for McLaren.**

▼ **James Hunt in the McLaren M23, finished in third place in the 1976 Japanese Grand Prix, securing him the title by one point.**

Technology 1977

Renault RS01

When the 3-litre formula was announced for 1966, there was a clause in the technical regulations stipulating that forced-induction engines could be no bigger than 1.5 litres. It was assumed that such a penalty would prevent anyone building a supercharged or turbocharged engine, the costs of which were expected to be exorbitant. Supercharged engines – whereby a mechanically-driven compressor compresses the fuel/air mix into the cylinders, massively increasing the power – had last been seen in Formula One in 1951. But at that time, exotic alcohol-based fuels that kept the extreme internal temperatures in check were permitted. Since 1958, only

▲ The 1.5-litre V6 was very compact, albeit heavy, thanks to ancilliaries needed for the turbo and its cooling.

▼ Jean-Pierre Jabouille gave the RS01 its first race at Silverstone in 1977, qualifying 21st and retiring in the race.

conventional pump-fuel had been allowed. Despite this, Renault reckoned they could make a success of the turbo engine – whereby exhaust gases rather than a mechanical device drive the compressor. In its initial form, the 1.5-litre V6 produced 500bhp – slightly more than most conventional 3-litre engines were giving. As if the engine were not innovation enough, the Renault was also the first Formula One car to feature radial tyres rather than

was trapped inside. Some fellow drivers pulled him out but he had suffered critical lung damage through inhalation of the flames. For days his life hung in the balance, and he was even granted the last rites. But, remarkably, he made a rapid recovery. Facially scarred, he returned three races later and finished fourth at Monza in one of the most astonishing performances ever seen in any sport.

He pulled out of the final race in Japan after one lap, unwilling to risk his life in conditions of virtually zero visibility. Hunt finished the race third, taking the Drivers' title by one point.

The story was made even better when in 1977 Lauda succeeded in regaining his crown. Better still, one

of his key victories came in Germany, albeit at a different track; his 1976 accident had ensured that the famous Nürburgring – recognized as the most demanding Grand Prix track of all since being built in 1926 – would never again host a Formula One race.

The 1977 British Grand Prix marked a key moment in Formula One history in the form of an unconventional yellow car that qualified only 21st fastest. It was the first Grand Prix start in 69 years for Renault. More significantly, it signified the arrival in Formula One of turbo-powered engines.

◄ The battle-scarred Niki Lauda returned to retake his World Championship title in 1977, and then he promptly left Ferrari.

The Magic of Ground Effect

The Lotus 78 of 1977 had a magic trick within it, one that took Formula One technology down a new road and would soon increase grip exponentially. In the process, it enabled the band of British constructors that had dominated Formula One for two decades to have a fighting chance against the return of the factories that Renault's entry to the sport now represented.

Lotus Innovations

With the 78 model, Lotus brought the concept of "ground effect" to Formula One. When air is funnelled through a small aperture that then opens out into a wide expanse, it creates a negative pressure. Give this area a seal with the ground and it will suck down. This in essence is how the Lotus worked, giving it a big grip advantage over its closest rivals.

Only car unreliability kept Mario Andretti from comfortably winning the 1977 World Championship with the Lotus 78. For 1978, the Lotus 79 represented an evolution of the concept, and this time the performance advantage it brought was massive. Andretti's only rival for the world crown was his team-mate Ronnie Peterson, but Peterson was contracted to be in a support role to Andretti,

▶ **American racing legend, Mario Andretti, won the 1978 World Championship using the ground-effect Lotus 78 and 79 models.**

▲ **Swede Gunnar Nilsson won the 1977 Belgian Grand Prix in the ground-effect Lotus 78. He died from cancer in 1978.**

and on a couple of occasions finished a dutiful second to him when he could conceivably have passed.

Andretti clinched the title at the Italian Grand Prix, but it was in tragic circumstances. Peterson died as a result of injuries sustained in a startline collision. His car slid beneath a barrier in the force of impact, breaking one of his legs. He was hospitalized but died later that evening from a brain embolism triggered by the broken bone. It was a tragic end to Lotus' glorious season.

▼ **Andretti winning the 1977 Italian Grand Prix in the Lotus 78. Its slow straightline speed was corrected in the 79 model.**

▲ The aftermath of the first lap crash which claimed the life of Ronnie Peterson at Monza on 10 September, 1978.

▶ Ronnie Peterson tragically succumbed to his Monza injuries after a fine season. He was lying second in the Championship.

Technology 1978

Lotus 79

The previous year's Lotus 78 had been the first Formula One car to utilize ground effect. Contained within its side pods were venturi channels, small apertures opening out into a bigger area. When air flowed through these, channels it created a negative pressure, which was sealed off via skirts running along the bottom of the pods, thereby sucking the car to the ground.

The problem with the 78 model was that the centre of pressure was too biased towards the front of the car, necessitating a bigger rear wing to balance the handling, at the cost of straightline speed. In its layout, the 79 addressed this problem, and more fully exploited the potential of the concept. Quite by chance, ground effect also

brought the decade-old Cosworth DFV engine back into play as the most suitable engine for the job. Since the mid-1970s, Ferrari had taken full advantage of the lower centre of gravity endowed by their flat-12 motor to produce the fastest cars in the competition. But efficient ground effect demanded side pods with plenty of open space behind them, in order to

▲ Ronnie Peterson followed Mario Andretti home in the Spanish Grand Prix of 1978, both Lotus 79-propelled.

speed up the airflow and increase the suction. This meant that the cylinder banks of the Ferrari were now in the worst possible place, while those of the DFV, angled upwards in a vee-shape, were perfectly situated.

Safety: Still a Way to Go

Ronnie Peterson's fatal accident at the 1978 Italian Grand Prix illustrated just how far there was still to go, over a decade after Jackie Stewart initiated the safety campaign. Peterson was the only Formula One driver to be killed on-track that year, suggesting some improvement since 1970 when three drivers succumbed. But the average for the decade was still slightly more than one driver death per season. The figures also showed that there would be a death or serious injury for every 40 accidents – a big improvement over the 1960s, but still far too high.

Taking Safety Seriously

Professor Sid Watkins, a British neurologist and motor racing fan, had been asked by Bernie Ecclestone to attend some races with a view to making suggestions about how to improve medical facilities. He was present that day at Monza but had no position of authority. His observations of events there indicated many areas where big improvements could be made relatively easily. Soon after,

▲ *(above and inset right)* John Watson in the carbon-fibre McLaren MP4/1, in which he survived unscathed from a huge accident at Monza.

▼ Catch fencing halts the errant cars of Jochen Mass and Nelson Piquet in the 1980 Belgian Grand Prix.

▲ Sid Watkins, FISA Doctor, is swarmed by the Coca-Cola girls at the Brazilian Grand Prix, Rio de Janeiro, in 1981.

▼ Denny Hulme leads Jackie Stewart through a newly-installed chicane at Monza in 1972, designed to keep speeds in check.

Watkins was made chief medical officer for all Grands Prix, which gave him absolute authority. He can bring a meeting grinding to a halt if he is not satisfied with any aspect of safety. The medical facilities of the circuits have since improved immeasurably.

Safety vs Advantage

In terms of car design, new regulations for 1973 stipulated that the space between the monocoque skins had to be filled with hardened foam to provide a deformable structure, and the fuel tanks had to be better insulated. But thereafter, the advent of ground effect cars made it more desirable from an aerodynamic performance point of view to have the cockpits far forward within the wheelbase, even to the extent that drivers' feet were sometimes ahead of the axle line of the front wheels, making them especially vulnerable. A regulation banning this practice didn't come into effect until 1988.

Circuit safety improved throughout the decade. Greater run-off areas were beginning to be provided on the fast corners, tyre barriers were erected, as was catch fencing, which would wrap itself around an errant car and thereby slow its progress. This, however, created a secondary hazard in that the poles to which the fencing was attached could strike a driver's head. The 1980s would see the catch fencing replaced by gravel traps. As a downside to the safety movement, several demanding corners – highlights of the track – were lost from the circuits as chicanes were installed before them to slow cars down to a safer cornering speed.

▲ Safety crusader Jackie Stewart in his post-retirement role of TV commentator talks viewers through a Lotus 79.

▲ Alan Jones and Gilles Villeneuve make use of the catch fencing at the British Grand Prix at Silverstone in 1981.

TV: Spreading the Word

The fairytale story of the 1976 Lauda vs Hunt epic was probably the spark that got television companies interested in Formula One. The British Broadcasting Corporation televised the championship finale – something of a departure from its previous policy of screening the Monaco and British Grands Prix only. In 1978, the BBC began televising every race.

Formula One Goes Global

If Hunt's performances can be said to have been responsible for bringing the BBC in, it was a pattern repeated as drivers of other nations were successful. Australia's Alan Jones began winning races on a regular basis in 1979, triggering Channel Nine's season-long coverage for the following year.

Emerson Fittipaldi's success in the early to mid-1970s saw interest in Formula One soar in Brazil, and the television companies responded appropriately. In each case, the broadcasts were such a success that they remained regular fixtures even after those drivers had left the sport or ceased to be successful. France was an early television convert, thanks to the success of the Elf programme in backing the nation's promising junior drivers until they reached Formula One; by 1978, there were seven French drivers there.

The rights to broadcast Formula One were – and are – negotiated by Bernie Ecclestone. Initially the terms were not too fierce, as he sought to lead them into the sport gently and thereby make it a more attractive place for sponsors

▲ *(left)* James Hunt's 1976 epic title race with Niki Lauda, and his glamorous profile, generated lots of interest from racing fans.

◄ Arguably the dice of the decade unfolded as Gilles Villeneuve and René Arnoux fought over second, France 1979.

▼ Jody Scheckter won the 1979 World Championship after taking his Ferrari to victory three times.

▼ Clay Regazzoni takes the flag at Silverstone 1979 to give the Williams team its first Grand Prix victory.

to be. But steadily, the process snowballed and, as the money rolled in, so the sport became bigger news, and so the fee increased. The television companies happily paid up, as the sport was attracting ever-more television advertising revenue.

Television and Live Drama

By the end of the 1970s, it was all just beginning to take off. There was some particularly good footage to show in 1979, most memorably in the French Grand Prix where Gilles Villeneuve's Ferrari and René Arnoux's Renault fought one of the most desperate and thrilling wheel-to-wheel battles ever seen, frequently trading rubber or running wide onto the grass in the closing laps of the race. In all the excitement, it was easy to overlook the fact that this was a fight for second place; some way ahead of them, Jean-Pierre Jabouille was himself making a bit of history. In winning the race for Renault, he gave the turbocharged engine its first ever Formula One victory.

At Silverstone for the next race, Clay Regazzoni gave the British Williams team its first win, initiating a lineage of success for them that continues to this day. His team-mate Alan Jones dominated the second half of the season in the ground-effect FW07 model. But it was Ferrari's Jody Scheckter who took the title thanks to three victories and superbly consistent finishing in between.

▼ Clay Regazzoni's Williams in action.

Entente Incordiale: The Battle for Control

Bernie Ecclestone's increasing power and influence through the 1970s had made the sport's nominal governing body, the FIA (Fédération Internationale de l'Automobile), very nervous. When the body elected a new president, Jean-Marie Balestre, in 1978 he vowed that he was going to wrest control of the sport back where it belonged. He included in that mission statement financial control as well as sporting and technical.

David vs Goliath
The body headed by Ecclestone, the FOCA, represented the interests of the independent teams, most of whom were British. It didn't include Ferrari, nor the car-producing factories of Renault and Alfa Romeo, both of whom had recently joined Formula One. Balestre, an outrageously manipulative politician, succeeded in exposing a fault line of conflicting interests between the FOCA and non-FOCA teams.

For 1980, Balestre attempted to ban the sliding skirts used on the sidepods of the cars that were a critical part of their ground effect performance. His stated objection was that they made the cars so much faster that circuits were having to be constantly changed, with ever-greater run-off areas, just to keep pace.

The British constructors, all of them relying on the venerable bought-in Cosworth DFV engine, felt that it was only their superior chassis technology

▲ *(top)* Jean-Marie Balestre, FISA President, talks with Bernie Ecclestone, Brabham team owner and FOCA member.

▼ Jody Scheckter finished second at the United States Grand Prix (West), Long Beach, Florida, in 1979.

▲ *(above)* Pole sitter Nelson Piquet, in the Brabham BT49, took his first Grand Prix win at the USA (West) Grand Prix in 1980.

▼ Max Mosley, March team owner, at the Canadian Grand Prix, Mosport Park, October 1977.

▼ Carlos Reutemann in the Williams FWO7B finished third at the Belgian Grand Prix at Zolder in 1980.

that was preventing Formula One being dominated by a small number of money-no-object factory teams, with their own more powerful engines. The sliding skirts were an essential element to this chassis superiority.

On the Brink of Divide

The argument bubbled on throughout 1980 before the sport split into two camps during the off-season of 1980–81. FOCA announced its own Championship and published a series of dates. Six teams, including Ferrari, Renault and Alfa Romeo, stayed loyal with the governing body, and it looked for a time as if there would be two conflicting World Championships. A South African Grand Prix took place in January with just the FOCA teams. It was a sure recipe for a complete commercial disaster.

Shapers

Jean-Marie Balestre

Noted as bombastic and highly controversial during his time as president of FISA, the sporting arm of the FIA, Balestre did many positive things for the sport during his time at the helm.

After serving in the war as an undercover agent for the French Resistance – posing as a member of the French SS – he established a successful French racing motor magazine, *Autojournal*. He is also given credit for popularizing kart racing, and founded the world karting commission. He rose to a position of authority within French national motorsport and this led to his presidency of the Paris-based world governing body. It was Balestre who established specific crash test requirements for Formula One cars and in so doing raised safety standards enormously. He was re-elected in 1987 and stayed in charge until the 1991 elections when he lost to Max Mosley, who for years had been Ecclestone's key partner in FOCA.

It was a farcical situation and a compromise was finally brokered by Enzo Ferrari. In a meeting at the Ferrari base of Maranello, Balestre and Ecclestone both signed an agreement – called the Concorde Agreement – that is, essentially, the basis on which the sport of Formula One runs today. FOCA was granted the commercial negotiating rights on the FIA's behalf, while the FIA retained control of all sporting and technical regulations.

Many years later Ecclestone revealed that he had been about to telephone Balestre to surrender when Balestre called him to suggest a compromise! At last, the racing could get under-way again, though feelings of distrust between the two sides continued to flare up from time to time.

▼ Jean-Pierre Jabouille, Renault RE20, retired on the first lap with clutch failure. Belgian Grand Prix, Zolder, 1980.

Specialists vs The Factories

Ground effect had arrived just in time to give the British specialist teams a weapon against the exotic turbo engines of the returning factory outfits. It did not take long for Renault to devise their own ground-effect chassis though, and so while the British teams were fighting to have turbos banned, they were also researching avenues through which they could get their own.

On Even Ground

There was a brief window – before Renault had made their engines fully reliable and before the specialist teams had sourced turbos – where a competitive equilibrium between the two was established. That window comprised the 1980 and 1981 seasons.

Alan Jones gave Williams its first World Championship in 1980, pushed hard by the Brabham of Nelson Piquet. The Renaults by now were running close to 600bhp – an advantage of around 100bhp over the DFV cars – and won three races in the hands of René Arnoux and Jean-Pierre Jabouille, but their chassis, despite featuring ground effect, lagged behind those of the best specialist teams and their engines repeatedly blew up.

▲ Alain Prost in the Renault RE30, en route to his first victory and on home soil at the French Grand Prix, Dijon-Prenois, in 1981. It was the first of 51 wins for the Frenchman.

◀ 1980 World Champion Alan Jones retired at the end of 1981 after another great season with Williams. He later returned, but without the same level of success.

▼ Prost's Renault dices hard with Jones' Williams in the 1981 German Grand Prix. It was a classic factory vs specialist team fight: the Renault had superior horsepower, but the Williams had a better chassis.

▼ Nelson Piquet took his Brabham to victory in the 1981 World Championship, defeating the less reliable Renaults.

▼ John Watson took McLaren out of the doldrums with victory in the 1981 British Grand Prix, a first for a carbon-fibre car.

It was a similar story in 1981 when Piquet took his Brabham-DFV to the title, though Alain Prost's Renault was frequently the quickest car and won three times between blow-ups. Ferrari now had their own turbo engine and

with it Gilles Villeneuve took two spectacular victories. McLaren, under the new management of Ron Dennis, came back into the reckoning after a few years in the doldrums as John Watson won the British Grand Prix in

the MP4/1, the first carbon-fibre Formula One car. Lotus attempted to take ground effect onto the next level with their twin-chassis 88 model, but the governing body banned the car from ever competing.

Technology 1981

McLaren MP4/1

The aerodynamic loads that the ground effect cars put upon their chassis was enormous. The Williams FW07 had been successful because designer Patrick Head had realized that the chassis needed to be massively rigid in order to take full advantage of ground effect forces. But there was a conflict for designers: the bigger the side pod venturis could be made, the more ground effect could be generated; but at the same time, the wider the sidepods, the narrower the central tub of the car, which limited its rigidity.

McLaren designer John Barnard realized the solution would be to make the tub in a material inherently stiffer but no heavier than the widely-used aluminium. Helped by American aerospace supplier Hercules, he made the MP4/1's monocoque from carbon-fibre. Strands of carbon-fibre were laid out into the required shape, bonded together and then oven-baked to make an immensely strong and stiff structure. For the same weight as an aluminium tub, its stiffness was double. It was also much stronger in an impact than

aluminium, as lead driver John Watson demonstrated with an enormous crash at Monza in 1981, from which he improbably climbed out unhurt. Soon, all Formula One cars would be made this way. As with the development of the monocoque chassis in the 1960s, the search for performance had brought with it unexpected benefits in car and driver safety too.

▼ Niki Lauda pilots the MP4/1 McLaren to victory in the 1982 British Grand Prix, his second victory with the car.

Partners Not Enemies

Competitive tension between the specialist teams and the "grandees" (Renault, Alfa and Ferrari) continued into the 1982 season as they fought off-track over the direction the sport was taking, as well as on the track over race victories.

Shady Tactics

Brabham and Williams were disqualified from first and second places in the Brazilian Grand Prix for running their cars underweight. They thought they had identified a loophole in the regulations that allowed them to do this so long as the cars complied when replenishable fluids were added post-race. The ruse they devised were big water tanks for "water-cooled brakes". They ran the race with the water tanks empty, then filled them post-race. It allowed the underpowered DFV-engined cars to run as much as 60kg under the minimum weight, something out of the reach of the turbo-engined machines with their heavy ancillaries. The governing body was not impressed.

Following the disqualification, the FOCA teams boycotted the San Marino Grand Prix. The rules were clarified and both sides were back together in time for the following Belgian Grand Prix. It was in qualifying for this race that Gilles Villeneuve was killed after his

Ferrari hit a slow-moving car, got airborne and crashed nose-first into the ground. The French-Canadian had been favourite to lift the 1982 Championship crown, as the Ferrari's powerful turbo engine was now mated to an efficient British-style chassis, and was generally the fastest car of the year.

▼ Fifth place finisher Derek Daly (*by rear wing*) discusses the demands of the new Detroit circuit as mechanics work on his Williams FW08 at the United States Grand Prix, Detroit, in 1982.

▲ Nelson Piquet (Brabham) (*centre*) was on the verge of collapse at the Brazilian Grand Prix, Rio de Janeiro, in 1982. To add to his woes, both he and second place finisher Keke Rosberg (Williams) (*left*), were subsequently disqualified, leaving Alain Prost (Renault) (*right*) as the eventual race winner.

▼ The Brabham team were embroiled in the "water-cooled" brakes controversy that led to the disqualification of Nelson Piquet (Brabham BT49D) from second place in the 1982 Brazilian Grand Prix.

Achieving Compromise

As it was, Keke Rosberg and Williams gave the old DFV engine its final championship glory as the Renaults again proved insufficiently reliable. But the message was clear: turbos were the future. Bernie Ecclestone's Brabham team had recognized as much and had gone into partnership with BMW, thereby merging specialist constructor chassis expertise with big factory financial and technical resources. It was to prove the way of the future, and the two types of entrant finally found peace as they flourished in Formula One together. The war was over.

As part of their imaginative campaign, Brabham also reintroduced the tactical pit stop to Formula One racing after a 25-year absence. Designer Gordon Murray realized that a low fuel/soft tyre compound car would more than make up for time lost in the pits by greater pace on the track. Soon everyone would be doing it, introducing a new competitive element to the races. Bosch introduced electronic engine management to the BMW engine, a critical step in making the turbo motor reliable, while BMW pioneered car-to-pits telemetry.

In 1983, Piquet took his Brabham-BMW turbo to a final race title

showdown with Renault's Alain Prost, and won. The Renault team stuttered on for another two seasons, but those doing the winning (McLaren-Porsche, Williams-Honda) were based on the blueprint of the Brabham-BMW partnership. Many years later Renault would finally win its first World Championship in partnership with Williams. Mutual success for specialists and factories was the new way.

▲ *(left)* Keke Rosberg drove for Fittipaldi, but failed to score any points over the 1981 season.

▲ *(right)* Alain Prost's Renault RE40 took pole position and won on Formula One's return to the Belgian circuit at Spa in 1983.

▼ Nelson Piquet's Brabham-BMW BT52 retired from the German Grand Prix at Hockenheim in 1983.

Changing of the Guard I

S oon after losing out in the 1983 title fight with Nelson Piquet, Alain Prost was sacked from Renault. It came at a moment when McLaren had not finalized who was going to drive their new Porsche turbo-powered car alongside Niki Lauda. Prost was quickly snapped up.

The Emergence of Prost

It was a fortuitous chain of events for Prost because almost by chance it put him into the fastest car of 1984. It soon became clear that the only thing standing between him and his first world title was Lauda in the sister car. Their in-team battles rescued Formula One from what might otherwise have been a dull year, such was the advantage enjoyed by the McLarens.

Lauda, with two World Championship titles to his name, had retired at the

end of 1979, saying he was "bored with driving round in circles". But he could stand only two years away from the cockpit and McLaren's Ron Dennis had lured him back for 1982. He was fourth on his first race back and it took only two more events before he was winning again. Still relying on DFV engines, the McLarens had been outpowered by the turbos in 1983 and Lauda had suffered a barren season. There were those who were wondering if he still had what it took, but in the

◄ **Alain Prost in 1984.**

▼ **Alain Prost's McLaren MP4/2 led the race, but a gearbox failure allowed his team-mate Niki Lauda through to take victory at the British Grand Prix, Brands Hatch, in 1984.**

final race of 1983, armed with the turbo, he had driven an extremely strong race, closing down on the leader before his engine expired.

Lauda Holds Off

As the 1984 season progressed, it soon became clear that Prost, as the younger, hungrier man, had a clear edge in speed. But Lauda had the guile and cunning of experience and he put it to superb use. They arrived at Estoril, Portugal, for the final round with nine points up for grabs and Lauda just 3.5 points ahead.

Prost qualified on the front row and quickly established a big lead in the race. Lauda had qualified a disastrous eleventh, and for much of the race was stuck in tenth, making no progress. As cars dropped out ahead, Lauda moved up to seventh. Assuming Prost was going to win this race, Lauda needed to finish second in order to clinch the title. He then began to get a move on, quickly disposing of Johansson, Alboreto and a young driver in his first season, Ayrton Senna. Now Lauda was third, with just Nigel Mansell's Lotus between him and a third world title. Lauda could make no gains on the Lotus, but at around three-quarter distance, Mansell was

suddenly lapping much slower – his brakes were failing. Lauda duly picked him off and cruised to his third title – five years after retiring!

The McLarens retained their dominant form into 1985, but Lauda suffered an appalling reliability record. By contrast, Prost glided from win to win, and took his first title by a comfortable margin. Only in Zandvoort, for the Dutch Grand Prix, was there an echo of 1984, when Lauda resolutely

held off a charging Prost in the closing stages to take his 25th – and final – Grand Prix victory. At the end of the season, Lauda retired once again, and this time he stayed out for good. It was a remarkable end to a remarkable two-part career.

▼ Niki Lauda's McLaren MP4/2B leads second-placed team-mate Alain Prost to take his twenty-fifth and final Grand Prix victory at Zandvoort, Holland, in 1985.

Prost vs Williams

By the tail-end of 1985, with Alain Prost well on his way to winning the title, the pace of the McLaren-Porsches was finally overcome by that of the Williams-Hondas, which won the final three races. For 1986 Williams enlisted double World Champion Nelson Piquet to partner Nigel Mansell, and thus made themselves favourites for the title. But that was to reckon without an intense personal battle between the two Williams drivers – and also the supreme skills of Prost.

The Race for Pace

The McLaren-Porsche successes had been built on a compact, fuel-efficient engine, the specification of which was largely laid down by McLaren designer John Barnard. As a paying customer that had exclusively commissioned the

▲ The Williams-Honda mechanics work on Nelson Piquet's car at the 1986 British Grand Prix at Brands Hatch.

engine from Porsche, McLaren were able to dictate what they needed rather more effectively than Williams, whose engines were supplied free of charge by Honda.

The Porsche's compact dimensions had allowed Barnard to design an aerodynamically efficient car. Since 1983, ground effect side venturis and skirts had been banned and so the emphasis came back to upper bodywork and maintaining a good balance between low drag and high downforce. Barnard's McLarens were tightly waisted around the engine, giving a healthy airflow to the rear wing of the car.

Fuel stops had been banned since 1984 and a fuel limit of 220 litres imposed. The trick for engine designers was to reach an efficiency level that still allowed a reasonable amount of turbo boost to be used. In this, the Bosch electronic control of the Porsche was supreme, and very much key to McLaren's world titles of 1984 and 1985. By 1986, however, Honda had caught up – and even surpassed – Porsche in this respect. Their engines were giving over 900bhp for the races and an astounding 1200bhp in high-boost qualifying trim. Williams had also begun to use the underfloor of the car,

◄ The dominance of the Williams-Hondas in 1987 was emphasized at the British Grand Prix. They were over a lap clear at the end.

▼ Nelson Piquet's Williams FW11B leads at the start of the 1987 Austrian Grand Prix at the Osterreichring. He finished second.

aft of the regulated flat-bottom area that extended to the rear axle line, to create more downforce. A sharp upwards sweep of the underbody formed a "diffuser" that created ground effect.

The Guile of Prost

Williams' year got off to a terrible start even before the season began as team boss Frank Williams was crippled in a road accident. He missed most of the year as designer Patrick Head stepped up to run the show. Mansell and Piquet fought like demons, fuelled by an intense dislike of each other. Prost's car wasn't usually as fast, but he won whenever the Williams faltered and sometimes – such as at Imola and Monaco – he simply out-drove and out-thought the Williams drivers. Going into the final round at Adelaide, Mansell had a six point lead. By lap 63, the three title contenders were in the

▶ Nigel Mansell wrestles his Williams FW11 back under control after his rear tyre blew on the Brabham Straight costing him the 1986 World Championship crown.

first three positions in the order of Piquet, Mansell, Prost. If it stayed like this Mansell would be Champion. But with 19 laps to go, Mansell's rear tyre exploded at around 300km/h (190mph). He wrestled the car to a stop, but his title was gone. Piquet was called in for a precautionary tyre change, leaving Prost to win the race and an unexpected second Championship.

The End of Turbo

In 1987, Williams extended their speed advantage over McLaren, and this time the title fight was between Piquet and Mansell, even though in winning the Portuguese Grand Prix, Prost broke Jackie Stewart's record of 27 wins. Piquet won the title after Mansell injured his back in a crash during practice for the penultimate round in Japan.

Changing of the Guard II

In a surprising development, Honda switched its supply of engines for 1988 from Williams to McLaren. As part of the deal, McLaren acquired the services of Ayrton Senna, who had driven a Honda-powered Lotus in 1987. In Senna and Prost, McLaren had possibly the most explosive driver line-up of all time. In Gordon Murray's MP4/4, it also had one of the greatest car designs. The combination produced the most dominant season enjoyed by any team in the modern era of Grand Prix racing. McLaren won 15 of the 16 races comprising the Championship.

It was the final year in which turbocharged engines would be allowed. The governing body had introduced a 3.5-litre non-turbo class in 1987 and then limited the turbos

yet further for 1988. They were not allowed to run any more than 2.5-bar boost (it had been limited to 4-bar in 1987) and they had to do a race distance on no more than 150 litres of fuel. For the non-turbo engines there was no fuel limitation. By 1989 the turbos would be outlawed. Controlling costs was put forward as the rationale behind this, but more likely it suited both the manufacturers and appeased the smaller teams, who had been calling for a turbo ban for years.

◀ Ayrton Senna in 1988.

▼ Senna's McLaren MP4/5 prepares to head out on to the track as team-mate Alain Prost waits in the pits.

▼ Gerhard Berger's Ferrari F187/88C leads team-mate Michele Alboreto to an emotional 1-2 home finish at the Italian Grand Prix, Monza, in 1988.

Although it had been the turbo-charged format that had attracted Renault to Formula One in 1977, and their subsequent success that had enticed other big manufacturers into the sport, those manufacturers had no intention of leaving Formula One just because of a return to normally-aspirated motors. Indeed, turbocharging was beginning to fall out of fashion for road-going engines as a new emissions law loomed, so the change of formula suited them fine. The turbo era had introduced them to Formula One and changed the scale of money in the sport, but its increasing global reach and image had more than justified the investment.

The massive financial investment by manufacturers had allowed the top teams to grow quickly in size and resources. Teams invested in wind tunnels and research and development programmes, and as quickly as new regulations were issued to control performance so new research-led solutions appeared. McLaren and Honda demonstrated as much in 1988 when even with the severe turbo engine restrictions, they dominated and easily eclipsed the non-turbo runners. Resources were now everything.

▲ Enzo Ferrari, racing driver from a different era and founder of the Ferrari marque, photographed c.1983.

Senna vs Prost

Senna clinched the Championship from Prost at the last round. In a parallel to the Lauda-Prost McLaren line-up of 1984, the younger, hungrier Senna was the quicker driver, but Prost had guile. It was an uneasy relationship from the start and would develop into a hostile one the following season.

The only 1988 race not won by McLaren was the Italian Grand Prix, where Senna, leading, was tripped up lapping a backmarker. With Prost already out, it gifted Ferrari a 1-2 result on home soil. Just a few weeks earlier, the team's founder, Enzo Ferrari, had died at the age of 90. He had been the last link to a very different age.

Prost Makes a Stand

The new non-turbo 3.5-litre era made little difference to McLaren and Honda's form. Like the returning Renault, who supplied the Williams team, Honda opted for a V10 engine, judging it the ideal compromise between the all-out power of a V12 and the compact packaging and economy of a V8.

Bitter Inter-team Rivalry

With up to 685bhp, the Honda was the most powerful engine in the field in 1989, leaving Senna and Prost to once again fight for the title. At Imola, the second round of the Championship, the pair fell out over a pre-race agreement not to fight into the first corner. Senna led clearly at the start and Prost didn't force the issue, but then the race was restarted after an enormous fiery accident for Gerhard Berger's Ferrari brought out the red flags. On the restart Prost led cleanly away, but this time Senna forced his way down the inside on his way to winning the race. Prost was furious, and from that moment on the pair were sworn enemies. The advantage see-sawed between them as the season played

out and, into the penultimate round in Japan, Prost was ahead on points. Senna needed to win here to keep the title fight open until the final round. The Frenchman dominated the first half of the race, but gradually Senna began to reel him in. On lap 47, just six from

▲ The moment when Alain Prost and team-mate Senna tangle to a standstill at the Japanese Grand Prix, Suzuka, 1989.

▼ After their collision, Alain Prost walks away mistakenly believing his car had been damaged in the accident.

▼ Senna pits for a new nosecone after his collision with Prost at Japan in 1989. Prost had already retired from the race.

the end, Senna made a move under braking into the chicane from a long way back. Essentially, it gave Prost the choice: either he gave way or had a collision. In no mood for compromises, Prost deliberately turned in on Senna and they tangled. They sat gesturing to each other in their stationary cars before Prost jumped out, falsely believing his machine had suffered suspension damage.

Senna restarted, returning to the track via the escape road, then pitted for a new nosecone, and came back to win the race. But he was subsequently disqualified for his use of the escape road, and the title went to Prost. Senna was furious, as was McLaren team boss Ron Dennis because Prost had already announced he was leaving McLaren for Ferrari in 1990. This result meant he would be taking the number one (reserved for the World Champion), with him. But the war between Prost and Senna was not over yet.

Technology 1989

Ferrari 640

Ferrari came back strongly in 1989, with a radical new John Barnard-designed car that Nigel Mansell and Gerhard Berger took to three victories. Powered by a V12 engine, its biggest innovation was a semi-automatic clutchless gearbox worked by electro-hydraulics.

Gear paddles on the back of the steering wheel – one for up, the other for down the box – replaced the conventional gear lever. It meant the cockpit could be narrower, to the benefit of the aerodynamics, and the mechanism could change the gears

faster than any driver. It also meant the driver could have two hands on the wheel at all times, which on certain types of corner with heavy braking into a tight apex, found him a lot of time.

It was an innovation that was widely copied, and it is now a standard feature of all Formula One cars.

◀ Gerhard Berger was thankful for the Ferrari 640's strength after surviving a huge impact at Imola in 1989.

▼ Berger didn't enjoy quite the same success with the 640 as Nigel Mansell. The car proved quick but unreliable initially.

Prost and Senna: War

he separation of Prost and Senna into separate teams did nothing to dilute the intensity of their battles in 1990. On the contrary, it now gained an even sharper edge. It was a finely-matched season between the two of them. Senna was the world's fastest driver aided by the Honda V10, still the most powerful engine. His nemesis Prost enjoyed the benefits of a Ferrari that was a little down on power but which had a clear handling advantage.

Neck and Neck

Senna began the season strongly, but Prost hit back with three consecutive mid-season victories. One of these, in Britain, was at the expense of his team-mate Nigel Mansell who was commanding the race until his gearbox played up. In an emotional outpouring afterwards, Mansell announced that he was going to retire at the end of the

▲ Ayrton Senna (*left*) and Alain Prost end up in the gravel after their run-in at the Japanese Grand Prix, Suzuka, in 1990.

▼ Senna (*left*) goes down the inside of Prost at Suzuka in 1990 with no intention of lifting off for the looming corner.

▼ Senna (*right*) and Prost walk back to the pits after retiring from the 1990 Japanese Grand Prix.

▼ Ayrton Senna at Monaco in 1991. Victory here was part of a campaign that took him to his third – and final – world title.

year. He was unhappy at the way Alain Prost had walked into what had been Mansell's team and been able to centre it around him.

A win for Prost in Spain made it five victories to the six of Senna, and then came Japan, the scene of their famous altercation the year before. Senna set pole, slightly quicker than Prost. The Brazilian then complained that the grid layout left him on the dirty side of the track, which would make him potentially slower off the line than Prost. He asked that the sides be changed, so he could benefit from his pole position. He was livid when the request was refused.

With this and their accident the year before as a backdrop, Senna had a ruthless plan if, as he feared, Prost was able to out-accelerate him away from the lights. Prost duly got ahead at the start, and the pair of them headed down to the first corner, braking from around 225km/h (140mph). Or at least Prost braked. Senna did not even lift the accelerator, and in a cynical move hit the back of the Ferrari, taking them both off into the gravel trap and retirement from the race. Now, with just one race to go, Prost could no longer catch his rival's points score.

► Winner Nigel Mansell at Silverstone in 1991. He pushed Senna close for the Championship as preparation for 1992.

Senna was World Champion for the second time.

Mansell had since "unretired", having been talked into returning to the Williams team which had enjoyed a promising 1990, with Riccardo Patrese and Thierry Boutsen scoring a win apiece in the improving Renault-engined car. It was a good move: the Ferrari effort imploded in 1991, while

the Williams-Renault gradually emerged as the fastest car of all. Mansell was able to push Senna's now V12 Honda-powered McLaren hard, but Ayrton was able to hang on for title number three. After falling into complete disarray, the Ferrari team sacked Prost two races before the season finished for being publicly critical about his car. He took a sabbatical the following year.

Gizmos to the Fore

Williams had followed Ferrari's early lead in developing a semi-automatic electro-hydraulic gearbox in 1991. Their chief aerodynamicist Adrian Newey had also come up with a highly efficient chassis. What Newey wanted to do now was make the next step – active ride. After much haranguing of technical director Patrick Head, Newey was finally given the go-ahead to develop what would turn out to be the dominant machine of 1992.

Active Ride

As long ago as 1983 active ride had been tried by Lotus, but the technology of the control systems of that time were insufficiently sophisticated. In 1987, both Lotus and Williams had won races with active ride cars, but at the time there didn't seem to be enough benefit over conventionally-sprung cars, and the developments were shelved.

By the early 1990s, the control systems were much improved and the cars were more pitch-sensitive than ever before – their aerodynamic effectiveness varied a lot according to the pitch of the car. There was an

▲ Adrian Newey, Williams chief designer, who was responsible for the all-conquering Williams FW14B.

▼ Nigel Mansell, winner of the Brazilian Grand Prix, 1992. Mansell took the FW14B to victory in the first five races that season.

enormous increase in aerodynamic performance to be had by keeping the ride height of the cars constant at all times. Active ride was perfect for this. Instead of springs and dampers, the suspension featured computer-controlled hydraulic actuators that would react in a split-second to the loads put on the car, and keep the ride height constant at all times, eliminating pitch, dive and roll.

The resultant Williams FW14B was a devastating tool. Mansell won the first five Grands Prix of 1992 and took nine victories during the season, both record-breaking statistics. He clinched the world title at the Hungarian Grand Prix, with five races still to go.

Early in 1992 Williams had taken the precaution of signing Alain Prost for 1993, and Prost took over leadership of the team as Mansell failed to agree financial terms and left to go Indycar racing. Mansell was replaced by test driver Damon Hill.

Traction Control

Not only did every serious team have active ride by 1993, but traction control

was an almost universal feature too, whereby computers would cut power to the wheels when excessive wheelspin was detected. In some cars, notably the Benetton B193, this system was combined with an automatic "launch control" system; the driver just pressed buttons to "arm" the system, then another as the lights changed and the car would automatically make the optimum getaway. The Benetton also featured four-wheel-steer. Williams introduced anti-lock ABS braking to their cars part-way through the season, while McLaren was working on a programme that, when perfected, would give different chassis settings from corner to corner.

While the other teams may have caught up with Williams in 1993 in the number of electronic gizmos used, the aerodynamic efficiency of the FW15 and the power of its Renault V10 made it by far the fastest car, which enabled Alain Prost to clinch his fourth title fairly comfortably. He took his 51st and final Grand Prix victory at the German Grand Prix at Hockenheim to set a record that would stand for some years. At the end of that season Prost retired.

▲ Damon Hill in the Williams FW15C takes the chequered flag for his first Grand Prix victory at the Hungarian Grand Prix, Hungaroring, in 1993.

◀ Race winner Nigel Mansell at the Mexican Grand Prix, Meixco City, 1992. Mansell set a new world record that year of nine wins in one season.

▼ Race winner Alain Prost in the Williams FW15C at the San Marino Grand Prix, Imola, Italy, in 1993.

The Senna Tragedy

yrton Senna, the world's greatest driver, was killed live on television on 1 May 1994. Just the previous day, Roland Ratzenberger had perished at the same Imola track. These were the first driver fatalities at a Grand Prix for 12 years. While this emphasized the great safety strides that had been made, the shocking events of Imola shook Formula One into a new safety initiative as the sport's right to exist came under scrutiny in a way unseen since the Le Mans tragedy of 1955.

De-humanizing the Sport

The 1994 season had started on a controversial note with the banning of "driver aids". Traction control, launch control, ABS braking, active suspension, and pits-to-car telemetry that enabled settings to be changed from the pits while the car was on the track, were all deemed illegal. The governing body, headed by Max Mosley, felt that the gizmos were de-humanizing the sport, damaging its public appeal. Concurrently, refuelling pit stops were reintroduced.

Senna, newly signed for Williams-Renault, had struggled in the opening two races against the Benetton-Ford of Michael Schumacher. Ever since making a startling Formula One debut at Spa in 1991, the German had been considered the man most likely to inherit Senna's

▲ Ayrton Senna in the Williams FW16 follows the painfully slow safety car after the startline crash at the San Marino Grand Prix.

▼ Senna embarks on his final lap before tragically losing his life in an accident on lap six at Imola, 1 May 1994.

▼ Roland Ratzenberger lost his life the day before Senna, at Imola. The Austrian was in his first season of Formula One.

Shapers:

Max Mosley

As President of the sport's governing body, the FIA, since 1991 Mosley has been extremely pro-active on the safety issues of the sport, and has successfully fended off an EEC initiative that threatened to wrest exclusive control of the sport away from the FIA. Through the FIA, Mosely has also initiated a vigorous safety testing procedure for road car manufacturers in an effort to transfer safety lessons learnt in racing to the road.

An urbane lawyer, he is the son of former English Fascist leader, Sir Oswald Mosley. He took up racing in the 1960s, competing as high as Formula Two, and in 1969 he co-founded March Engineering, which entered Formula One the following year. The team won three Grands Prix in the 1970s, and the company became a highly successful customer race car producer.

▲ Max Mosley, President of the FIA. He pushed through extensive safety measures after Imola in 1994.

Mosley was a key member of FOCA, and in the early 1980s fought hard alongside Bernie Ecclestone, wrestling the FIA for control of the sport. The poacher became gamekeeper when he was elected as former foe Jean-Marie Balestre's replacement in 1991.

throne as the world's number one. The early races of 1994 confirmed as much as Senna struggled with a car suffering an aerodynamic flaw and lacking the traction and stability of Schumacher's car. The change in regulations appeared to have slowed Senna's car more than Schumacher's.

Death at Imola

Senna was leading Schumacher at Imola when the race came under the jurisdiction of the safety car, soon after the start, in order that debris from a startline accident could be cleared up. Upon the resumption of racing, Senna was pushing extremely hard to keep Schumacher at bay when he lost control through the flat-out kink of Tamburello. He hit the retaining wall

at around 210km/h (130mph), and a suspension part flew off and pierced his helmet, inflicting fatal injuries.

At the Monaco Grand Prix, where Karl Wendlinger went into a coma following impact with a protective barrier, Max Mosley announced a series of regulation changes to address the safety issue. Stepped-bottom regulations limiting ground effect were imposed from the very next race, together with a pit lane speed limit.

From 1995, engine capacity would be reduced to 3 litres and cockpits had to feature protective raised sides. The FIA's safety programme has been ongoing since the deaths at Imola in 1994, with a series of ever-tougher crash tests and compulsory safety features introduced on a regular basis.

▼ A scorching start helped Michael Schumacher's Benetton to victory in the 1994 French Grand Prix.

Damon's Debacles

Following the death of Ayrton Senna, the 1994 season distilled into a controversial duel between Benetton's Michael Schumacher and Williams' Damon Hill. The German was widely acknowledged now as Formula One's greatest exponent, while the early aerodynamic problems of the Williams were quickly sorted to make it Formula One's fastest car.

Life After Senna
Schumacher had taken victory in the first four rounds before Hill made his seasonal breakthrough, with victory in Spain. Spookily, it echoed his late father Graham's achievement of 1968, when victory at the same race had acted as a much-needed tonic for a team devastated by the loss of its number one driver. Here, Damon did much the same thing for Williams. For all that, Schumacher astonished by finishing second in a car that for much of the race was stuck in fifth gear.

At the British Grand Prix that year, Schumacher was given a draconian race ban for the relatively minor infringement of overtaking on the warm-up lap. This was later changed to a two race ban! Combined with his disqualification from victory in the Belgian Grand Prix – because the underfloor wooden plank, which ensured the regulation stepped-bottom rules were met, had been ground away

▲ Damon Hill (*left*) and Michael Schumacher in the midst of a robust battle for the lead, Belgium, 1995.

◄ Schumacher's professional foul on Hill, Adelaide 1994, ensured the German took his first world title.

▼ Michael Schumacher tries a daring move inside Damon Hill at the 1995 Portuguese Grand Prix at Estoril.

▼ Race winner Michael Schumacher in the Benetton B195 at the 1995 Monaco Grand Prix, Monte Carlo.

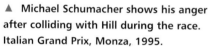

▲ Michael Schumacher shows his anger after colliding with Hill during the race. Italian Grand Prix, Monza, 1995.

when he spun on a kerb – it somewhat artificially made the final round in Australia a title-decider.

Schumacher and Hill quickly pulled away from the rest of the field, both stretching themselves to their very limits. It was Schumacher who cracked first, glancing the wall before rejoining the track. This had happened out of Hill's sight, and as he then made a dive for the inside at the next corner, Schumacher turned in on him and terminally damaged the Williams' suspension. Schumacher was champion

▲ Schumacher discusses tactics with technical director Ross Brawn (*centre*) and Pat Symonds (*left*) at Silverstone in 1994.

▼ Schumacher and Benetton completely dominated the 1995 championship, frequently humiliating Hill and Williams.

under the most controversial circumstances in what had been an intensely controversial season.

There was to be no doubting the outcome in 1995 though. Benetton was newly equipped with a Renault engine like that in the Williams, which nonetheless retained its status as Formula One's fastest car. Despite this, Schumacher and the Benetton team consistently out-performed Hill and Williams, taking nine victories on the way to a comfortable title. Schumacher and Benetton technical director, Ross Brawn, repeatedly won races through superior pit stop strategies, as they formed an incredibly close working relationship.

Schuey Joins Ferrari

After winning two consecutive World Championships with a relatively unfancied team, what next was there for Michael Schumacher? It would have been quite straightforward to have negotiated a place at Williams, who had the fastest car and biggest depth of technical talent. It would probably have been the work of a moment to make himself part of Mercedes-Benz's ambitious Formula One plans in partnership with the mighty McLaren team. What he did instead was accept motorsport's biggest challenge: he transferred to Ferrari, the biggest name in Formula One, but a team in disarray that hadn't been a championship contender for years.

▲ Ferrari President Luca di Montezemolo (*left*) and team manager Jean Todt (*right*): architects of the Ferrari revival.

Ferrari Steadies Ship
Scuderia Ferrari had been through some turbulent times since the death of its founder Enzo Ferrari in 1988, but a measure of management stability seemed to arrive following Luca di Montezemolo's appointment as president of the company in late 1991. A man close to the Agnelli family of parent company Fiat, Montezemolo had been Ferrari's Formula One team manager in the 1970s, but since then had risen through the corporate ranks. No longer could he devote his time

▼ Despite an uncompetitive car, Michael Schumacher won three times in the 1996 Ferrari, aided here by the rain at Barcelona.

▼ Michael Schumacher with Ferrari technical director Ross Brawn (*left*) at the 1997 French Grand Prix at Magny-Cours.

to the running of the Formula One operation, and for this role he recruited Jean Todt, a man with a brilliant reputation as a team organizer honed first in rallying, then with the Peugeot sportscar squad.

The Long Road to Success

With money no object, Todt wanted the best available and so he recruited Schumacher. What the German found when he arrived was a team still rebuilding. By the standards of a top Formula One team, the on-site technical facilities were lacking. Technical director John Barnard had set up a satellite operation in Britain where he designed and built the cars. When Schumacher tested the new V10-engined F310 model he realized immediately he was in for a difficult season. Its handling was woeful, and its reliability worse. Somehow he managed to win three races with it in 1996, but at no stage that season was he or the Ferrari team in Championship contention. For 1997, Barnard had produced a much better

car but his Ferrari contract was coming to an end. Schumacher pushed to have the team recruit the man with whom he had shared success at Benetton, Ross Brawn. With him came Benetton chief designer Rory Byrne. The triangle was reunited. From that moment, Ferrari just got better.

▲ Michael Schumacher in the Ferrari F310B took second at the 1997 German Grand Prix.

▼ Ferrari's line-up (*left to right*): Paulo Martinelli (engine chief), Michael Schumacher, Ross Brawn (technical director), Jean Todt (sporting director), Rubens Barrichello, and Rory Byrne (chief designer).

▼ Michael Schumacher's Ferrari F310B finished second at the San Marino Grand Prix at Imola in 1997.

Second Generation Champions

With Michael Schumacher struggling in his first year at Ferrari, 1996 represented Damon Hill's best chance yet for a world title, equipped as he was with the latest Williams-Renault model, the FW18.

Damon Comes Good
He made full use of the opportunity with a series of very polished performances, but often he was made to work very hard by his new team-mate, a Formula One rookie by the name of Jacques Villeneuve. It made for a fascinating inter-team battle, two second-generation Formula One drivers fighting not only each other but the memory of their late and legendary fathers, Graham Hill and Gilles Villeneuve.

Villeneuve Jr had already created a sensation in the United States, where he had won the Indycar championship and the Indy 500. He made a startling Formula One debut in the Australian Grand Prix, bagging pole position and looking set to win until a late slide across the grass damaged a radiator and handed victory to Hill. Damon's greater experience showed over the season with a more consistent level of competitiveness, and he clinched the Championship in Japan with a mature drive to victory. Villeneuve, though, created some moments of spine-

▲ Jacques Villeneuve and Damon Hill at the British Grand Prix, Silverstone, in 1996.

tingling drama, never more so than at Estoril's final corner, when he did the unthinkable by overtaking Michael Schumacher round the outside.

Villeneuve vs Schumacher
Controversially, Williams didn't renew Damon Hill's contract for 1997, and he was replaced by Heinz-Harald Frentzen. This left Villeneuve to battle

with Schumacher's Ferrari for the world title. Their fortunes see-sawed through the season, and the showdown came in the final at Jerez, Spain. There, Schumacher was leading but Villeneuve, on new tyres, was catching fast after his pit stop. Electing to surprise the Ferrari driver, he made a move down the inside from a long way back. By the time Schumacher realized what was happening, it was too late. He turned in on the Williams, but succeeded only in bouncing off it and landing beached in the gravel trap. It left Villeneuve free to cruise to the title, though there was controversy in that he allowed the McLarens of Mika Häkkinen and David Coulthard to pass him in the late stages in exchange for their help earlier in the race, when they did not attack him in the midst of his battle with the Ferrari.

Ironically, one of the chief architects of this Williams World Championship, chief aerodynamicist Adrian Newey, had already left the team and headed for McLaren. This coincided with Renault withdrawing from official participation in the sport, leaving the Williams team's strength much reduced for the future. It would be some time before it recovered from such a double blow.

◄ "I've made it at last!", Damon Hill in the Williams FW18 becomes the 1996 World Champion at the Japanese Grand Prix.

▲ Hill with the 1996 World Championship trophy after winning the Japanese Grand Prix at Suzuka, 1996.

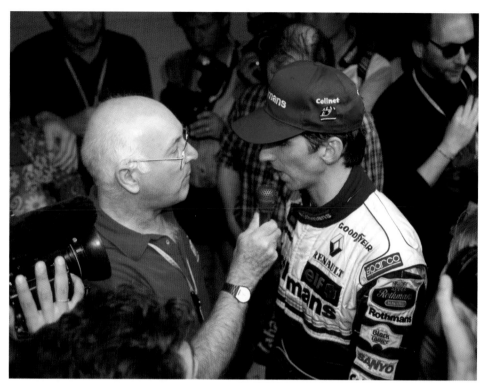

▲ Murray Walker (*left*), in his final Formula One race commentary for the BBC, interviews Hill, the new 1996 World Champion.

▼ Michael Schumacher turns his Ferrari into the passing Williams of Jacques Villeneuve, in a vain attempt to take his rival out of the race.

The McLaren Wonder Years

Everything conspired in McLaren's favour for the 1998 season. Formula One's technical regulations were radically altered just as brilliant aerodynamicist Adrian Newey arrived at the team. The Mercedes engines powering the cars were at the peak of their development, and the Bridgestone tyres gave them a performance advantage over the Goodyears on Michael Schumacher's Ferrari.

McLaren Overcome Restrictions

The FIA had been concerned about rising lap speeds, and their solution for 1998 was two-fold. Firstly, the maximum width of the cars was reduced from 2 metres to 1.8, so reducing the available ground effect-generating under-floor area, as well as limiting the mechanical grip. Secondly, slick tyres were outlawed and replaced by grooved tyres, giving a smaller surface area of rubber on the track. The effect was to make the cars more

▲ McLaren designer Adrian Newey.

▼ The McLarens of Häkkinen and Coulthard lead at the first corner of the Australian Grand Prix, Melbourne, in 1999.

skittery, and initially they were as much as 2 seconds per lap slower than they had been in 1997, though further technical development soon began to reduce this deficit.

The Cool Finn

McLaren's MP4-13 model brilliantly resolved the issues arising from the new regulations, and gave Mika Häkkinen and David Coulthard a flurry of victories. Ferrari fought back though, and came on very strong in the second half of the season. Michael Schumacher went to the final round in Japan with a chance of the title, but a dominant drive from Häkkinen sealed it for the Finn and his team.

Mika had a rather easier time of it in 1999 when Schumacher broke a leg in a crash at Silverstone. However, the strength of Ferrari showed when their number two driver, Eddie Irvine, took the title battle all the way to the final round. But again Häkkinen sealed it.

▼ David Coulthard in the McLaren MP4–14 at the Monaco Grand Prix in 1999.

▲ Mika Häkkinen and the McLaren MP4-13 took third place at the French Grand Prix at Magny-Cours in 1998.

▼ Häkkinen took third at the Malaysian Grand Prix at Sepang in 1999, this time driving the McLaren MP4-14.

Technology 1998

McLaren MP4-13

The new narrow-track/grooved tyre regulations of 1998 gave designers the chance to fundamentally re-evaluate the requirements rather than fine-honing existing themes. The McLaren design team, led by Adrian Newey, did this better than anyone else.

The tyre grooves substantially reduced the amount of rubber in contact with the track surface, placing mechanical grip at much more of a premium than before. Previously, aerodynamic performance had over-ruled all else, but McLaren actually surrendered some of that in order to claw back mechanical grip lost to the new regulations. In partnership with tyre suppliers Bridgestone, they opted for bigger front tyres, which more than made up in terms of grip what had been lost through increased drag. They gave the car a lower nose section too, reasoning that the limitation of under-body airflow would be more than compensated by the lowering of the centre of gravity.

Powered by a Mercedes-Benz V10 engine that produced 800bhp, it was the fastest car, and gave the McLaren team its first world title for seven years.

▼ Häkkinen's McLaren MP4-13 at the Hungarian Grand Prix in 1998.

The 21-year Itch

Michael Schumacher's dream of bringing world championship glory back to Ferrari finally came true in 2000, five years after joining. In each of those years the team were successively more competitive, as designer Rory Byrne and technical director Ross Brawn fine-honed their use of the huge resources at their disposal. The Ferrari F1-2000 was the first car to be created from the on-site wind tunnel. A 90-degree vee angle in its V10 lowered the centre of gravity from the previous motor's 80-degree angle. New materials enabled the cylinder heads to be smaller and lighter.

For each of the previous three years, Ferrari had to develop their way to mid-season competitiveness after beginning the season trailing either Williams or McLaren on speed. This car was fast right from the off – and that made the critical difference. Schumacher won the first three Grands Prix of the year and over the course of the season took a

▲ Ferrari's Michael Schumacher is elated after winning at Japan in 2000, while Mika Häkkinen (*far left*) and David Coulthard (*right*), for McLaren, look somewhat less so.

▼ The start of the Japanese Grand Prix, 2000. Häkkinen gets the jump on Schumacher.

further six. He clinched the title by winning an incredibly tense duel in Japan against his only rival, McLaren's Mika Häkkinen.

This was the first time since Jody Scheckter's 1979 success that a Ferrari driver had won the world title. The

▼ Luca di Montezemolo (*right*), president of Ferrari, talks with Hiroshi of Bridgestone tyres at the San Marino Grand Prix, 2002.

team president Luca di Montezemolo was present in Japan to witness the culmination of the work he had begun when he took up the post nine years earlier, when the team had been in

complete disarray. His dream had converged with that of Schumacher, Brawn and Byrne, the three men who had already won world titles together at Benetton.

▲ Michael Schumacher, in the Ferrari F1-2000, leads team-mate Rubens Barrichello at the British Grand Prix, Silverstone, in 2000. Schumacher took third place in the race.

Shapers

Ross Brawn

Brawn became best-known as the man whose brilliant pit strategies at both Benetton and Ferrari won countless races for Michael Schumacher. But as technical director of Ferrari, he was also an organizational genius with the necessary technical background to structure the Italian team in a way that brought the longest period of sustained success in its long history.

Brawn had been a highly successful designer before his partnership with Rory Byrne enabled him to step back. He began his motor racing career in 1976 as a research and development engineer at Williams. There, he learned an enormous amount from resident design chief Patrick Head in all aspects of Formula One car design. After spells as chief designer at Beatrice and

Arrows, he was recruited by Tom Walkinshaw's TWR team and designed the fabulously successful Jaguar XJR-14 sports racer. When Walkinshaw bought into the Benetton Formula One team, Brawn went with him, and worked alongside Rory Byrne for the first time. Here, the golden partnership took form. When Michael Schumacher joined the team, the triangle was complete.

For only one year – 1996, when Schumacher joined Ferrari but Brawn and Byrne stayed at Benetton – was the partnership broken up. Never have three such brilliant individuals worked together for so long in Formula One. That in itself goes a long way to explaining their success.

◄ Ferrari technical director Ross Brawn.

Ferrari Break All Records

Ferrari and Michael Schumacher actually strengthened their hold on Formula One during 2001 and 2002. The German superstar gave the Italian marque the greatest run of sustained success in its long and glorious history, and in the process he made himself the most statistically successful Formula One driver of all time.

In the 2001 Hungarian Grand Prix he clinched his fourth world title and equalled the record of 51 Grand Prix victories secured by Alain Prost eight years earlier. At the very next race, at Spa in Belgium, Schumacher surpassed that record. By the end of 2002 he had secured his fifth World Drivers' Championship, equalling the all-time record of Juan Manuel Fangio, and his career race win tally stood at an astonishing 64. Ferrari also took its fourth consecutive World Constructors' Championship in this year, a feat it had never before achieved. In winning 11 Grands Prix in 2002 alone, Schumacher also set the benchmark for the number of victories during a season, beating a record he had previously shared with Nigel Mansell.

◀ Ferrari's Michael Schumacher makes his trademark victory leap on the podium after winning the Spanish Grand Prix in 2002. McLaren's David Coulthard (*right*) finished in third place.

▼ (*left*) Rubens Barrichello's Ferrari F2002 (*below*) inches past team-mate Michael Schumacher to take an unexpected victory at the United States Grand Prix, Indianapolis, 2002.

Behind the awesome numbers lay Ferrari's ever-greater technical resource, and the brilliant use made of it by Rory Byrne and his design team. But in 2001 the Ferrari, while the fastest all-round car, was frequently out-powered by the BMW motor in the Williams chassis. When Formula One rookie Juan Pablo Montoya aggressively took his Williams past Schumacher's Ferrari to lead the Brazilian Grand Prix, many heralded the arrival of a new challenge to Schumacher's dominance. But despite several more exciting dices with the champion, Montoya's competitive circumstances actually declined in 2002 as the Williams FW24 proved no match for the F2002 Ferrari.

At the 2002 Italian Grand Prix, BMW proudly announced that its engine was the first in Formula One to break the 19,000rpm barrier. At this astronomical speed, the 3-litre V10 motor was achieving around 880 horsepower, making it the most powerful engine in Formula One.

BMW had re-entered Formula One with Williams in 2000. Also returning at that time was French tyre company Michelin, absent since 1984 and looking to break Bridgestone's dominance. With Williams in 2001 and 2002, and McLaren in 2002, Michelin returned to the race winner's circle, but the dominance of the Bridgestone-shod Ferrari meant such victories were perhaps fewer than their product warranted, a situation Michelin shared with BMW.

It was an illustration of how the various facets of the sport were being dwarfed by the scale of Ferrari's dominance – to the extent that calls were being made to liven up what was becoming an overly predictable show. Ferrari had courted controversy in Austria in 2002 when it instructed its second driver, Rubens Barrichello, who had led all the way, to move over in the last few hundred yards and hand victory to Schumacher. After the championship was sewn up several other races were stage-managed between the Ferrari drivers, such was their dominance. It was a development that did not go down well with fans of the sport.

Among moves being considered by the governing body were weight penalties for success and a new system of driver contracts that could see them change team for each race. That such radical departures were being contemplated illustrated the staggering extent of Ferrari's superiority.

▲ Juan Pablo Montoya in the Williams-BMW FW24 *(left)* and team-mate Ralf Schumacher, *(right)* squeeze out Schumacher's Ferrari F2002.

▼ Michael Schumacher *(left)* collects his Drivers' Championship Trophy at the FIA Prize Gala, while Jean Todt *(centre)* collects the Constructors' Trophy for Ferrari.

Schumacher Leads the Way

Ferrari's Michael Schumacher broke the all-time World Championship record in 2003 by scoring his sixth title. The previous record – Juan Manuel Fangio's five – had stood for 46 years. However, in contrast to the one-way dominance of Ferrari in 2002, the 2003 season was a classic, with a superbly tight battle for the World Championship between four drivers from three different teams.

Schumacher's 2002 dominance had led to falling television viewing figures. The governing body's response was a new set of sporting regulations for 2003. The points scoring system was revised, with a smaller gap between first and second and points down to eighth place instead of sixth – all designed to keep the title fight running longer. One-lap qualifying, whereby each driver took to the track on his own and had only one chance in which to set a time that would determine his grid position, was introduced. Furthermore, fuel could not be added to the car between qualifying and the race – meaning that there was a trade-off to be made between qualifying speed and pit stop strategies. These latter two changes had the effect of mixing the grids up slightly. But the

biggest contribution to the closely-matched 2003 competition was the improvement in the speed of the Williams-BMW and McLaren-Mercedes teams, aided considerably in both cases by the big advances made by their tyre supplier, Michelin. The rival Bridgestone

▲ **Juan Pablo Montoya's win at Monaco kick-started the Williams team's 2003 season.**

◄ **McLaren's Kimi Raikkonen took his first Formula One victory in the 2003 Malaysian Grand Prix, and pushed Michael Schumacher for the world title throughout the season.**

tyres, so dominant the year before, were left trailing, and this left Ferrari facing up to a very tough job.

At the halfway point, with five victories, Schumacher appeared to be on course to correct his shaky start. As it transpired, he didn't win again for some time. The Williams team had raced its new FW25 model from the beginning of the year. The breakthrough came at Monaco, where Juan Pablo Montoya took an impressive victory. From this point onwards, Williams was usually the fastest car around. In fact, the biggest problem for the team was that its two drivers, Montoya and Ralf Schumacher, were so closely matched that they were taking points from each other as well as from rival drivers.

Meanwhile, McLaren's Kimi Raikkonen kept scoring high places, adding to his victory in Malaysia. McLaren had modified their 2002 car, with which to start the season, and the plan had been to replace it with the radical MP4/18. Development hitches with that car, and the continued success of the MP4/17D, meant that it never did appear. Raikkonen's strong finishing record kept him in Championship contention right until the final round.

Ferrari's Rubens Barrichello won the British Grand Prix in a superlative display and sealed Schumacher's title by winning in the final round in Japan. In the two races prior to this, Schumacher had returned to winning form.

Giancarlo Fisichella gave Jordan a freak victory in a wet, accident-shortened Brazilian Grand Prix. The season's other winner was newcomer Fernando Alonso, driving for Renault. Aged just 22 years and 26 days, Alonso became the youngest ever Grand Prix winner, and the first from Spain, when he won at the Hungaroring. Having withdrawn as an engine supplier after winning the 1997 World title with Williams, Renault had returned as a team in 2000 when it bought out Benetton. Under the control of former Benetton boss Flavio Briatore, Renault became increasingly competitive, and Alonso's result marked its first team victory for 20 years.

2004: Schuey Still Unstoppable

Ten years after his first Championship, Michael Schumacher enjoyed his most dominant season yet to take world title number seven. Armed with Ferrari's new F2004 and much improved rubber from Bridgestone, Schumacher won all but a handful of the races, smashing his own record for the number of victories in one season.

There was disappointment for 2003 title contenders Williams-BMW and McLaren-Mercedes as they each came up with sub-standard cars. McLaren put this to rights in the second half of the year with a revised MP4/19B, and Kimi Raikkonen ended the drought for the team by winning the Belgian Grand Prix.

Renault's Jarno Trulli took his first Grand Prix victory after many years of trying with a dominant victory at Monte Carlo, but his later performances were disappointing and he was released from his contract before the season ended, paving the way for the return of former champion Jacques Villeneuve.

Villeneuve's former team-mate Jenson Button enjoyed a competitive season for BAR-Honda. He led several races and finished in third place in the World Championship, the highest-placed non-Ferrari driver.

▲ Fernando Alonso in the Renault R24 at the inaugural Bahrain Grand Prix, the third round of the 2004 World Championship.

▼ Michael Schumacher's Ferrari F2004 during qualifying for the Monaco Grand Prix, Monte Carlo, in 2004.

Alonso Advances, Schuey Stymied

The Schumacher/Ferrari era came shuddering to a close during the 2005 championship as the Italian team struggled to adapt their car to a new set of regulations that prohibited tyre changes during the races. Michelin appeared better able to cope with the demand for long-life tyres than their rival manufacturer Bridgestone, and with Ferrari the only leading team on the latter brand, its performance suffered. Instead there was a thrilling contest for the driver's championship between two young heir apparents to Michael Schumacher's long-held throne – Renault's Fernando Alonso and McLaren's Kimi Raikkonen.

Alonso eventually secured the title with two races remaining and – at 24 years, one month and 27 days – became the youngest world champion in the sport's history, beating the record held by Emerson Fittipaldi for the previous 33 years. This added to Alonso's existing records as the youngest ever Grand Prix winner (set in 2003) and youngest ever pole position setter (also 2003). He also became the first world champion from Spain.

Along with the change in tyre regulations came further restrictions on the aerodynamics as part of the

▲ **Renault's Fernando Alonso celebrates with the team after becoming the youngest ever champion. His third place at the 2005 Brazilian Grand Prix was enough to secure the title with two races remaining.**

▼ **David Coulthard gets Red Bull's inaugural season off to a surprise start. After qualifying fifth on the grid at the Australian Grand Prix in 2005, he finished fourth in his RB1.**

ongoing effort to control the speeds of the cars. Front wings had to be mounted higher, rear wings mounted farther forwards, restricting their efficiency, while the downforce-inducing diffusers on the underfloor of the cars were also restricted. It resulted in much more intricate upper body surfaces as aerodynamicists desperately clawed back the lost downforce and by the end of the season the cars were lapping almost as quickly as in 2004.

McLaren's resident aerodynamics genius, Adrian Newey, resolved the new demands brilliantly and the McLaren-Mercedes MP4-20 was the fastest car of the season by a comfortable margin. However, it was also quite frail, and Raikkonen retired or was penalized in far too many races because of the reliability problems of the new car. By contrast Alonso's Renault R25 wasn't quite as fast but had bullet-proof reliability built in. Furthermore, the former Benetton team was strategically brilliant, often conjuring up results that flattered the car in much the same way it had when Schumacher was its driver in the mid-1990s.

Schumacher and Ferrari won just once and in the most controversial circumstances imaginable. They were the victors in the American Grand Prix

▶ Michael Schumacher shows his displeasure after Takuma Sato drove his BAR-Honda into the back of the former champion's Ferrari at the Belgian Grand Prix, 2005.

at Indianapolis, which was severely tarnished by the enforced withdrawal of all but six of the cars because of a potentially dangerous problem with the Michelin tyre through the high speed banking of turn 13. Enraged spectators ripped up their tickets and left in their thousands as the race got underway and the 14 Michelin-shod cars drove from the dummy grid direct to their garages to retire. The incident seriously threatened to once again end the on/off relationship between the United States and Formula One, and caused much ill-feeling towards the sport.

Every other race apart from the anomalous American event was won by either a Renault or McLaren-Mercedes and the respective team-mates to Alonso and Raikkonen – Giancarlo Fisichella and Juan Pablo Montoya – each contributed towards their teams' victory tallies. Montoya's year was compromised by an early-season shoulder injury but he came on ever-stronger towards the end of his first season with McLaren.

At the end of an under-achieving season, Williams and BMW ended their five-year partnership. The German car manufacturer bought out the independent Sauber team and set up as a Formula One constructor in its own right, hoping to achieve more success. This left Williams to continue into 2006 with a non-factory engine from Cosworth. It all underlined the renewed tension between road-car

manufacturers and a governing body that wished to see Formula One remain with independent teams at its core. As such, and with the covenant by which the sport is run – the Concorde agreement – coming up for renewal at the end of 2007, there was much jockeying for position between the two factions and their conflicting visions of how the sport should progress into the future.

◀ Kimi Raikkonen's McLaren-Mercedes MP4-20 (centre) takes the lead from Renault's Giancarlo Fisichella (left) and comes under pressure from Fernando Alonso (right) at the first Turkish Grand Prix, 2005.

▼ The start of the controversial United States Grand Prix, 2005. The withdrawal of the Michelin-shod cars due to safety concerns left only the six cars using Bridgestone tyres.

A–Z
Constructors

In 1895, Panhard-Levassor took one of the pioneering, new-fangled motor cars it was trying to sell to the public, and modified it with an override switch on its engine-speed governer. Thus was created the first winning racing car.

Although a divergence quickly formed between road cars and racing machines, for many decades racing car constructors tended to be the same teams as those who built customer cars for the public. In the late 1920s, specialist teams began to form, relying on racing for their existence. Some, like *Scuderia Ferrari*, relied on the hardware of manufacturers. Others, like Maserati, began building their own machines. But still the factories were the dominant constructors.

But by the end of the 1950s, Formula One was being dominated by a new breed that were constructors in a more literal sense. Pioneered by Cooper, these teams assembled their cars using bought-in components. This formed the blueprint for Formula One constructors for the next 20 years. But with the commercial success of Formula One came the return of the big car-producing factories – but this time with a difference; they usually entered the sport in partnership with an existing specialist team.

This mix of specialist understanding with factory financial clout characterizes the Formula One constructor of today.

◀ The drama of the pit stop.
Mika Salo's Toyota lays rubber.

Alfa Romeo

Within months of producing its first road-going cars in 1910, this Turin-based company was involved in racing to publicize its products. It reached the front rank of the sport in the 1920s when, aided by one of its drivers, Enzo Ferrari, it poached key racing technical staff from the bigger Fiat concern.

Chief among these staff was the brilliant designer, Vittorio Jano, who created the company's first successful Grand Prix car, the P2. Introduced in 1924, it won the inaugural World Manufacturers' Championship the following year. Jano's P3 of 1930 was the first genuine single-seater Grand Prix car and remained successful for many years, sealing its immortality

◄ The Alfa 158 "Alfetta" was conceived pre-war as a voiturette racer but had a successful post-war career as a Championship Grand Prix winning car.

▼ Bruno Giocomelli's Alfa leads the 1980 USA Grand Prix. He was dominating the race until the coil failed at three-quarter distance.

Alfa Romeo

Country of origin	Italy
Date of foundation	1910
Active years in Grands Prix	1924–39, 1946–51, 1979–85
Grand Prix victories	10 (+ 42 pre-championship)

when Tazio Nuvolari took it to victory against the far more advanced German cars in the 1935 German Grand Prix.

The German domination eventually led to Alfa concentrating on voiturette ("small car") racing in the late 1930s, with an elegant 1.5-litre machine dubbed the "Alfetta". Designed by Giocchino Colombo under the direction of Alfa's now racing manager, Enzo Ferrari, it got a new lease of life post World War II when Formula One

was created along the lines of the old voiturette formula. It won Giuseppe Farina the inaugural World Drivers' Championship in 1950, with team-mate Juan Manuel Fangio following up with the 1951 title.

Thereafter the company withdrew from Formula One. It returned as an engine supplier to Brabham in 1976 before committing itself to an unsuccessful constructors role from 1979 to 1985.

Auto Union

T his company was created in 1932 with the merger of four German car manufacturers. Its boss, Baron Klaus van Oertzen, was a racing fan and took the company into Grand Prix racing after the Nazi party offered subsidies for any company representing the Fatherland in the sport.

Van Oertzen commissioned former Mercedes engineer Ferdinand Porsche to design a car for the new 750kg formula of 1934, and he came up with a stunning mid-engined V16 design. Like the rival Mercedes, its independent suspension was a novelty and proved to be the trigger that allowed previously unheard of horsepower to be utilized. Hans Stuck won races in the car's first season and a development of it dominated 1936 with Bernd Rosemeyer. When the latter driver was

Auto Union	
Country of origin	Germany
Date of foundation	1932
Active years in Grands Prix	1934–39
Grand Prix victories	15 pre-championship

killed attempting a world speed record for the company, he was replaced by the legendary Tazio Nuvolari, who enjoyed much success in 1938 and 1939 in new V12 supercharged versions.

However, World War II left the constituent parts of the company in different countries, under different regimes, splitting it up. Today's Audi is one of the descendants.

▲ H. P. Muller in an Auto Union V16 during the European Mountain Championship round at Grossglockner in 1939.

▶ Tazio Nuvolari in action at Donington Park, England, in 1938, winning the 250-mile International Grand Prix at an average speed of 129.53km/h (80.49mph).

Benetton

The famous Italian fashion clothes manufacturer first appeared in Formula One as a sponsor of the British Tyrrell team in 1983; founder Luciano Benetton was attracted by the image-boosting profile of the sport.

After a further spell sponsoring the Alfa Romeo team, Benetton decided to become a Formula One constructor in its own right when the opportunity of purchasing the British former Toleman team presented itself in time for the 1986 season. This, it was felt, represented better value than simply being a sponsor, and the team itself was already up and running. The resident designer Rory Byrne proved himself a highly gifted man and his BMW turbo-powered B186 was competitive enough to give the team – and its driver Gerhard Berger – their first Grand Prix success at Mexico 1986.

Sporadic success followed until the team was put on a more solid footing with the recruitment in 1989 of Flavio Briatore, a friend and business associate of Luciano Benetton. In partnership with Ford, competitiveness grew. For 1990, racing entrepreneur Tom Walkinshaw bought a share in the team, bringing with him designer Ross Brawn. Although Walkinshaw subsequently left, the technical partnership of Brawn and Byrne proved exceptionally fertile, especially so when blended with the driving gifts of the startling newcomer Michael Schumacher. The German won his first Grand Prix for the team in 1992, and two years later

▼ Gerhard Berger gives Benetton its first Grand Prix victory at Mexico in 1986.

Benetton

Country of origin	United Kingdom
Date of foundation	1986
Active years in Grands Prix	1986–2001
Grand Prix victories	27 (+ 1 Constructors' Cup)

the team secured the World Drivers' Championship. This feat was repeated in 1995, this time with Renault power in place of Ford.

For the 1996 season, Schumacher left Benetton for Ferrari, and within a year Brawn and Byrne had followed him there. This rather decimated the team, despite the return of Gerhard Berger. The Austrian took Benetton's final Grand Prix victory at Hockenheim in 1997. The team continued for another four years, but in 2000 it was bought by Renault. In 2002, the Benetton tag was dropped in favour of the name of the parent company. The Renault Formula One cars are still built in the former Benetton premises in England.

◄ Michael Schumacher celebrates victory in the 1995 Pacific Grand Prix.

▼ Schumacher's 1995 win at Aida clinches Benetton's second successive championship.

Brabham

▼ Jack Brabham at the 1966 French Grand Prix, becoming the first man to win in a car bearing his own name.

After winning two World Championships with Cooper in 1959 and 1960, Jack Brabham found the team's impetus running out in the seasons that followed. For 1962, he decided to branch out on his own, and his Brabham team became one of the core British teams – using bought-in components in the way Cooper had pioneered – that came to dominate the sport in that era.

Brabham initially built customer racing cars for the lower formulae, partly to fund the Formula One team. The cars were all designed by Ron Tauranac, a friend of Jack Brabham's from their days in Australian dirt-track racing. They soon proved highly effective. Dan Gurney gave the team its first Grand Prix victory in France in 1964. In the same country two years later, Jack became the first man to win a Grand Prix in a car bearing his own name. This was the foundation for winning the World Drivers' and Constructors' Championships of that year. In 1967, Brabham's second driver Denny Hulme gave the team its second successive championship double.

◄ The Brabham BT3 made its Grand Prix debut in the hands of the team owner, Jack Brabham. He retired on lap nine of the 1962 German Grand Prix with a broken throttle linkage.

Brabham retired at the end of 1970, and returned home to Australia. The team was initially bought by Tauranac, but soon after it was sold again, this time to Bernie Ecclestone, who had managed the late Jochen Rindt, a former Brabham driver. Ecclestone gave the team a new lease of life, aided by the brilliant young South African designer, Gordon Murray.

In winning the 1981 world title, Nelson Piquet gave the Ecclestone-era Brabham its first title success. It was a feat the team repeated in 1983, this time in partnership with BMW. This association saw Brabham pioneer the use of electronic engine management and pits-to-car telemetry. Furthermore, in 1982, Murray re-introduced the tactical pit stop to Formula One racing, after a gap of three decades.

Ecclestone sold the team in 1987. It stuttered on, ever less successful, until going out of business in 1992.

Brabham	
Country of origin	United Kingdom
Date of foundation	1962
Active years in Grands Prix	1962–92
Grand Prix victories	35 (+ 1 Constructors' Cup)

◄ Brabham reintroduced tactical pit stops to Formula One, as here, with Nelson Piquet making a stop at Silverstone in 1983.

BRM

British Racing Motors was the brainchild of Raymond Mays, a successful racing driver of the 1930s, who had also initiated the ERA company of that time. With the post-war BRM project, Mays devised the idea of a motor racing trust, with financial and resource contributions from British industry. The resulting car would advertise British engineering excellence to the rest of the world through the medium of Formula One racing. To this end, designer Peter Berthon came up with a hugely complex machine, with an engine of 16 tiny cylinders, which complied with the 1.5-litre supercharged regulations for Formula One.

The engine was said to have a power potential of up to 600bhp, which, if true, would have made it a match for the all-conquering Alfettas of the time. Unfortunately, the car proved horrifically unreliable and, after interminable delays, it fell into obsolescence when the technical regulations were changed. What had been billed as a world-beater became a laughing stock.

In the mid-1950s, industrialist Alfred Owen bought out the company, retaining Mays as a consultant. For the 2.5-litre formula a much simpler car, the P25, was built, and Jo Bonnier won the team's first Grand Prix in Holland 1959. The 1.5-litre formula of 1961–65 marked the team's glory years. With the

▲ **Graham Hill, here in the 1962 French Grand Prix, gave BRM its one and only world title in 27 years of trying.**

BRM	
Country of origin	United Kingdom
Date of foundation	1948
Active years in Grands Prix	1950–77
Grand Prix victories	17 (+ 1 Constructors' Cup)

▼ **Jo Siffert dominated the 1971 Austrian Grand Prix for BRM. It was the team's last fully competitive season.**

mid-engined V8 P57 of 1962, Graham Hill won the World Championship. In 1965 Jackie Stewart took his first Grand Prix victory with the team after a dramatic dice with team-mate Hill.

Early mistakes were repeated when the 3-litre formula was introduced in 1966, as the team produced a heavy and inefficient H16. A V12 engine originally designed for sports car racing brought a measure of respectability back to the team in the early 1970s, but by the middle part of that decade, the team – under the direction of Owen's brother-in-law Louis Stanley – was under-funded and lacking direction. Its last Grand Prix appearance came in 1977.

Bugatti

Ettore Bugatti was an eccentric self-trained Italian artist-cum-engineer who gave the world the fabulous and beautiful Bugatti line of cars, built in Molsheim in the Alsace region of France in the 1920s and 1930s. These were exquisite and exotic machines to which the rich and famous aspired. Ettore also designed and built devastatingly successful racing cars, notably the Type 35, introduced in 1924 and still winning Grands Prix in the early 1930s.

Before setting up Bugatti cars in 1910, Ettore had received commissions from manufacturers such as Peugeot and de Dietrich, and during World War I he designed a 16-cylinder aero engine, the internal design of which influenced racing car builders in the early 1920s. The Type 35 was the first truly successful Bugatti Grand Prix car, taken to major victories by a whole host of drivers. Its twin-cam derivative, the Type 51, continued the winning lineage. But the German domination of the mid-1930s left Bugatti unable to respond, at a time when it was going through internal difficulties.

▲ The type 59 model took over from the 35/51 late in 1933 but was soon overwhelmed by the new German cars.

◄ Driver Maurice Trintignant (in white hat and raincoat) at the new Bugatti T251 Formula One car tests in 1956.

Ettore's son Jean, a talented stylist for the company, was seen as Ettore's natural heir but was killed testing a sports car in 1939. Ettore himself died in 1947. The company continued from one financial crisis to another but managed to create a radical mid-engined Formula One car, the 251, in 1956. However, the car was under-developed and, ultimately, unsuccessful and the company died soon after.

Bugatti	
Country of origin	France
Date of foundation	1909
Active years in Grands Prix	1921–39 and 1956
Grand Prix victories	35 pre-championship

◄ Bugatti's type 35/51 ran at the frontline of Grands Prix from 1924 until 1933. For a time the car formed the backbone of Grand Prix racing.

Cooper

T he Cooper team forever changed the convention of where a Formula One car's engine was situated – and a lot more besides. After a breakthrough victory with a tiny mid-engined car at the Argentina Grand Prix in 1958, the days of front-engined cars were numbered. It also heralded the domination of Formula One by specialist British assemblers, using bought-in components, making the sport less reliant on road car-producing factories.

Father and son Charles and John Cooper ran the team from a garage in Surbiton, near London. They initially set up in the early post-war years as manufacturers of cars for the then new Formula 500 series, a low-cost formula for cars powered by 500cc motorcycle engines. With engines designed for chain-drive, the logical place to put the engine was in between the driver and the rear wheels. The Coopers took this F500 convention all the way to Formula One, the breakthrough for them being when engine suppliers Coventry Climax came up with a twin-cam engine, giving the Cooper reasonable power for the first time.

Jack Brabham took works Cooper-Climaxes to victory in both the 1959 and 1960 World Championships, and Formula One changed forever. No

▲ In winning the 1960 British Grand Prix, Jack Brabham put Cooper well on the way to its successive World Championship.

Cooper	
Country of origin	United Kingdom
Date of foundation	1948
Active years in Grands Prix	1952–68
Grand Prix victories	16 (+ 2 Constructors' Cups)

▼ Cooper's final race victory came with Pedro Rodriguez in 1967 in South Africa.

longer would the sport's health be at the whim of road car manufacturers, as Cooper's method divorced the technicalities of the cars from road car convention, and at the same time opened up Formula One to specialists lacking the financial resource to fund engine design and build programmes.

Ironically, other British specialist constructors created in a similar vein, such as Lotus, Brabham and McLaren – the latter two companies created by former works Cooper drivers – leapfrogged Cooper. Using Maserati engines, the team took its final race victory with Pedro Rodriguez in South Africa in 1967, and withdrew at the end of the following year.

Delage

This French constructor sealed its place of immortality within the sport when, in 1927, it won all four major Grands Prix comprising the season, with its lead driver Robert Benoist.

Founded in 1905 by Louis Delage, the former chief of development at Peugeot, the company began by producing road-going cars. It then entered voiturette ("small car") racing for publicity. The company's first Grand Prix car came in 1912, and was highly sophisticated for the time, with desmodronic valve actuation and a five-speed gearbox. Two years later, René Thomas took a Delage to victory in the Indianapolis 500.

Delage	
Country of origin	France
Date of foundation	1905
Active years in Grands Prix	1912–27
Grand Prix victories	7 pre-championship

Grand Prix success came in the 1920s, first with a V12-engined car and later with the straight-8 that came to dominate in 1927. However, the development costs of these cars came close to bankrupting the company and it withdrew from the sport. It was later bought-out by Delahaye, and Louis Delage was pensioned off. He died in relative poverty in 1947.

▲ Robert Benoist in the 1924 French Grand Prix held in Lyons. He drove the 2-litre V-12 Delage 2LCV to third place. Note the driver's protective face mask.

▼ The Delage 1.5 litre model in action at the 1927 British Grand Prix at Brooklands.

Duesenberg

By winning the French Grand Prix in 1921, Jimmy Murphy made Duesenberg the first American manufacturer to triumph in a major European race. But the company's racing credentials had already been established by success in America, notably the Indianapolis 500. The cars were the beautifully-engineered creations of the brothers Fred and August Duesenberg. Unusually, they began in racing before diversifying into road car production, with some of the most luxurious and sought-after machines of the 1920s and 1930s.

Divergence in technical regulation between American and European racing after 1921 meant that Duesenberg did not stay around to build on its successful European foray, and instead went on to dominate the Indy 500.

Duesenberg	
Country of origin	USA
Date of foundation	1914
Active years in Grands Prix	1921
Grand Prix victories	1 pre-championship

▲ *(top)*
The Deusenbergs shocked France by winning the French Grand Prix at Le Mans in 1921.

▲ *(above)*
Jimmy Murphy in a Deusenberg at the French Grand Prix, Le Mans, 1921.

◄ **Tommy Milton in a Duesenberg at Indianapolis in 1920.**

Ferrari

Enzo Ferrari had been a works driver with Alfa Romeo in the early 1920s, and subsequently became its general "fixer", recruiting key technical staff from Fiat, for example. He took an Alfa Romeo dealership and formed a race team, Scuderia Ferrari, which for a time became the official race entrant of Alfa Romeo. He finally split from Alfa in 1939, with the intention of building his own cars.

In 1948, the first Grand Prix Ferrari appeared. It enjoyed some success in 1949, but this was largely due to the absence of the previously dominant Alfa Romeo. When the latter team returned in 1950, Ferrari was again reduced to also-ran status. The breakthrough came the following year, when Ferrari's designer Aurelio Lampredi came up with a 4.5-litre normally-aspirated car that, through its fuel-thriftiness, was able to defeat the supercharged Alfas at the British Grand Prix, driven by José Froilán González.

The first World Championships came in 1952 and 1953 with Alberto Ascari, and there followed further titles for Juan Manuel Fangio in 1956 and Mike Hawthorn in 1958. A new 1.5-litre formula for 1961 saw Ferrari more prepared than anyone else and the red cars dominated the championship, driven by Phil Hill and Wolfgang von Trips. John Surtees took another title for the team in 1964. There was then a barren period until the mid-1970s, when the combined forces of designer Mauro Forghieri and driver Niki Lauda brought a four-year sequence of victories

◄ The Monaco Grand Prix was one of five victories that Niki Lauda took in 1975 on his way to the first Ferrari World Championship for 11 years.

Ferrari	
Country of origin	Italy
Date of foundation	1946
Active years in Grands Prix	1948–present
Grand Prix victories	182 (+ 13 Constructors' Cups)

that yielded two Drivers' and three Constructors' World Championships.

Jody Scheckter and Gilles Villeneuve brought the team another Constructors' title in 1979, with Scheckter also taking the Drivers' honours. Ferrari then took the 1982 and 1983 Constructors' Championships before another barren period, as the British teams overtook them in the depth of their technology.

Enzo died in 1988, after which the team came under the full control of Fiat, which had bought into it in 1969. A period of success came in 1989–90, with innovative John Barnard-designed cars, whose chassis were conceived and built in Britain, but it was the arrival of former manager Luca di Montezemolo in 1991 that led to more sustained success – and with cars that were once more of Italian manufacture.

Michael Schumacher joined in 1996, and with the arrival of his Benetton technical partners, Ross Brawn and Rory Byrne, a new era dawned. They clinched the 2000 championship, and dominated in 2001 and 2002. Record-breaking fifth and sixth consecutive world constructors' titles came in 2003 and 2004.

▼ Michael Schumacher's victory in the 2002 British Grand Prix helped Ferrari to its fourth consecutive constructors' title.

Fiat

▼ Felice Nazzaro driving for Fiat at Targa Florio in 1907.

Right from its birth at the turn of the 20th century, the Milan-based Fiat concern saw racing as essential to its image and its technical education. It graduated to international motor racing in 1904 and its ambitious philosophy was demonstrated when it pioneered the progression from side-valve to overhead-valve engines. It was later an early convert to the overhead-camshaft motor.

In 1907, Fiat won all three major races of the season with their lead driver Felice Nazzaro, backed up by Vincenzo Lancia, both of whom had been inherited when Fiat bought the Ceirano company in 1900. Fiat remained a major force in Grand Prix racing up until the outbreak of World War I.

Newly informed by the technology drive of war, Fiat again set the technological pace in the early 1920s, thanks to a brilliant group of engineers, directed by Guido Fornaca but also including Vittorio Jano. The philosophy

Fiat	
Country of origin	Italy
Date of foundation	1900
Active years in Grands Prix	1904–24 and 1927
Grand Prix victories	12 pre-championship

behind their straight-eight engine of 1921 proved highly influential for decades to come. Fiat was the dominant Grand Prix force in 1922 and 1923 (when it was the first to win a Grand Prix with a supercharged engine), but by 1924 rival teams had begun to poach its technical staff. This triggered the company's withdrawal at the end of the year. It made a brief –

and victorious – comeback in 1927, but generally concentrated on its production range thereafter. In 1969, the company acquired Ferrari as one of its specialist satellites.

▼ David Bruce-Brown in his Fiat 14.1-litre model at the 1912 French Grand Prix at Dieppe.

Hesketh

▼ James Hunt ended his and Hesketh's first year of Formula One with second place and a lap record in the USA Grand Prix.

The British Lord, Alexander Hesketh, brightened up the Formula One scene in the mid-1970s with his eccentric but successful team that was built around the talents of designer Dr Harvey Postlethwaite and leading driver James Hunt.

Hesketh himself projected the image an of an aristocratic dilettante – and his team remains the only one to have included a grand piano as part of its race weekend cargo – but Postlethwaite and Hunt were gifted and committed. The three parties found themselves thrown together by circumstance. Separately, neither Hesketh nor Hunt had enjoyed great success in the junior categories of the sport but decided to graduate to Formula One together in 1973. To this end, a car was purchased from the March team, and with it came promising March boffin, Postlethwaite.

With Postlethwaite's modifications, the March performed far better than the similar cars of the works team, culminating in second place and a lap record for Hunt in the 1973 American Grand Prix. For the following year Postlethwaite designed a new "Hesketh" car. At the 1975 Dutch Grand Prix Hunt took the Hesketh to a fairy tale victory over the mighty Ferrari of that year's World Champion, Niki Lauda.

But it was close to the final hurrah. Even a Lord didn't have money to burn indefinitely and, with no significant commercial backers, the team released Hunt and Postlethwaite and resorted to running pay-drivers for a further couple of seasons before pulling out completely.

Hesketh	
Country of origin	United Kingdom
Date of foundation	1972
Active years in Grands Prix	1973–78
Grand Prix victories	1

▼ Hunt withstood pressure from Lauda's Ferrari to win the 1975 Dutch Grand Prix.

Jordan

▼ Damon Hill gave Jordan its first Grand Prix victory at a wet 1998 Belgian Grand Prix.

G uided by the entrepreneurial Irishman Eddie Jordan, this team made what seemed at the time to be a financially suicidal bid to graduate to Formula One in 1991, and, remarkably, they made it work.

With lots of wheeling and dealing and a very respectable car from designer Gary Anderson, Jordan made its mark during its first Formula One season of 1991 after a successful decade in the junior ranks of Formula Three and Formula 3000. In between scoring points that took them to fifth place in the Constructors' Championship, Jordan took a lap record in Hungary, had one of its drivers, Bertrand Gachot, jailed for assault, introduced Formula One to the talents of Michael Schumacher – and then immediately lost him to a bigger team.

Hovering for the first few years on the brink of financial disaster, Jordan steadily built itself up, helped by partnerships first with Yamaha then Peugeot. Rubens Barrichello gave the team its first pole position at Spa in 1994. Four years later this was the

◄ Giancarlo Fisichella won the team's fourth victory in the rain of Brazil in 2003.

venue of Jordan's first Grand Prix victory, as Damon Hill and Ralf Schumacher drove their cars to a Jordan 1-2.

Heinz-Harald Frentzen scored two more victories for the team in 1999 and was an outside championship contender until the penultimate race of the year. The team never quite recaptured such form and in 2004 Eddie Jordan sold out to new owners who one year later re-named the team and thereby brought the history of Jordan Grand Prix to a close.

Jordan	
Country of origin	United Kingdom
Date of foundation	1991
Active years in Grands Prix	1991–2005
Grand Prix victories	4

◄ Bertrand Gachot giving the Jordan team its Formula One baptism at the 1991 USA Grand Prix in Phoenix, Arizona.

Lancia

ounded by former Fiat racer Vincenzo Lancia in 1906, this company initially concentrated on road-going cars. By the time it first entered Grand Prix racing in 1954, Vincenzo's son Gianni was running it.

Gianni Lancia commissioned legendary design genius Vittorio Jano to create a car for the new 2.5-litre Formula One regulations of 1954. This machine, dubbed the D50, showed beyond doubt that the elderly Jano's creative flair was still very much intact. He favoured an engine with the then highly unusual V8 format and used it to form part of the car's structural stiffness – the first time this had been done in Formula One and not to be seen again for another 12 years. He also gave the car long and low pannier fuel tanks, separate from the main

▼ Alberto Ascari won the 1955 non-championship Valentino Grand Prix, the Lancia team's only victory.

Lancia	
Country of origin	Italy
Date of foundation	1906
Active years in Grands Prix	1954–55
Grand Prix victories	0 (1 non-championship)

body, keeping changes in the centre of gravity to a minimum as the fuel load decreased.

Alberto Ascari gave this car its debut at the 1954 Spanish Grand Prix, the final race of the season, and set pole position by over a second. He was leading the race comfortably when the car broke down. Lancia began 1955 as joint favourites with Mercedes for the world title, but financial problems and the death of Ascari in a testing accident with Ferrari meant it all turned sour. Lancia withdrew at the end of the year, never to return. The assets of the Grand Prix project were then handed over to

Ferrari, who, using modified versions of the D50, dominated the 1956 World Championship. The cars continued into 1957 before being replaced by a model of Ferrari's own design.

▲ Ferrari used the Lancia D50 to win the 1956 World Championship with Fangio.

▶ The 1954 Lancia D50 was the most technically advanced car of its time, but its full potential was never realized.

Ligier

▼ Jacques Lafitte got Ligier off to a flying start in 1979 with victories in the first two races of the season.

This all-French team entered Grand Prix racing in 1976 after serving its apprenticeship in sports car racing. It was the project of Guy Ligier, a colourful character who had been a rugby international as well as a privateer Formula One driver in the 1960s.

Backed by French tobacco company Gitanes and using the Matra V12 engine, Ligier enjoyed a surprisingly competitive first season, thanks largely to the design talents of former Matra engineer Gerard Ducarouge and the driving of Jacques Laffite. Together they won their first Grand Prix in Sweden 1977.

A switch to the Cosworth DFV engine and a superb new ground-effect chassis from Ducarouge gave the team a fantastic start to 1979, as Laffite dominated the opening two races. Team-mate Patrick Depailler then won in Spain and at the halfway point of the year both drivers were in contention for the championship. But Depailler was then injured and the car lost its form, leaving Laffite fourth in the championship. Further success came in 1980, Laffite and Didier Pironi often showing the

Ligier	
Country of origin	France
Date of foundation	1970
Active years in Grands Prix	1976–97
Grand Prix victories	9

▼ Lafitte in the first Formula One Ligier "teapot" taking fourth place at the USA Grand Prix West, Long Beach, in 1976. This was the team's first points finish.

JS11/15 model to be the fastest around, but consistency again proved elusive. Laffite was a championship contender in 1981, now with Matra power once more, but again ended up fourth.

A liaison with road car producer Talbot lasted from 1981 until the end of 1982 after which the glory days of the team were effectively over. It went through several changes of ownership and even won one more race – with Olivier Panis at Monaco 1996 – but was never again a competitive force. At the end of 1996 the team was acquired by Alain Prost and renamed after him.

Lotus

▼ Stirling Moss gave Lotus the first of its 79 Grand Prix victories at Monaco in 1960.

Colin Chapman was the founding genius of Lotus, arguably the most influential and innovative team in Grand Prix history.

The team entered Formula One in 1958, and Stirling Moss took the marque's first victory at Monaco in 1960 in a car privately owned and entered by Rob Walker. Shortly afterwards, Moss was badly injured when his suspension broke at Spa, and a reputation of frailty would dog Lotus for much of the next couple of decades. The cars tended to either break or win.

The Lotus 25 of 1962 was the first Formula One car to feature monocoque construction. Jim Clark took it to Lotus' first World Championship in 1963 and followed it up with another in 1965, while a development of the car also won Clark the Indy 500 that year.

The Lotus 49 of 1967 used the new Cosworth DFV engine as a structural part of the car, another highly progressive feature. Small winglets and an upward-sweeping rear body on this car at Monaco in 1968 signalled the arrival of downforce in Formula One. Within a few races most of the field carried huge front and rear wings on stilts. The wedge-shaped Lotus 72 of 1970 resolved the conflicting requirements of downforce and low drag. The Lotus 78 of 1977 brought another quantum leap in aerodynamic downforce through the application of the ground-effect principle. The follow-up Lotus 79 dominated the 1978 World Championship. Five drivers – Clark, Graham Hill, Jochen Rindt, Emerson Fittipaldi and Mario Andretti – won world titles with Lotus.

▲ Jim Clark, here in the 1967 Belgian Grand Prix, won two World Championship titles for the Lotus team.

Lotus	
Country of origin	United Kingdom
Date of foundation	1956
Active years in Grands Prix	1958–94
Grand Prix victories	79 (+ 7 Constructors' Cups)

Chapman died from a heart attack late in 1982. The team never fully recovered, though it did subsequently enjoy a spell of success with Ayrton Senna in a Renault turbo-engined car. The last win came at Detroit in 1987. Once Senna left, success dried up, and the team went downhill before going out of business at the end of 1994.

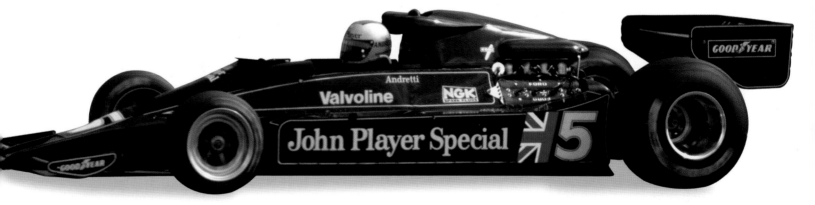

Maserati

Alfieri Maserati was the guiding force behind this specialist race car constructor, aided by four of his brothers. He established his Bologna garage and tuning business in 1914 but didn't build a "Maserati" car until 1926. This was when the Diatto company, which had commissioned him to design and build them a Grand Prix car, got into financial trouble, leaving him to take over the project. A gifted driver as well as engineer, Alfieri scored well with the car. Developments of it were ever-more competitive and by the early 1930s, Maserati was enjoying considerable success with drivers such as Achille Varzi and Tazio Nuvolari. Alfieri himself died in 1932 from a prostrate injury he received while racing, leaving the running of the business to brother Bindo.

The German domination of the mid- to late-1930s led Maserati to leave Grand Prix racing and compete instead in the voiturette ("small car") category. After World War II, this became Formula One, bringing Maserati back into Grand Prix competition. By this time, the company had been bought out by the Orsi family and relocated to Modena. After serving a

10-year service contract, the Maserati brothers left in 1947 and founded a new racing outfit, OSCA.

Maserati hardware formed the mainstay of early post-war racing as their cars proved highly popular with privateers. The works team enjoyed

Maserati	
Country of origin	Italy
Date of foundation	1926
Active years in Grands Prix	1926–39, 1946–58
Grand Prix victories	9 (+ 11 pre-championship)

considerable success in the pre-World Championship era with Alberto Ascari and Luigi Villoresi. It wasn't until 1953 that the team scored its first championship-status Grand Prix victory, with Juan Manuel Fangio in Italy.

For 1954's 2.5-litre formula, Maserati designer Giocchino Colombo designed the 250F. It won races immediately and, although it did not take the title until 1957, the car established itself as one of the all-time greats. Maserati was in financial difficulty by 1958 and withdrew from the sport to concentrate on the production of its exotic road-going sports cars, a line initiated by the Orsis earlier in the decade.

▲ The 1926 Maserati type 26.

◄ Juan Manuel Fangio in the Maserati 250F. The Argentinian ace served two spells with Maserati from 1952–1954 and 1957–1958. He took Maserati's first and only World Championship win in 1957.

Matra

▼ A puncture deprived Chris Amon's Matra MS120D of victory in France in 1972.

This French missile manufacturer entered the sport in 1964 when it took over the ailing Bonett sports car constructor, the founder of which was a friend of Matra chief, Marcel Chassagny.

Matra put engineer Jean-Luc Lagardère in charge of the new subsidiary and he enthusiastically committed to a long-term programme of competition, comprising Formula Three, Formula Two, and eventual graduation to Formula One. Backed by Elf, this came in 1968. The company had designed a new V12 engine for the project but hedged its bets by supplying a car to Ken Tyrrell, who fitted it with the dominant Ford Cosworth DFV V8 and had it driven by Jackie Stewart. The Cosworth-engined car proved more competitive than the Matra-powered one and Stewart only narrowly missed out on the World Championship that year.

For 1969 Matra withdrew its own team to further develop the V12, but Stewart and Tyrrell enjoyed a dominant season in the Matra-Ford, making Matra World Constructors' Champion in only its second year of Formula One. Ironically, it proved to be the team's final flourish of Formual One success.

A marketing tie-up with Chrysler France for a road car made the Matra-Ford politically unacceptable, and the Tyrrell arrangement came to an end.

▲ Jackie Stewart scored his fourth victory in five races in a Matra 1–2 finish at the French Grand Prix, Clermont Ferrand, 1969.

▼ Jean-Pierre Beltoise sits on the grid and finished in ninth place at the French Grand Prix, Rouen-les-Essarts, 1968.

Matra	
Country of origin	France
Date of foundation	1964
Active years in Grands Prix	1968–72
Grand Prix victories	9 (+ 1 Constructors' Cup)

Matra reintroduced its V12 engine but despite several competitive showings from 1970–72, it failed to win a Grand Prix. The company withdrew from the category at the end of 1972 to focus on sports car racing. Some years later, the V12 Matra engine got a taste of Formula One success, powering Jacques Laffite's Ligier to victories on three occasions between 1977 and 1981.

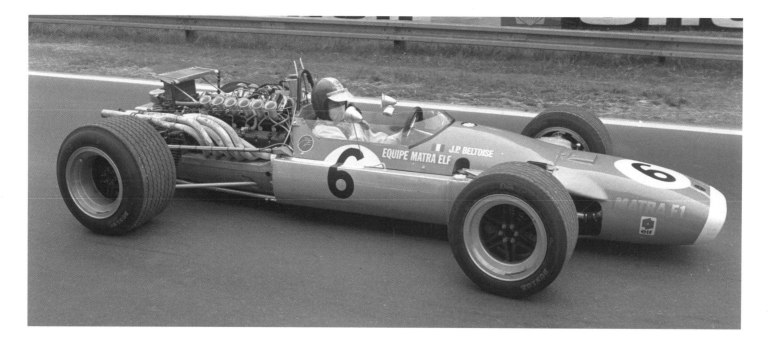

Mercedes

▼ German constructors Mercedes and Auto Union together dominated Grand Prix racing from 1934–39.

Gottlieb Daimler is co-credited with the invention of the motor car. He did not live to see the completion of the "Mercedes" model he was working on at the turn of the century. Mercedes was the name of the daughter of Emile Julinek, the Austrian importer for the company. The car's name change from Daimler came in recognition of how big a progression this 1901 model was over anything previously seen. When Mercedes officially entered competition in 1903, it quickly ended the domination of the French Panhard and Mors marques.

The company regularly came in and out of the sport as it developed new technologies that fed its production car and aero-engine programmes. It was the first team to race an overhead-cam engined car, in 1906, and it won the French Grand Prix of 1908 and 1914.

In 1923, Mercedes introduced the supercharger to racing but its next period of sustained success didn't come until the inauguration of the 750kg

Mercedes

Country of origin	Germany
Date of foundation	1901
Active years in Grands Prix	1903–08, 1914, 1926–39, 1954–55
Grand Prix victories	9 (+ 29 pre-championship)

formula of 1934 when, with Nazi party backing, Mercedes rewrote the rules of Grand Prix technology. With ever-more powerful cars that were soon reaching over 322km/h (200mph), the "silver arrows" – so named because of their bare aluminium bodies – dominated until the outbreak of World War Two.

It was 1954 before the company re-entered Grand Prix racing. It did so with the highly progressive W196, with Juan Manuel Fangio taking the car to victory on its debut in France. Fangio and Mercedes took the World title that year, and in 1955. Indeed, during two seasons of racing, the W196 was beaten on only three occasions. But at the end of the 1955 season, the company was forced to withdraw from the sport after one of its cars was launched into the crowd at the Le Mans 24 Hours sports car race, killing more than 80 of the spectators.

Following that catastrophe, it was to be a very long time before the company felt comfortable re-entering the sport. It did so first in sports car racing in the late 1980s, before entering Formula One with Sauber from 1993. After two years it switched its engine supply to the long-established McLaren team, and eventually this became one of the sport's greatest liaisons. McLaren-Mercedes dominated Formula One in 1998 and 1999, and continues to be a major force.

◄ Mercedes-Benz team-mates Stirling Moss (6) and Juan Manuel Fangio (2) lead the 1955 Monaco Grand Prix into the first corner.

Mors

Mors was one of the most successful pioneer racing manufacturers at the dawn of the sport in the late 19th and early 20th centuries.

Emile Mors, chief of one of France's leading telegraph equipment companies, founded the company in the 1890s and competed himself in some of the early city-to-city races. An injury in one of these events caused him to retire from competitive driving, but he employed others to do so for him. Using ever-more monstrous engines, Mors came to vie with Panhard as the fastest racing car of them all.

The Mors of Fernand Gabriel was victorious in the tragic Paris–Madrid

Mors	
Country of origin	France
Date of foundation	1897
Active years in Grands Prix	1897–1908
Grand Prix victories	11 pre-championship

race, in 1903, that caused city-to-city racing to be banned for all time. It was never to win a major event again. Mors built its last Grand Prix racing car in 1908 after failing to keep pace with technology advances introduced by more progressively engineered cars from the likes of Mercedes, Renault and Fiat. The company was later bought out by Citroën.

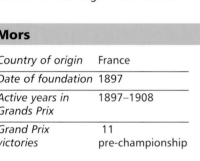

▲ *(right)* **The 1902 Paris–Vienna type Mors, drivern by Augières at Archères, near Paris. He set a new land speed record of 123.4km/h (77.13mph).**

▶ **The 1903 Mors "Dauphin" shows an early attempt at steamlining.**

McLaren

Kiwi Bruce McLaren left Cooper to form his own team in 1966. Within two years he had joined his former Cooper team-mate Jack Brabham in the exclusive club of men who have won Grands Prix in cars bearing their own name.

Tragically, Bruce never lived to see the colossus that his team came to be. He was killed testing a Can-Am sports car at Goodwood in 1970. His partner Teddy Mayer took over the running of the team – which was highly successful in Indycar and Can-Am racing, as well as Formula One – and steered it to its first World Championship, in 1974, with Emerson Fittipaldi and the Gordon Coppuck-designed M23 model. Two years later, James Hunt used an M23 in his dramatic title victory over Niki Lauda.

By the late 1970s, the team had lost its technical impetus, and its sponsor

◄ Bruce McLaren – here in third place – eventually won this race at Spa in 1968 for the team's first Formula One victory.

Marlboro arranged for a merger between McLaren and Marlboro's Formula Two team, Project 4, run by Ron Dennis. Dennis brought with him designer John Barnard who then produced the first carbon-fibre Formula One car, the McLaren MP4/1. This won a race in its first season and established the new era McLaren as a serious competitive force. World Championships followed with

TAG-Porsche power in 1984, 85 and 86, and with Honda in 1988, 89, 90 and 91. During the 1980s and 1990s McLaren, together with Williams, dominated the sport, with Niki Lauda, Alain Prost and Ayrton Senna bringing championship glory. A new partnership with Mercedes yielded titles in 1998 and 1999 with Mika Häkkinen. Since Häkkinen's retirement at the end of 2001, another Finn, Kimi Raikkonen, has led the team's challenge and he only narrowly lost out on the world titles of 2003 and 2005.

◄ Mika Häkkinen won the 1998 Monaco Grand Prix on his way to his first, and the team's tenth, drivers' title.

▼ Ayrton Senna leads eventual winner Alain Prost in the 1988 French Grand Prix. Their MP4/4s won 15 out of 16 races that year.

McLaren	
Country of origin	United Kingdom
Date of foundation	1966
Active years in Grands Prix	1966–present
Grand Prix victories	148 (+ 8 Constructors' Cups)

Panhard

A Panhard-Levassor was the very first winning race car, taking the finish of the 1895 Paris–Bordeaux–Paris more than five hours ahead of its nearest competitor. It was driven by one of the partners in the business, Emile Levassor. The other partner was Louis-René Panhard.

A friend of Levassor's had gained the French commercial rights to the German Daimler engine, leading to Panhard and Levassor diversifying from their core engineering business to car manufacture. Racing was recognized as essential in both improving technology and advertising the capability of the automobile in general. Indeed, Emile Lavassor was one of the driving forces in the early days of the sport.

Using ever bigger, more powerful engines, Panhard dominated the early city-to-city events, though eventually it

began to be challenged hard by rival, Mors. Like that company, Panhard failed to keep up with advances introduced by more progressive companies and, again like Mors, it built its last Grand Prix racer in 1908, the year that Louis-René Panhard died. Thereafter, guided by Panhard's sons, it concentrated on production cars until the 1960s, when Citroën bought it out.

Panhard	
Country of origin	France
Date of foundation	1895
Active years in Grands Prix	1895–1908
Grand Prix victories	22 pre-championship

▲ The very first winning racing car won the 1895 Paris–Bordeaux–Paris race but wasn't eligible for the prize money on account of it having only two seats!

▼ Lebron's Panhard in the Circuit des Ardennes race in 1905.

▲ Henry Farman in a Panhard-Levassor passing through Criel-sur-Mer, Dieppe, in the 1908 French Grand Prix.

Peugeot

Peugeot was already a very old company when the motor car was first invented, having begun as a steel works, producing everything from steel rods for insertion into fancy dresses to bicycles. It produced a steam car in 1889, but was soon converted to the benefits of the petrol engine by Gottlieb Daimler. Using Daimler-engined cars, Peugeot took part in the very first city-to-city races and later produced its own power units, designed by Louis Rigolout, who was also the company's nominated race driver.

Peugeot then lost interest in racing as it built up its production facilities. In 1906, a splinter group was formed, Lion-Peugeot, to produce bicycles and light cars. This company entered the new voiturette ("small car") class of racing, and became the dominant force there, with drivers Jules Goux, Georges Boillot and Paulo Zuccarelli. A 1911 reorganization brought the two companies back together and the racing core of the former offshoot planned its first full-size Grand Prix car. Designed by Ernest Henry, the 1912 Peugeot L76 model broke new technical ground in having twin overhead camshafts driving four valves for each engine cylinder.

It was a revolutionary concept, making up in technology what it conceded to its rivals in engine size – at 7.6 litres it was just over half the size of the 14.1-litre Fiat. After a closely matched race against the Fiat, Boillot took the car to victory in the 1912 French Grand Prix, and so brought the era of the racing monster to an end. Peugeot won again in 1913 and also took the American Indy 500 that year – something it repeated in 1916 and 1919. Henry left the company during

◄ **Dario Resta won at Indianapolis for Peugeot in 1916. The progressive design of the car influenced a whole generation of imitators.**

▼ *(left)* **Goux took fourth at Indianapolis in 1914 but had won the event at his and Peugeot's first attempt in 1913.**

▼ **René Thomas in the Peugeot L3 won the Coupe de la Meuse at the Circuit des Ardennes, Belgium, in 1912. This car was a voiturette version of the Grand Prix car.**

the war, Boillot was killed and then Goux departed too, leaving Peugeot bereft of racing experience. There was an attempt on the Indy 500 in 1921 with a radical but hopelessly unreliable machine. This triggered a retirement from frontline racing.

It returned to sports car racing in 1990 and made a Formula One engine for McLaren in 1994. This partnership lasted just one year and in six subsequent seasons with the Jordan and Prost teams, it failed to win a race. Peugeot withdrew from the sport at the end of the 2000 season.

Peugeot	
Country of origin	France
Date of foundation	1889
Active years in Grands Prix	1895–1902 1906–14
Grand Prix victories	13

Renault

The son of a button manufacturer, Louis Renault first got into car manufacture after devising a successful improvement to the gearbox of his own de Dion car in the 1890s. Backed by his brothers Fernand and Marcel, he set up a factory to produce Renault cars. Louis and Marcel raced these machines in the early city-to-city events.

The brothers and the little Renaults were brilliant performers, often beating cars massively more powerful. But in the catastrophic 1903 Paris–Madrid race, Marcel was one of the fatalities. Louis finished second, but retired from competitive driving thereafter. The new Grand Prix competition of 1906 led Renault back to the sport, producing a new car for Ferenc Szisz – formerly Louis's riding mechanic – to drive. He took it to victory. The company continued racing until 1908.

It returned, 69 years later, with a car that changed the face of Formula One: the turbo-charged RS01. Jean-Pierre Jabouille's Renault won the 1979 French Grand Prix, and before long the rest of the grid was forced to follow suit. After missing out on the 1983 world title, Renault withdrew as a works team at the end of 1985, though it continued to supply engines to other teams.

▲ The winning car of the first ever Grand Prix was this Renault, driven by Ferenc Szisz.

This continued after the turbo era. In 1989, it debuted its V10 engine with the Williams team. This configuration was as widely copied as the earlier turbo. Renault V10s powered Williams and Benetton to five World Drivers' titles between 1992 and 1997, after which it withdrew once more. It returned as a works team in 2002, having bought out the Benetton team. Fernando Alonso's victory in the 2003 Hungarian Grand Prix marked a return to winning ways, and two years later Alonso was triumphant in giving Renault its first World Championship as a team.

Renault	
Country of origin	France
Date of foundation	1898
Active years in Grands Prix	1901–08, 1977–85 2002–present
Grand Prix victories	25 (+ 1 Constructors' Cup)

▼ Jarno Trulli in the Renault R202 retired from the 2002 Malaysian Grand Prix. The team had re-entered Formula One that season.

Sunbeam

Victory in France in 1923 made Sunbeam the first British constructor to win a Grand Prix.

First and foremost a production car company, its technical director Louis Coatalen was a big believer in racing and took the company into voiturette ("small car") competition in 1910. With third, fourth and fifth places overall, Sunbeams took the first three places in the voiturette class of the 1912 French Grand Prix. The class victory was repeated a year later.

Coatalen recruited former Peugeot designer Ernest Henry to produce a Grand Prix car for the new 2-litre formula of 1922. It proved ineffective against the new Fiats, leading to

Sunbeam

Country of origin	United Kingdom
Date of foundation	1904
Active years in Grands Prix	1911–26
Grand Prix victories	3 pre-championship

Henry's replacement by one of the Fiat's designers Vincent Bertarione. For 1923, the Italian produced a car so similar to the 1922 Fiat that it was instantly dubbed "the green Fiat". It proved very effective and enabled Henry Segrave to come through for victory in France – ironically after the faster, newly-supercharged Fiats had retired when dominating.

For 1924, Sunbeam development engineer Captain Jack Irving devised Sunbeam's own supercharger, and in compressing the fuel/air mixture rather than merely the air, it allowed for lower internal temperatures and therefore more power. So equipped, the 1924 Sunbeam dominated the French Grand Prix from the start but retired with electrical trouble.

Soon afterwards, poor financial performance forced the termination of the company's racing programme, though it was later successful in securing world speed records.

▼ Henry Segrave in the Sunbeam 2-litre at the French Grand Prix in 1925.

Tyrrell

Ken Tyrrell was a timber merchant who had been moderately successful as a driver in the British Formula 500/Formula Three series in the 1950s. But he found his true vocation as a team entrant. In 1964, he teamed up with a promising young Scottish driver, Jackie Stewart, and together they stormed to victory in the British Formula Three Championship.

Stewart immediately graduated to Formula One, leaving Tyrrell to find further success as an entrant in Touring Car and Formula Two racing. Stewart continued to drive for Tyrrell in between his Formula One commitments, and for 1968 the pair were reunited properly in Formula One. Tyrrell had arranged that he be provided with a Matra chassis in which he would install the Ford Cosworth DFV engine. With Stewart driving, the team were close runners-up in the World Championship that year. Still with a Matra-Ford they went one better in 1969, dominating the season.

The Matra association then ended, and after purchasing a March for 1970 as a stop-gap, the first "Tyrrell" car appeared at the end of that season. Designed by Derek Gardner, the chassis had clear Matra influences. Powered by the ubiquitous Ford Cosworth DFV, it dominated the 1971 season as Stewart took his second world title. Tyrrell took the corresponding constructors' title in its first full season of racing.

The team remained a major force for the remaining two years of Stewart's career, but Jackie retired from the sport after securing title number three in 1973. Stewart's intended replacement, François Cevert, was killed practising for what was due to be Stewart's final race, a body blow to the team. Tyrrell instead recruited Formula One new boys Jody Scheckter and Patrick Depailler and enjoyed some success, but the glory days of Stewart were over.

A six-wheeler in 1976 gave the team lots of publicity as well as a 1-2 at the Swedish Grand Prix, but it was never repeated. The four-wheel replacement, the 008, won the 1978 Monaco Grand Prix with Depailler, but the team was struggling to generate commercial backing as Formula One entered a

▲ Jody Scheckter leads second-placed team-mate Patrick Depailler to take the first and only victory for a six-wheeled car.

▼ Jean Alesi – here in the 1990 Mexican Grand Prix – gave the team its last strong year. He scored second at Phoenix.

Tyrrell	
Country of origin	United Kingdom
Date of foundation	1970
Active years in Grands Prix	1970–98
Grand Prix victories	23 (+ 1 Constructors' Cup)

slicker, more expensive age. There were some bright spots – Michele Alboreto won a couple of races in the early 1980s, and Jean Alesi showed that the 1990 Tyrrell 019 was perhaps the best chassis on the grid – but overall the trend was downward.

The team was bought out at the end of 1997 by British American Tobacco. Ken Tyrrell died in 2001, aged 77, and the Formula One world mourned one of the last direct links to an earlier era.

Vanwall

▼ 1958 Vanwall Formula One car. Its sleek aeronautic-inspired lines helped make it the quickest car in a straight line.

Vanwall won the inaugural Formula One World Constructors' Championship in 1958, and so achieved the ambition of its founder Tony Vandervell, the British industrialist who had vowed to one day beat Ferrari.

Vandervell was the proprietor of Vandervell Bearings, whose patented "thinwall" bearing had been a major breakthrough for several manufacturers – including Ferrari – in making their engines more efficient. Vandervell had originally been part of the BRM trust, but left in frustration at the "management by committee" of that team in its early days. Instead, he persuaded Enzo Ferrari to sell him a series of Formula One cars that were then modified and raced as "Thinwall Specials".

The natural progression from this was a fully Vandervell car. This first appeared in 1955 and was labelled the "Vanwall". In place of the Ferrari engine was a four-cylinder unit derived from the single-cylinder Norton motorcycle race engines. Vandervell later commissioned de Havilland aerodynamicist Frank Costin to design a highly advanced low-drag body for it. Costin, in turn, suggested that Vandervell commission Lotus' Colin Chapman to make modifications to

Vanwall

Country of origin	United Kingdom
Date of foundation	1955
Active years in Grands Prix	1955–58
Grand Prix victories	9 (+ 1 Constructors' Cup)

▼ Tony Vandervell (*left*) with mechanics at Pescara, Italy, in 1957.

the chassis and suspension. The combined result of all this development was that the Vanwall was the fastest car of 1957, and Tony Brooks and Stirling Moss gave it its first victory in the British Grand Prix of that year.

Brooks and Moss won six Grands Prix for the team in 1958, ensuring the Constructors' title. But in the final race of the season, at Morocco, third team driver Stuart Lewis-Evans crashed and received fatal burns. Vandervell, in failing health anyway, was devastated by the loss of his driver and he announced his retirement from the sport. The team did struggle on for another couple of seasons, appearing sporadically, but the serious challenge was over. Vandervell died in 1967.

▲ Stirling Moss and Tony Brooks in 1957. These two gifted drivers ensured Vanwall's first Grand Prix win at Aintree that year.

Williams

▼ Alan Jones in the Williams FW06 ran a sensational race at Long Beach in 1978, to firmly establish the team for the first time.

Frank Williams founded the team that came to dominate Formula One for much of the 1980s and 1990s in 1977. A keystone to its success was his chief designer Patrick Head.

Prior to this, Williams had eked out an existence on the fringes of Formula One, grabbing the occasional result but being perpetually underfunded. With the Head-designed Williams FW06 of 1978, the team's form enabled it to attract decent backing. The follow-up FW07 of 1979 gave the team its first victory, at the British Grand Prix, with Clay Regazzoni. Team-mate Alan Jones went on to dominate the second half of the season before giving the team its first World Championship in 1980.

Williams driver Keke Rosberg took the last ever DFV-powered World Championship in 1982. From the end of 1983, Williams went into partnership with Honda, a combination that yielded World Constructors' Championships in 1986 and 1987; Williams driver Nelson Piquet took the World Champion title in the latter year. After being surprisingly

Williams

Country of origin	United Kingdom
Date of foundation	1977
Active years in Grands Prix	1977–present
Grand Prix victories	113 (+9 Constructors' Cups)

dropped by Honda, Williams took up with Renault, and this led to an even more dominant spell. A Williams-Renault driver was Champion in 1992, 1993, 1996 and 1997.

From 2000, the team's engine partner was BMW but despite several Grand Prix wins together the partnership was dissolved at the end of 2005.

◄ Nelson Piquet leads Nigel Mansell as the two Williams fight over victory in the 1987 British Grand Prix. Mansell won.

▼ Juan Pablo Montoya tests the BMW Williams FW24 on an artificially wet track at Valencia, Spain, in 2002.

Constructors: The Current Challengers

Today's Formula One grid comprises ten teams. Five of these – Ferrari, Jordan, McLaren, Renault and Williams – have winning pedigrees. The remaining five aspire to join their ranks. These are the challengers.

◀ Minardi at the German Grand Prix, 2003.

▼ Sauber at the Hungarian Grand Prix, 2003.

Ready for Battle

In recent years, major road car producing manufacturers have entered Formula One, sometimes as engine suppliers, as in the case of Mercedes, BMW and Honda, and sometimes as fully formed teams, as with Jaguar, Renault and Toyota. Formula One has provided the manufacturers with a superbly effective global marketing platform.

At the same time, the level of financial investment they have brought to their Formula One programmes has increased the cost of competing for everyone. For those few teams not in partnership with one of the major manufacturers, these are very tough times indeed.

This was emphasized at the beginning of both 2001 and 2002, when the Prost and Arrows teams respectively went out of business. The three remaining teams not aligned to manufacturers – Jordan, Minardi and Sauber – are striving to be the Davids to the manufacturers' Goliaths.

The team names at the forefront of Formula One – Ferrari, McLaren and Williams – have been the same for some time, and joining their winning circle is not easy. But, in 2003, Renault showed that it could be done, breaking back into that elite group by taking its first victory in 20 years. Toyota is fancied as the next manufacturer to make that breakthrough.

▲ The challenger teams in action in 2003: *(from top)* Jaguar, BAR-Honda, Minardi, *(left)* Sauber, *(right)* Toyota.

BAR

Guided by Craig Pollock, the manager of 1997 World Champion Jacques Villeneuve, the tobacco giant British American Tobacco decided to create its own Formula One team. To this end it bought out the Tyrrell team and renamed it British American Racing, shortened to BAR.

The team was formed around Villeneuve, who drove the first BAR car in the 1999 Australian Grand Prix. It proved a difficult debut season as the team failed to score a single point.

Changing to Honda works engines, it improved during 2000. Pollock resigned at the end of 2001 to be replaced by David Richards. Completing the new-broom era, Villeneuve was replaced for 2004 by the Honda-favoured Takuma Sato. During that year BAR took a major step forwards, scoring its first pole position with Jenson Button, and fighting hard for second place in the World Constructors' Championship.

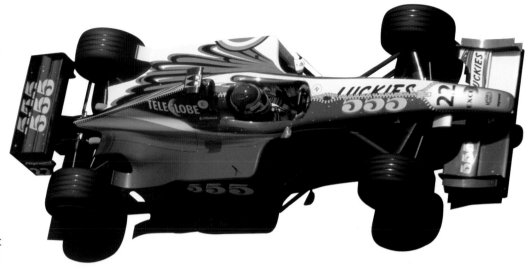

BAR	
Country of origin	United Kingdom
Date of foundation	1999
Active years in Grands Prix	1999–present
Grand Prix victories	0

▼ Olivier Panis driving the BAR-Honda 004 at the Canadian Grand Prix, Montreal, Canada, in 2002.

▲ *(top)* Jacques Villeneuve at the Spanish Grand Prix, Barcelona, in 1999. The team suffered a dismal first year.

▲ *(above)* Jacques Villeneuve drove the BAR Honda 003 to third place in Barcelona in 2001. It was the team's first podium.

Red Bull

After first appearing in Formula One as a sponsor of the Sauber team, Red Bull became a constructor in 2005 when it bought out the Jaguar Racing team along with its UK base and existing staff.

Red Bull owner Dietrich Mateschitz sees the sport as an effective marketing tool. He recruited former F3000 team owner Christian Horner to run the new team. David Coulthard was chosen as lead driver with Christian Klien alongside him. They raced the RB1, a development of Jaguar's 2004 R5, to promising effect, with Coulthard a regular points scorer.

The team's 2006 plans included a new car powered by a Ferrari-sourced engine, and a junior team – a result of Mateschitz's purchase of the former Minardi team.

Red Bull

Country of origin	United Kingdom
Date of foundation	2005
Active years in Grands Prix	2005–present
Grand Prix victories	0

▲ **David Coulthard in action in Red Bull Racing's first Formula One car, the RB1, during qualifying for the Italian Grand Prix at Monza in 2005.**

▼ **Christian Klien's RB1 trails David Coulthard during the Italian Grand Prix, 2005. Klien finished the race in thirteenth, two places ahead of his team-mate.**

Minardi

Italy's "other" Formula One team after Ferrari, Minardi, has been part of the sport since 1985, when Formula Two constructor Giancarlo Minardi graduated to the upper echelon.

It has been a struggle for the tiny, underfunded team, but in the USA in 1990, Pierluigi Martini did give Minardi a front row qualifying position. He also scored the team's best-ever result with fourth in the 1991 Portuguese Grand Prix. Team founder Minardi sold his stake in the 1990s to Gabriele Rumi who sold out to airline boss Paul Stoddard in 2001. He kept the team running for five years until selling out to drinks firm Red Bull, who rebranded the team for 2006 thus ending the Minardi name in the sport.

Minardi	
Country of origin	Italy
Date of foundation	1985
Active years in Grands Prix	1985–2005
Grand Prix victories	0

▲ Pierluigi Martini – Minardi's most successful driver – leads Stefan Bellof's Tyrrell in the 1985 Dutch Grand Prix.

▼ Mark Webber in the Minardi Asiatech PS02 during practice for the Austrian Grand Prix at the A1-Ring in 2002.

Sauber

After a successful campaign in sports cars that included World Championships and victory in the Le Mans 24 Hours, the Swiss-based Sauber team graduated to Formula One in partnership with Mercedes in 1993.

The Mercedes link came to an end in 1995. After a short partnership with Ford, Sauber found a level of stability using customer Ferrari engines from 1998.

The team improved to the point that it finished fourth in the World Constructors' Championship of 2001, ahead of many teams with factory engine partnerships.

With Kimi Raikkonen in 2001 and Felipe Massa in 2002, team boss Peter Sauber earned a reputation as a talent scout. Both drivers had highly impressive Grand Prix seasons with Sauber as rookies.

Midway through the 2005 season it was announced that car manufacturer BMW had bought the team along with its base in Switzerland. BMW had supplied engines to the Williams team but with this move became a constructor in its own right for the first time.

▲ *(top)* Sauber versus Sauber. Jean Alesi and Johnny Herbert tangle at the Argentine Grand Prix, Buenos Aires, in 1998.

▲ *(above)* J.J. Lehto in the Sauber-Mercedes C12 at the Italian Grand Prix, Monza, in 1993. The team was in partnership with Mercedes during its first season of Formula One.

◀ Nick Heidfeld qualified only 17th in the 2002 Monaco Grand Prix, but he had helped to take the Sauber team to fourth place in the previous year's title chase.

Sauber	
Country of origin	Switzerland
Date of foundation	1970
Active years in Grands Prix	1993–2005
Grand Prix victories	0

Toyota

▼ Allan McNish in the Toyota TF102 at the 2002 Monaco Grand Prix in Monte Carlo.

The world's third biggest motor manufacturer entered Formula One for the first time in 2002. Bravely, it decided to do so on its own rather than in partnership with an existing specialist team. Having enjoyed great success in the sport of rallying, it used the same Cologne base to establish its Formula One operation, although the impetus comes very much from the parent company in Japan.

Chief designer Gustav Brunner – a veteran of several Formula One teams, including Ferrari – designed the TF102 chassis into which the all-new Toyota V10 engine was installed. The car created a good impression immediately, with straightline speed as good as that of the top teams. It was also uncannily reliable for a brand new design, with Mika Salo scoring World Championship points in two of its first three races.

The facilities and investment behind Toyota's first season left few onlookers in any doubt that this would in time become a serious force. Former Renault technical director Mike Gascoyne was recruited in 2003 and the first car under his direction did well in 2005, with Jarno Trulli achieving the team's first podiums and its first pole position. A first victory seems to be just around the corner.

▲ Mika Salo's Toyota TF102 finished sixth in the debut race for Toyota at the Australian Grand Prix, Melbourne, in 2002.

Toyota	
Country of origin	Japan
Date of foundation	2001
Active years in Grands Prix	2002–present
Grand Prix victories	0

▼ Both Toyota drivers Mika Salo and Allan McNish get involved in a first corner accident at Melbourne in 2002.

A – Z
Drivers

The same competitive urge to drive a machine faster than the next man has produced over a century of heroes. Through the ages of wildly differing machinery and circumstance, that basic urge has remained the same, as has the basic technique of balancing grip against power through steering and throttle control.

It was always a dangerous sport and despite the elimination of many unnecessary perils, it remains inherently so. Many of these heroes didn't get to live out the natural span of their lives. Here then are the men who excelled in a sport with the highest of stakes.

◄ The start of the Monaco Grand Prix, Monte Carlo, 2002.

Jean Alesi

A spectacular Formula One career that lasted for over 12 years yielded only one victory but produced countless moments of high drama and astonishing car control.

Alesi graduated to Formula 3000 in 1988 as the French Formula Three Champion, and the following year he clinched the Formula 3000 crown with Eddie Jordan Racing. That season he made his Formula One debut with Tyrrell, making a big impression by coming home fourth in his first event. He created an even bigger impact in the first race of 1990, at Phoenix, when after leading in the Tyrrell and being passed by Ayrton Senna, he cheekily re-passed the great Brazilian before surrendering to the inevitable and finishing second.

Such performances led to a string of offers from top teams for 1991, among them Williams and Ferrari. In a decision of dubious wisdom, he chose the latter, then spent five years in a sequence of Ferraris that were rarely as quick as the top cars. His sole victory came in Canada in 1995, his final year with the Italian team.

Alesi spent the next six seasons in a succession of ever-less competitive cars from Benetton, Sauber and Prost. A mid-2001 switch to Jordan was a last gasp opportunity to regain form and rescue his career, but he was dropped at the end of the year.

Jean Alesi	
Nationality	French
Seasons	1989–2001
Teams driven for	Tyrrell, Ferrari, Benetton, Sauber, Prost, Jordan
Number of major victories	1

◄ Jean Alesi celebrates his first Grand Prix victory at Montreal, Canada, in 1995.

▼ (*below*) Alesi came second for Ferrari at the San Marino Grand Prix at Imola in 1995.

▼ (*bottom*) Jean Alesi, in the Ferrari 412T2, took second place at the German Grand Prix, Nürburgring, in 1995.

Fernando Alonso

In winning the 2005 World Championship, Fernando Alonso became the sport's youngest ever champion. He was just 24 years old when he clinched the title in Brazil. This followed on from being the youngest ever Grand Prix winner (22 years old in Hungary 2003). He is also the first champion to hail from Spain

The 2003 season was Alonso's first with a competitive team, though he had made his debut with Minardi in 2001 as a 19-year-old. At age six he had been encouraged by his father – himself a keen amateur kart racer – to take up karting in Spain. Over the following years he became one of the country's top exponents of the sport, and this led to his graduation to car racing in 1999, when he won the Spain-based Formula Nissan Championship.

This gave him a test drive with Minardi which led to a seat in the F3000 category, the stepping stone to Formula One. During this time Alonso's talent was noticed by Renault boss, Flavio Briatore, who gave him a long-term contract.

After his debut Formula One season with Minardi, he took up the position of test driver for the Renault team, and from there he graduated to a seat with the race team in 2003. His sensational form has led many to mark him out as the future successor to Michael Schumacher as the sport's number one driver, and Spain's new sporting hero.

Fernando Alonso	
Nationality	Spanish
Seasons	2001–present
Teams driven for	Minardi, Renault
Number of major victories	8

◀ Alonso has ignited Formula One interest in his native Spain.

▼ Alonso became the youngest-ever Grand Prix winner, at 22 years 26 days, when he triumphed in Hungary in 2003.

▲ Fernando Alonso's Renault has a comfortable lead at the 2003 Hungarian Grand Prix.

Chris Amon

The brilliant New Zealander has the unfortunate reputation as the greatest driver never to win a Grand Prix. He began his Formula One career as a 19-year-old in 1963 – for many years he held the record as the youngest driver to start a Grand Prix – and ended it as a disillusioned 32-year-old in 1976. In between, he gave some virtuoso performances that stood comparison with any of the greats of the sport, but he added to his natural bad luck by a sequence of poor career moves.

Indulged by his farming father, Amon began racing in New Zealand, where he was spotted by Formula One team owner Reg Parnell, who took him into Formula One with his privateer team. Amon won the Le Mans 24 Hour sportscar race of 1966 in partnership with Bruce McLaren, but not until he signed with Ferrari for 1967 did his potential become clear. He took fourth in that year's championship, but in 1968, with a more competitive car, he was often the fastest man around. He retired from a 40-second lead in Spain and an even more dominant position in the closing stages in Canada. It seemed only a matter of time before such form gave him the world title.

▲ Chris Amon in 1968.

▼ Chris Amon's Ferrari 312 took second place at the British Grand Prix, Brands Hatch, in 1968.

Chris Amon	
Nationality	New Zealand
Seasons	1963–76
Teams driven for	Parnell, Cooper Ferrari, March, Matra, Tecno, Tyrrell, Amon, BRM, Ensign, Wolf
Number of major victories	0

In the non-championship Tasman series of 1967–68, he raced wheel-to-wheel with the great Jim Clark. In the same competition the following year, he triumphed over future champion, Jochen Rindt. He left Ferrari at the end of 1969, just as the team came good, and left March at the end of 1970, as it was on the verge of producing the car that would take Ronnie Peterson to second in the 1971 World Championship. In France in 1972, he drove one of the greatest races of all time when, after leading comfortably in his Matra, he suffered a puncture then came back to take third. After retiring in 1977 he returned home to New Zealand.

Mario Andretti

Often cited as the most versatile racing driver of all time, Andretti was a champion in Formula One and Indycar racing, and he has won in everything from dirt-track racing to NASCAR stock cars.

Of Italian descent, Andretti moved to America as a child. Together with his twin brother Aldo, he began racing dirt-track midget cars, leading eventually to a full-time drive in the USAC Championship that included the famous Indianapolis 500 race. As a rookie, he won the USAC Championship in 1965. At Indianapolis that year he came to the attention of Lotus boss Colin Chapman, who promised him a Formula One drive whenever he felt he was ready.

Mario Andretti	
Nationality	American
Seasons	1968–82
Teams driven for	Lotus, Ferrari, Parnelli, Alfa Romeo
Number of major victories	12

◀ **Mario Andretti won the 1978 World Championship driving for Lotus – taking six victories along the way.**

▼ **Mario Andretti took pole position and finished in third place as a Ferrari stand-in at the Italian Grand Prix, Monza, in 1982.**

He felt ready by the end of 1968 – and promptly put his Lotus on pole position on his Formula One debut at the American Grand Prix. He didn't race in Formula One full-time until 1976, but in between he won the 1971 South African Grand Prix for Ferrari. In 1976, he returned to Lotus, and together they won the final race of the year. This was a prelude to a brilliant two-season run with the ground-effect Lotus 78 and 79 models, culminating in the 1978 World Championship. Lotus' competitiveness went downhill subsequently, and Andretti spent his final Formula One season in 1981 with Alfa Romeo. Ferrari called him up as a stand-in at the 1982 Italian Grand Prix – and he responded with pole position, showing that at the age of 42, he still had it.

Thereafter, he finished off his career in American Indycar racing, winning for many years before finally retiring from motorsport at the end of 1994.

◀ **Winner Mario Andretti leads Jo Siffert at the South African Grand Prix, 1971.**

René Arnoux

Arnoux was one of the generation of French drivers of the 1970s who began their careers at the Winfield Racing Drivers' School and succeeded in each category as they moved up the ladder. Arnoux's progress wasn't as smooth as those of some of his peers, but when he got his big Formula One break in 1979, with Renault, he made maximum use of it. In a Formula One career lasting 11 years, he took 18 pole positions and seven race wins with Renault and Ferrari.

After winning the 1977 Formula Two Championship with the Martini team, they graduated to Formula One together in 1978. It was an underfunded effort and they struggled, but for 1979 Renault wanted to expand to running two of its radical turbocharged cars, and Arnoux's promise and nationality made him a shoe-in for the drive. He won his first Grand Prix in Brazil in 1980, and driving alongside Alain Prost in the

▼ *(below)* Winner René Arnoux in the Renault RE20 at the South African Grand Prix in 1980. It was his second victory.

following two years he proved every bit as fast, if not as calculating. After famously disobeying team orders to win the 1982 French Grand Prix, his days at Renault were numbered. For 1983 he was recruited by Ferrari.

He took three victories in his first season with the Italian team, entering the final round with an outside chance of taking the world title but ultimately finishing third. After performing erratically, he was sacked by Ferrari early in 1985 and this signalled the end of his frontline career. He returned with Ligier in 1986 and served out four more Formula One years before quietly retiring at the end of 1989.

◀ René Arnoux was one of the fastest drivers of the early 1980s.

▼ *(bottom)* Arnoux, here in his final full season with Ferrari, at Austria in 1984. He won three times for the Italian team.

René Arnoux

Nationality	French
Seasons	1978–89
Teams driven for	Martini, Renault, Ferrari, Ligier
Number of major victories	7

Alberto Ascari

The man who would be 1952 and 1953 World Champion was just seven years old when his father, Antonio, was killed while leading the 1925 French Grand Prix. Alberto subsequently began racing motorcycles and, just prior to the outbreak of World War II, he made his car racing debut.

Post-war, he was signed by Maserati and enjoyed considerable success there in 1948 and 1949. His senior team-mate Luigi Villoresi adopted him as his protégé and guided his subsequent career. In 1950, the pair were recruited by Ferrari, where they stayed for the next four years.

Ascari quickly demonstrated that he was the only driver on the same level as the legendary Juan Manuel Fangio, and the two had some epic dices. For 1952, the World Championship was changed from Formula One to Formula Two regulations, and Ferrari produced the fastest machine. It was under these circumstances that Ascari reeled off the most dominant championship display ever seen. He missed the first race to compete in the Indianapolis 500, but won every single subsequent round of the contest. Despite increased pressure from Fangio's Maserati in 1953, he took his second title quite comfortably. For 1954, he was recruited by Lancia but

Alberto Ascari	
Nationality	Italian
Seasons	1947–55
Teams driven for	Maserati, Ferrari, Alfa Romeo, Lancia
Number of major victories	15

◀ Alberto Ascari, driving a 2-litre Ferrari 500, celebrates his win at Silverstone, 1953.

▼ (left) Alberto Ascari and and Luigi Villoresi.

▼ Alberto Ascari led the 1951 French Grand Prix in the Ferrari 375.

delays in readying the new D50 model meant he did very little racing. Highly superstitious, it has been claimed he was obsessed with the idea that destiny would not allow him to live longer than the 36 years his father had enjoyed.

At 36 years old, he was lying in second place in the 1955 Monaco Grand Prix when he crashed into the harbour. He was only slightly injured. A few days later, he visited Monza to watch his friend Eugenio Castellotti test a Ferrari sports car, before asking if he himself might try the car. In an accident that has never been fully explained, Ascari left the road and was killed.

Antonio Ascari

Ascari worked his way into the racing seat through a succession of jobs as a mechanic and tester before World War I. Post-war, he established himself as an Alfa Romeo dealer in Milan, and through that connection began racing works Alfas.

This was at a time when the Milan-based company was just emerging as a serious Grand Prix force, and Ascari's arrival upon the international scene was sensational. In his first big-time event, Cremona 1924, he gave the brand new Alfa Romeo P2 a debut victory. He then came to within three laps of winning the French Grand Prix before going on to a dominant victory in Italy.

Within the space of a few months, Ascari had made serious claim to be the world's fastest Grand Prix driver. He opened his 1925 account with a start-to-finish victory in the Belgian Grand Prix. He was leading by a long way in the French Grand Prix of that year when rain began to fall, and everyone but Ascari reduced their pace considerably. But he pressed on, and eventually he slid wide. A rear wheel became entangled in some fencing, and the car flipped upside down. It was before the days of crash helmets or roll-over bars, and Ascari's injuries were fatal.

Antonio Ascari	
Nationality	Italian
Seasons	1924–25
Teams driven for	Alfa Romeo
Number of major victories	2

▲ *(left)* Antonio Ascari for Alfa Romeo at Monza in 1924, his first year in Grand Prix.

▲ *(right)* Antonio Ascari *(left)* with young Alberto, seated in the car, and Enzo Ferrari *(second from left)*.

▼ Antonio Ascari driving for Alfa Romeo at the French Grand Prix, Montlhéry, 1925.

Rubens Barrichello

As the other half to Michael Schumacher in the dominant Ferrari team in the first years of this century, Barrichello performed with distinction for six years alongside the champion. Although usually subservient to Schumacher, Barrichello scored nine victories during his time with Ferrari and finished runner-up in the 2002 and 2004 championships. He ended his stint with the team at the close of the 2005 season.

Prior to his stint at Ferrari, Barrichello had served a seven-year apprenticeship in Formula One with the Jordan and Stewart teams, showing regular flair and promise but never quite managing to win a race. After a successful karting career in Brazil, Barrichello came to Europe in 1990 and established a big reputation in the junior categories, winning the European GM Euroseries that year and following it up with victory in the 1991 British Formula Three Championship.

His Formula One debut came in 1993, with Jordan. In that year's European Grand Prix at Donington, he drove brilliantly to run in second position to

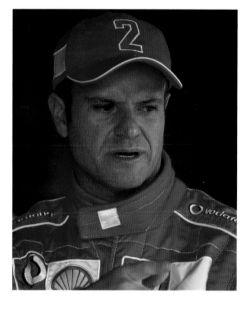

Rubens Barrichello	
Nationality	Brazilian
Seasons	1993–present
Teams driven for	Jordan, Stewart, Ferrari
Number of major victories	9

◀ Barrichello has been a critical part of Ferrari's success into the new millennium.

▼ Barrichello takes victory in the 2003 Japanese Grand Prix.

his countryman and idol Ayrton Senna before retirement. It took a long time to convert such potential into Formula One success, but he finally achieved his first win at Hockenheim in the 2000 German Grand Prix.

He was at the centre of the Ferrari controversy in 2002 when the team instructed him to give way to his team-mate Schumacher in the Austrian Grand Prix, despite having led the race from the start. He complied in the last few hundred yards of the race, triggering an outcry from those who felt the team were doing the sport a disservice. In 2003, he won both the British and Japanese Grands Prix and was a critical element in securing Schumacher's record sixth title.

Robert Benoist

Benoist's Grand Prix immortality is assured by his feat of winning all four Grands Prix of 1927 for Delage.

The son of a Rothschild gamekeeper, he began racing bicycles and worked for the Grégoire car company shortly before World War I. He volunteered as a pilot for the war and survived being shot down; he was also credited with shooting down one enemy plane. After the war, he began cyclecar racing and was a dominant champion in 1923. This brought him to the attention of Delage, with whom he made his Grand Prix debut in 1924. He finished third in that year's European Grand Prix at Lyons. He then shared victory with team-mate Albert Divo in the 1925 French Grand Prix, after the Alfa team withdrew following the death of Antonio Ascari.

As the Delage became ever-more competitive, so Benoist's career flowered, culminating in his victorious 1927 season. Delage then withdrew from racing, leaving Benoist to serve the rest of his career with Bugatti, for whom he won the Le Mans 24 Hours sports car race in 1937.

Robert Benoist	
Nationality	French
Seasons	1924–36
Teams driven for	Delage, Bugatti
Number of major victories	5

During World War II Benoist was a leading member of the French resistance against German occupation, and he received training in Britain. Working in collaboration with fellow Grand Prix drivers William Grover-Williams and Jean-Pierre Wimille, he was highly successful in the field before being captured and executed by the Gestapo.

▲ Louis Chiron (left) and Benoist in 1928.

◄ Benoist in action at the European Grand Prix, San Sebastian, Spain, in 1926.

Gerhard Berger

In a Formula One career stretching from 1984 to 1997, Berger took victories with Benetton, Ferrari and McLaren, though he never managed a sustained challenge for the world title.

The Austrian's rise through the sport's junior ranks was rapid, and partly funded by his father's transport company. He made a big step from Renault Five racing to Formula Three in 1983, and was immediately competitive. By the end of 1984, he was making his Formula One debut in an ATS-BMW with over 800 horsepower. His abundant natural ability meant he adapted comfortably.

After a season driving for Arrows in 1985, he was recruited by the new Benetton team for 1986. At the end of that season he gave himself and the team their first victory, with a winning drive in Mexico. His performances had attracted the attention of Ferrari, with whom he scored two consecutive victories at the end of 1987.

In the early laps of the 1989 San Marino Grand Prix, a wing failure sent him into the wall at Imola's flat-out Tamburello corner. The impact was massive and the Ferrari erupted in flames. Remarkably, he was pulled out of the car with just slight burns to his hands, a broken rib and fractured shoulder blade. Two races later he was back behind the wheel.

▲ Gerhard Berger in 1987, during the first of two stints driving for the Ferrari team. He won the final two races of that year.

In 1990, he was recruited by McLaren to partner Ayrton Senna, but he wasn't the same standard as the Brazilian. He served three years alongside Senna before returning to Ferrari for a big money offer. He helped improve the team's performances and won the 1994 German Grand Prix. He left in 1996, when Ferrari recruited Michael Schumacher, and returned to Benetton, where he served out his career, winning the 1997 German Grand Prix before retiring. He later took up the post of motorsport director with BMW.

Gerhard Berger	
Nationality	Austrian
Seasons	1984–97
Teams driven for	ATS, Arrows, Benetton, Ferrari, McLaren
Number of major victories	10

▲ Berger's Benetton locks a wheel on the way to third place in the 1997 Brazilian Grand Prix in Sao Paulo.

▶ Berger's Ferrari (left) attempts to fend off Damon Hill's Williams in the 1994 Canadian Grand Prix. Berger finished fourth, two places behind Hill.

Georges Boillot

Boillot appeared like a meteor in Grand Prix racing, winning on his debut in France in 1912, and establishing himself as the fastest and most daring driver up to the outbreak of World War I. Serving as a pilot in the French Air Force, he was killed in action in 1916.

His car racing career began in the voiturette ("small car") class, with Lion-Peugeot, in 1908. He soon came to be the dominant driver of this category, and when Lion-Peugeot and the parent Peugeot company were reunited in 1911, he was central to the plan of building and racing a full-size Grand Prix car.

This car was the ground-breaking twin-cam, four-valve-per-cylinder L76. Boillot took it to victory on its debut at Dieppe. He repeated this result in the French Grand Prix of 1913, before setting pole position and a lap record

Georges Boillot	
Nationality	French
Seasons	1912–14
Teams driven for	Peugeot
Number of major victories	2

▲ Georges Boillot finished first in the 1910 Mont Ventoux hill climb in the Lion-Peugeot.

▼ (left) Boillot won the Mont Ventoux hill climb in 1913 in the Peugeot 5.7 litre.

▼ (right) Georges Boillot.

on his debut at the Indianapolis 500 in 1914. Later that year, in the French Grand Prix, he drove a heroic race in a Peugeot that was, by now, outclassed by the latest model from Mercedes. He kept the faster German cars at bay for almost all of the race's seven-hour duration, but retired on the final lap with engine failure.

He was shot down after attempting to take on seven German scout planes single-handed. He was awarded a posthumous *Legion d'Honneur*.

Pietro Bordino

▼ Pietro Bordino driving for Fiat in the 2-litre Grand Prix of 1924.

As the lead driver with the crack Fiat squad, Bordino was the man to beat in the early 1920s.

He had begun as a Fiat riding mechanic pre-war, alongside aces Felice Nazzaro and Vincenzo Lancia. His driving debut for Fiat was at the 1921 Brescia Grand Prix where his speed was sensational, leading comfortably until sidelined by mechanical problems.

Through 1922 and 1923, he won a whole flurry of major Grands Prix, and had there been a World Championship then he would have won titles in both

years. Fiat withdrew from Grand Prix racing at the end of 1924, and Bordino wasn't seen for a while. The company made a one-off comeback at the 1927 Milan Grand Prix, which Bordino completely dominated.

He was practising for the 1928 Targa Florio race in a Bugatti when he hit a dog, jamming his steering and causing him to crash into a river with fatal results.

◄ Bordino's new Fiat at the Monza Grand Prix of 1927.

Pietro Bordino	
Nationality	Italian
Seasons	1921–28
Teams driven for	Fiat, Bugatti
Number of major victories	3

▼ Bordino – in the Fiat 802 – retired from the 1921 Italian Grand Prix at Brescia but set a lap record of 150.35km/h (93.43mph).

Jack Brabham

This tough Australian who began his career midget-racing on the cinder tracks of his home country won three World Championships, the last of them in a car bearing his own name. This stands as a unique achievement in the history of the sport.

After a highly successful career in Australia, Brabham arrived in Britain in 1955 and hooked up with the Cooper team. A highly technical driver, Brabham was able to help Cooper develop its mid-engined cars, first of all in sports cars and subsequently in Formula One.

In 1959, Brabham in the mid-engined Cooper emerged victorious from a final-round championship showdown against Tony Brooks in the front-engined Ferrari. It was the final nail in the coffin for the traditional Grand Prix car. Brabham repeated his success in 1960 but the Cooper was about to be leapfrogged by Lotus.

Sensing that Cooper was a spent force, Brabham set up on his own, recruiting his friend from midget-racing, Ron Tauranac, to design the

▲ Jack Brabham, in the Brabham BT33, taking his 14th and final Grand Prix victory at Kyalami, South Africa, in 1970.

Jack Brabham

Nationality	Australian
Seasons	1955–70
Teams driven for	Cooper, Brabham
Number of major victories	14

Brabham BT3, which made its debut in 1962. Brabham seemed content to let his employed driver Dan Gurney lead the team and was planning to retire from the wheel at the end of 1965. But then Gurney left to set up *his* own team, leaving Brabham as the lead driver once again. This coincided with the new 3-litre formula, and Brabham's shrewdness of engine choice and cockpit skills gave him his third title.

He remained a front rank driver until his retirement at the end of 1970, when, at the age of 44, he sold up and returned home to Australia.

▲ Brabham at the Mexico Grand Prix in 1969, where he finished the race in third place after starting from pole position.

◄ Brabham retired from the 1966 Italian Grand Prix at Monza, but he won that year's championship regardless.

Tony Brooks

Brooks vies with Stirling Moss as the greatest driver never to have won the World Championship, though his quiet, less thrusting manner meant he has never achieved the same fame as his contemporary.

Brooks came to prominence in 1955 when, in only his second race outside the British club scene, he won the Syracuse Grand Prix for Connaught. Although it was a non-championship event, this was the first Grand Prix victory for a British car and driver for over 30 years. On his aeroplane flights there and back, he was studying for his final exams in dentistry.

Although Brooks received the qualification, he never did take up dentistry, as his huge talent made him much in demand within the sport. After a season with BRM in 1956,

▲ Tony Brooks, driver for Vanwall, Aston Martin and Cooper cars, in 1958.

▲ Brooks winning the German Grand Prix at the Nürburgring for Vanwall in 1958.

Tony Brooks	
Nationality	British
Seasons	1955–61
Teams driven for	Connaught, BRM, Vanwall, Ferrari
Number of major victories	6

he was recruited by Vanwall to drive alongside Moss in 1957. The pair proved extremely evenly-matched and took a shared victory in the British Grand Prix. Brooks won three times in 1958, helping Vanwall to the World Constructors' title.

For 1959, he moved to Ferrari and was unlucky to lose out in the title showdown with Jack Brabham. He

was hit from behind off the line by his team-mate and insisted on pitting for a damage inspection, unwilling to risk his life. He finished the race third, but otherwise would probably have won both the race and the championship.

It was his last competitive season. Wanting to return to Britain, he was obliged to take drives in inferior cars, and he retired at the end of 1961.

► Tony Brooks in his Ferrari during practice for the 1959 Italian Grand Prix. Clutch failure at the start of the race lost him a likely victory in the World Championship that year. He never came so close again.

David Bruce-Brown

As one of the stars of American racing, Bruce-Brown was recruited by the visiting European teams in the 1910 and 1911 American Grand Prize races. Against the cream of American and European racing combined, he won both times for Benz and Fiat respectively.

Highly impressed by his speed and intelligence, Fiat brought him over to Europe to compete in the 1912 French Grand Prix. He was leading the race against the Peugeot of Georges Boillot when he retired.

Commonly hailed as the best driver in the world at this time, he was killed during practice for the 1912 Vanderbilt Cup in Milwaukee.

David Bruce-Brown	
Nationality	American
Seasons	1910–12
Teams driven for	Benz, Fiat
Number of major victories	2

▲ David Bruce-Brown at the wheel of his Benz, at the Savannah Grand Prix, 1910.

▼ Bruce-Brown in the 1911 Vanderbilt Cup. He was killed in this event the following year.

Jenson Button

▼ Jenson Button in the Williams-BMW FW22 at the Japanese Grand Prix, Suzuka, in 2000.

Button burst onto the Formula One scene in sensational fashion in 2000 when, as a 20-year old, he was plucked from the junior ranks of racing to drive in Formula One for the mighty Williams-BMW team. By finishing sixth in Brazil 2000, his second race for the team, he became the youngest British Formula One driver ever to score a world championship point. He went on to several more stunning performances during his debut year, including out-qualifying Michael Schumacher on his first visit to the Belgian Grand Prix.

Despite generally out-performing his Williams team-mate, Ralf Schumacher, in the latter stages of the 2000 season, Button was moved aside to make way for Juan Pablo Montoya in 2001. The Colombian was already on a long term contract with Williams and Button had been used as a stand-in. Nonetheless,

it had enabled him to show his talent at the highest level, and he transferred to the Renault team for the next two seasons. In 2003, he drove alongside Jacques Villeneuve at BAR-Honda and proceeded to out-perform the former champion. With a more competitive car in 2004, Button began scoring pole positions and leading races. He remains Britain's brightest Formula One prospect.

Jenson Button

Nationality	British
Seasons	2000–present
Teams driven for	Williams, Renault BAR
Number of major victories	0

▼ Jenson Button in the Renault F1 R202 at the Monaco Grand Prix, 2002.

▲ Jenson Button in 2003.

Rudolf Caracciola

One of the all-time great Grand Prix drivers, Caracciola's career was intertwined with Mercedes in the 1920s and 1930s. He first made his reputation with some astonishing Grand Prix drives in the hopelessly heavy and unsuitable SSK sports car. With this he fought for victory in the first Monaco Grand Prix of 1929; twice he took the car to victory in the German Prix around the tortuous Nürburgring.

When Mercedes could offer him no racing programme for 1932, Caracciola switched to Alfa Romeo, where he instantly matched the speed of the legendary Tazio Nuvolari. He badly injured a leg in a practice accident at Monaco in 1933, and this came close to ending his career.

◄ Rudolf Caracciola in his Mercedes W163 during the 1939 French Grand Prix. He retired after hitting a wall.

He was tempted back by Mercedes as it re-entered Grand Prix racing under the Nazi regime in 1934. His silky touch had not deserted him and he was European Champion in 1935, '37 and '38. Rudi's greatest performances invariably came in the rain, where his uncanny feel led to the tag of "reinmeister".

After spending the duration of World War II in exile in Switzerland, Caracciola did not return to Grand Prix racing post-war. He died in 1959.

▲ Rudolf Caracciola, the European Champion of 1935, 1937 and 1938.

► Manfred von Brauchitsch and Caracciola, both driving for Mercedes, fight for the lead in the 1937 Monaco Grand Prix.

Rudolf Caracciola

Nationality	German
Seasons	1926–39
Teams driven for	Mercedes, Alfa Romeo
Number of major victories	17

François Cevert

C evert was being groomed by Ken Tyrrell as Jackie Stewart's heir, ready to take over as Tyrrell's lead driver after Stewart retired. With his talent, film star looks, intelligence and charm, he looked set to be a major star. He had spent three seasons under the combined tutelage of the two masters and looked set to be one of the elite of Formula One drivers. But in qualifying for the 1973 American Grand Prix – ironically due to be Stewart's final race – Cevert was killed attempting to secure pole position. Jackie withdrew, and the rest of the Formula One world mourned with him.

Cevert benefited from Elf's drive to promote young French talent. After winning a scholarship with the Winfield Racing School in 1968, he had proved very quick in Formula Three and

Formula Two, and he made his Formula One debut with the Elf-sponsored Tyrrell team in 1970. At the end of 1971, he won the American Grand Prix. In 1973, he dutifully followed Stewart home on three occasions, though the Scot later confided he believed Cevert could have passed him had he chosen to.

▲ François Cevert celebrates his first and only Grand Prix victory at Watkins Glen, USA, in 1971. It was the scene of his death two years later.

▼ Cevert at Montjuich Park, Spain, in 1973, where he finished second to his mentor, Jackie Stewart.

▲ Cevert in 1972: his film star looks belied talent and determination. A very bright future looked assured.

François Cevert	
Nationality	French
Seasons	1970–73
Teams driven for	Tyrrell
Number of major victories	1

Louis Chiron

▼ Chiron established himself as a frontline Grand Prix driver in Bugatti's type 35 model.

One of the major stars of Grand Prix racing in the late 1920s and 1930s, Chiron continued driving in Formula One until the mid-1950s.

A native of Monte Carlo, his early career was synonymous with Bugatti. He first began winning major races for this constructor in 1928, though not until 1931 did he finally manage to win his home Grand Prix.

He later transferred across to Alfa Romeo and produced what was arguably his finest drive when he took his Alfa P3 to victory in the 1934 French Grand Prix against the faster cars of Mercedes and Auto Union.

He continued his career post-war, but not with the same degree of success. After retiring, he was asked by Monaco's Prince Rainier to run the Monaco Grand Prix. He did so until his death in 1979, aged 78.

Louis Chiron	
Nationality	French
Seasons	1928–58
Teams driven for	Bugatti, Alfa Romeo, Mercedes, Talbot, Lancia
Number of major victories	14

◄ Chiron, here in his role of running the Monaco Grand Prix, talks to Juan Manuel Fangio.

▼ Chiron in a Scuderia-Ferrari Alfa Romeo P3 in 1934.

Jim Clark

The greatest driver of his era, Clark was World Champion in 1963 and 1965 and, at the time of his death in 1968, he had won more Grands Prix than anyone in the sport's history. He drove for Lotus throughout his Formula One career.

A Scottish farmer, he was adopted as a protégé by amateur racing driver Ian Scott-Watson. His early successes came in a variety of saloons and sports cars in local club racing. The break into the big time came after testing a Lotus Formula Two car at Brands Hatch, where he was trading times with the team's Formula One star Graham Hill. Lotus boss Colin Chapman was stunned when he subsequently learned that this was Clark's first ever drive in a single-seater.

Clark subsequently became a works Lotus Formula Two driver, and within a few months was making his Formula One debut in Holland in 1960. Chapman and Clark came to form a very close relationship, and as each man was a genius in their respective fields of design and driving, phenomenal success followed. As well as winning in Formula One, they also took the American racing world by storm with victory in the 1965 Indy 500.

Clark was 32 and at the height of his powers when he was killed in a Formula Two race at Hockenheim on 7 April 1968.

Jim Clark	
Nationality	British
Seasons	1960–68
Teams driven for	Lotus
Number of major victories	25

▲ Jim Clark dominating his final Grand Prix at South Africa in 1968.

▶ Jim Clark, World Drivers' Champion of 1963 and 1965.

▼ Clark gives the Lotus 25 its debut at the 1962 Dutch Grand Prix. He would win two world titles with this car and its derivative.

Peter Collins

Collins' place in motorsport folklore was guaranteed when he gave up his chance of winning the 1956 World Championship by handing his car over to title rival and team-mate Juan Manuel Fangio in the final round. In what was a cruel twist of fate, he was denied any subsequent challenge for the crown, suffering a fatal accident during the 1958 German Grand Prix.

Collins was part of a new generation of British talent to emerge from that country's pioneering Formula 500 Championship. After a few promising runs for a variety of British teams from 1954 to 1955, his big chance came when he was signed by Ferrari for 1956. He won the Belgian and French Grand Prix that year and would almost certainly have taken the crown were it not for his act of supreme sportsman-ship at Monza in the season finale.

He stayed at Ferrari in company with his close friend Mike Hawthorn for the rest of his time. Two weeks after winning the 1958 British Grand Prix, he was chasing Tony Brooks' race-leading Vanwall at the Nürburgring when his car left the road and overturned.

◀ Collins stayed loyal to Ferrari from 1956 until his demise in 1958. He was a firm favourite of Enzo Ferrari.

Peter Collins

Nationality	British
Seasons	1952–58
Teams driven for	HWM, Vanwall, Owen, Maserati, Ferrari
Number of major victories	3

◀ Peter Collins was just 20 years old when he made his Grand Prix debut, in 1952, and only 26 when he was killed.

▲ Peter Collins with his Ferrari in 1957. Ferrari were not fully competitive that year, and Collins' best finishes were third in France and Germany.

▶ Peter Collins in his Mercedes at Targa Florio in 1955. He was beaten by team-mate Stirling Moss after suffering an accident.

David Coulthard

T he Scot's big career break came under the tragic circumstances of Ayrton Senna's death. As Williams' test driver, Coulthard took over the seat of the legendary Brazilian and established himself as a regular Grand Prix winner. His first victory came in 1995 in Portugal.

From karting, Coulthard served an apprenticeship in the British junior categories. He was in the European Formula 3000 Championship when his Formula One chance came. After four consecutive pole positions for Williams at the end of 1995, he moved to McLaren.

Initially, this was a backward step in terms of competitiveness, but he began his winning sequence for his new team with victory in Australia in 1997. The McLarens of 1998 and 1999 were the fastest cars but Coulthard was outshone by team-mate Mika Häkkinen. He mounted a serious title challenge to Michael Schumacher in 2001 but by this time Ferrari had gained a performance advantage over McLaren. He continued to win races for McLaren through 2002 and 2003 and served the team for longer than any driver in its 35-year history.

He moved to the new Red Bull team for the 2005 season and became a regular points scorer for the fledgling constructor.

◀ David Coulthard in his Williams FW17 at the Spanish Grand Prix, Barcelona, in 1995. It was his first full season of Formula One.

David Coulthard

Nationality	British
Seasons	1994–present
Teams driven for	Williams, McLaren, Red Bull
Number of major victories	13

◀ David Coulthard has spent most of his Formula One career with McLaren after getting his first break with Williams.

▼ Coulthard took a great victory at Monaco in 2002. Here, he is chased by Juan Pablo Montoya and Michael Schumacher, neither of whom could break his defence.

Arthur Duray

Born in New York but a resident of France, Duray was one of the top drivers of the era of the sport before World War I. He enjoyed a long career that stretched from the turn of the 20th century to the late 1920s, though his halcyon days were with de Dietrich in 1905–07.

After establishing the land speed record at 134.31km/h (83.46mph) in 1903 for Gobron-Brille, Duray began racing with that company. De Dietrich then recruited him and they won the 1906 Circuit des Ardennes together.

After de Dietrich withdrew from the sport in 1912, Duray was left without a top drive but, undeterred, he continued in the small car class. He scored a stunning second place in the 1913 Indianapolis 500, having led for much of the distance, in a 3-litre Peugeot that was 2.5 litres down on the rest of the field. After the war, he continued racing in the voiturette and sports car categories, and continued to set speed records before his retirement in 1928.

▼ Arthur Duray in the Alcyon voiturette (small car) in the 1912 French Grand Prix. He continued in this class into the 1920s.

▲ Arthur Duray in 1908.

◄ Arthur Duray, with de Dietrich emblem, at the 1907 Moscow–St Petersburg race.

Arthur Duray

Nationality	French
Seasons	1903–14
Teams driven for	Gobron-Brille, de Dietrich, Delage, Peugeot
Number of major victories	1

Juan Manuel Fangio

This Argentinian legend was a five-time World Champion in the 1950s, and was commonly referred to as "El Maestro". His amazing Grand Prix career began when he was already in his late 30s, and he won his final title at the age of 46.

Hailing from a modest family background in Balcarce, his early racing exploits were on dirt roads in saloon cars, partly financed by whip-rounds among the people of his village. He quickly established a huge reputation in his homeland, but it was not until the leading European teams and drivers of the day visited Argentina for an off-season mini-series in 1948 that the phenomenon of Fangio was revealed to the wider world.

Jean-Pierre Wimille was acknowledged as the world's finest driver at that time. In the Rosario Grand Prix, he and Fangio were matched in identical Gordinis. They staged a superb duel. Wimille won but only after Fangio's car had begun to lose power. Fangio took the consolation of fastest lap. Afterwards, Wimille paid tribute to his rival and rightly predicted that great things awaited him.

The Argentinian Motor Club paid for a national team that included Fangio to race in European events in 1949. His form in the club's Maserati proved beyond all doubt his stunning

▲ **Fangio (18) starts the 1954 French Grand Prix in pole position, ahead of Karl Kling (20).**

Juan Manuel Fangio	
Nationality	Argentinian
Seasons	1949–58
Teams driven for	Alfa Romeo, Maserati, Mercedes, Ferrari
Number of major victories	24

speed, leading to his recruitment by Alfa-Romeo for the 1950 season.

Only unreliability kept him from victory in the inaugural World Championship that year, but he was a dominant champion in 1951. A neck-breaking accident kept him out for most of 1952 but he was back in his winning stride by 1953. He then won four successive world titles, a record that lasted 46 years. He retired in 1958 and returned to his homeland, where he ran a Mercedes-Benz dealership until his death in 1995.

◀ **Fangio became a legend through his exploits in the 1950s, when he won five world titles in eight years.**

▶ **Juan Manuel Fangio winning the International Trophy of 1951 at Silverstone for Alfa Romeo.**

Giuseppe Farina

Farina was already 44 years old when, in 1950, he won the inaugural World Championship. As a highly promising newcomer in the 1930s, his best years were probably lost to the war.

Farina had qualified to become a doctor of political science when at 26 years old he began his racing career. At Maserati he was taken under the wing of Tazio Nuvolari, but he really began to shine in voiturette racing with Alfa Romeo before the war intervened.

After a spell with Ferrari, he moved back to Alfa after the war in the new Formula One category. As a driver in the fastest car, he was well placed when the World Championship was inaugurated. His only competition for the title was team-mate Juan Manuel Fangio, whom he defeated through a superior finishing record. He won races in subsequent seasons with Ferrari, but retired at the end of 1955, having been troubled by leg burns incurred the previous year. He was killed in a road accident in 1966, while driving to the French Grand Prix.

◄ The 1950 World Championship title was the culmination of a long career for Giuseppe Farina.

▼ Farina became the sport's first World Champion with three victories in 1950.

▼ Farina winning the very first race of the World Championship at Silverstone in 1950.

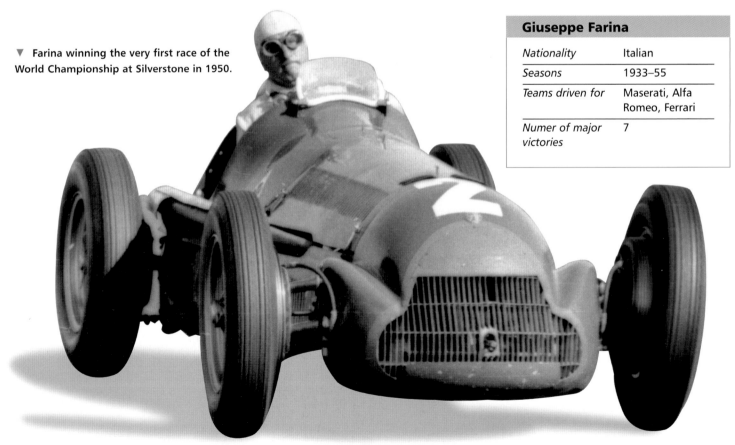

Giuseppe Farina

Nationality	Italian
Seasons	1933–55
Teams driven for	Maserati, Alfa Romeo, Ferrari
Numer of major victories	7

Emerson Fittipaldi

By moving from his native Brazil to race in Europe to further his career, and then becoming World Champion in 1972 and 1974, Emerson Fittipaldi blazed a trail that countless South American drivers have followed ever since.

The son of a sports journalist, Emerson raced karts from an early age, along with his elder brother Wilson. He arrived in Britain in 1968 to race in the junior Formula Ford category, and proved an instant sensation. Lotus' Colin Chapman shrewdly signed him to drive the team's Formula Three and Formula Two cars, and by 1970 he was making his Formula One debut.

In fairy-tale fashion, he won his fifth Grand Prix, this result in America ensuring that Lotus' recently-deceased Jochen Rindt became a posthumous World Champion. After a sequence of victories, he became the sport's youngest-ever World Champion in 1972, aged 25. He joined McLaren for 1974 and promptly won another title.

Surprisingly, he left McLaren at the end of 1975 to drive for the Brazilian Copersucar team that had been founded by his brother Wilson. It proved a frustrating venture, and in five years of trying Emerson never did find success with the cars. He retired for a time before making a glorious comeback in Indycar racing, winning two Indy 500s before his final retirement from motorsport in 1996.

▲ Fittipaldi's final podium came with third place in the 1980 USA West Grand Prix – from 24th on the grid.

Emerson Fittipaldi

Nationality	Brazilian
Seasons	1970–80
Teams driven for	Lotus, McLaren, Fittipaldi
Number of major victories	14

▼ Fittipaldi's victory at Watkins Glen in 1970 ensured that his late team-mate Jochen Rindt took the world title.

▲ Fittipaldi stands on top of the podium after his fifth Grand Prix, the USA, in 1970.

José Froilán González

The burly Argentinian, known as the "Pampas Bull", won Ferrari's first ever championship-stature Grand Prix, when he beat his friend Fangio's Alfa at Silverstone in 1951.

Fangio was instrumental in getting González an opportunity in Europe in 1950, and his form in a privately-run Maserati brought him his recruitment to Ferrari the following year. After a spell alongside Fangio at Maserati, he returned to Ferrari in 1954, again winning the British Grand Prix and finishing runner-up in the World Championship that season.

At the end of the year, he was injured in a sports car race and niggles from this led to his retirement from regular competition, though he continued to appear at his home Grand Prix until 1960. He concentrated thereafter on his garage business.

Froilan Gonzalez

Nationality	Argentinian
Seasons	1950–60
Teams driven for	Maserati, Ferrari
Number of major victories	2

◀ Froilián González at the Argentine Grand Prix in 1973, 13 years after his retirement.

▼ (right) Froilán González during the 1954 German Grand Prix in his Ferrari.

▼ (bottom) Silverstone and the start of the 1951 British Grand Prix, with González (12) racing head to head with Juan Manuel Fangio's Alfa Romeo. González won the race, and Fangio finished in second place.

▼ (left) Froilán González on his way to the first Championship-status Grand Prix win for Ferrari at Silverstone in 1951.

Dan Gurney

▼ Gurney took his first Grand Prix victory at Rouen in 1962. It stands as the only such win for the Porsche marque.

In a 12-year Formula One career that spanned spells at Ferrari, BRM, Porsche, Brabham and his own Eagle team, the American Gurney frequently displayed outstanding talent, but was never able to create the right circumstances for a title bid.

The son of an opera singer, he began racing sports cars in California in the early 1950s. The American Ferrari importer Luigi Chinetti was instrumental in getting Gurney a chance with the Ferrari sports car team in Europe in 1958. This opportunity led to his Grand Prix graduation with the team the following year. He made a great impression, running at the front in just his second race.

Uneasy about the politics within Ferrari, he moved to BRM for 1960, but the car proved less competitive than hoped, and this led him to accept an offer to lead Porsche's new Formula One effort for 1961. He gave the team its only Grand Prix victory at France in 1962, having narrowly lost out in the same race in 1961. The disappointing form of the cars led to the German company's withdrawal at the end of 1962, and this left Gurney to hook up with Jack Brabham, who was in the throes of establishing his own team.

Gurney, rather than double World Champion Brabham, proved to be the cutting edge of the driving squad, and in 1964 he gave them their first victory, in France. He won again in Mexico that year, but at the end of a relatively

Dan Gurney	
Nationality	American
Seasons	1959–70
Teams driven for	Ferrari, BRM, Porsche, Brabham, Eagle, McLaren
Number of major victories	4

▼ Two years after his success for Porsche, Gurney gave the Brabham team its first win.

barren 1965, he left to pursue the dream of creating his own team, Eagle. This cost him a real chance of the 1966 World Championship, as Brabhams proved the dominant cars that year.

Gurney won in Belgium in 1967 in the Eagle, but thereafter the car was left behind by the new DFV-powered machines and Gurney's interest in Formula One waned. He drove his last Grand Prix in 1970, as a stand-in at McLaren, and went on to enjoy considerable success as a team owner in Indy car racing.

▲ Dan Gurney celebrates his victory at Rouen in France in 1964.

Mika Häkkinen

The furiously fast Finn came back from near-death in 1995 to win the World Championships of 1998 and 1999 with McLaren-Mercedes.

Managed by former World Champion Keke Rosberg after early years in karting and Formula Ford, he was backed by Marlboro to pursue his career in Britain where he became Formula Three Champion in 1990. Lotus' Peter Collins had a sharp eye for new talent, and he signed Hakkinen for 1991. He performed with much promise, but the team's glory days were over. For 1993, he accepted a role as test driver with McLaren, reasoning that he needed to show his pace in a top car even if it meant not racing in the short term.

When McLaren dropped Michael Andretti near the end of the season,

Mika Häkkinen	
Nationality	Finnish
Seasons	1991–2001
Teams driven for	Lotus, McLaren
Number of major victories	20

after a series of disappointing performances, Häkkinen stepped up to replace him. In a sensational performance, he outqualified his team-mate, the great Ayrton Senna, and his future was seemingly assured.

In qualifying for the 1995 Australian Grand Prix, a puncture-induced accident left him critically injured, and only an

emergency tracheotomy, track-side, saved his life. Remarkably, he seemed to have lost none of his speed when he returned for the start of 1996.

The breakthrough came at the end of 1997 in Jerez, though Häkkinen's victory there was gifted to him by Williams' Jacques Villeneuve, as thanks for McLaren co-operation in not attacking him in the early stages of the race as he fought for the world title with Michael Schumacher.

It was the prelude to a devastating run of victories in the superb McLaren-Mercedes of 1998 and 1999. Häkkinen only narrowly lost out on a third title in 2000. He retired at the end of 2001, though left the door open for a future possible return. In 2002, he announced his retirement was permanent.

▲ *(right)* Mika Häkkinen in the Lotus 102B at the rain-shortened Australian Grand Prix.

▲ *(left)* Häkkinen at the Melbourne Grand Prix in 2001. It was here he made the decision to retire from Formula One.

▶ Häkkinen driving his McLaren MP4-14 to victory in the Brazilian Grand Prix at Interlagos in 1999.

Mike Hawthorn

Hawthorn became the first British World Champion when he took the title for Ferrari in 1958. He immediately retired from what was then a lethally dangerous sport, but ironically was killed in a road accident just a few months later.

After a lightning quick rise through British club racing in the early 1950s, aided by his former bike-racing father, Hawthorn found himself on the international stage in 1952, when Formula Two was made the World Championship category. Some great performances in a Cooper-Bristol caught the eye of Enzo Ferrari, who signed him for 1953. In the French Grand Prix of that year, Hawthorn scored his first victory after a stirring wheel-to-wheel battle with Juan Manuel Fangio's Maserati.

It would be another five years before Hawthorn was once again in a fully competitive Ferrari, and although he won only the French Grand Prix in 1958, he scored highly everywhere and secured the title in the final round – with some help from team-mate Phil Hill, who moved aside to hand him second place.

After retiring to his garage business, Hawthorn fatally crashed his road car near Guildford in January 1959.

Mike Hawthorn	
Nationality	British
Seasons	1952–58
Teams driven for	Ferrari, Vanwall, BRM
Number of major victories	3

◄ Blonde and dashing, Hawthorn captured the public's imagination.

▼ Mike Hawthorn takes over the car of Ferrari team-mate José Froilán González on lap 16 of the 1954 German Grand Prix.

▲ Hawthorn in the Ferrari model 246 at the Monaco Grand Prix. The car won him the 1958 World Championship title.

▲ Hawthorn and Stirling Moss battled hard over the destiny of the 1958 world title. Hawthorn narrowly won.

Damon Hill

The 1996 World Champion Hill graduated from the role of test driver to racer for the mighty Williams-Renault team, following the departure of Nigel Mansell. It was a gifted opportunity, and it led to a fruitful association for all concerned.

The son of double World Champion Graham Hill, Damon began racing on motorbikes, and did not progress to cars until he was well into his 20s. A front runner in British Formula Ford and Formula Three racing, he was competing in Formula 3000 in 1991 when he was offered the chance by Williams to test-drive for Formula One.

He made his Grand Prix debut with the uncompetitive Brabham team in 1992. It proved useful experience for when he gained his first big break with Williams the following season. Alongside the great Alain Prost, he acquitted himself well, and he won his first Grand Prix in Hungary.

In 1994, he stepped up as team leader following the death of Prost's replacement, Ayrton Senna. His nemesis proved to be Benetton's Michael Schumacher, and the championship battle distilled into a final round shoot-out between the two men. Schumacher and Hill pulled well away from the rest in Adelaide, and Hill pounced when Schumacher was slowed after an off-track moment, but the German turned in on him, damaging Hill's suspension. With both out, Hill had lost the title. He was comfortably beaten by Schumacher in 1995, but put this to rights in 1996. With his new team-mate Jacques Villeneuve as his only serious rival, Hill clinched the title in Japan.

Controversially, Williams dropped Hill for 1997, leaving him to drive for the smaller Arrows team with which he came within an ace of winning the Grand Prix in Hungary. For 1998, he switched to Jordan, winning the team's first – and his 22nd – Grand Prix, at Belgium. He retired after a disappointing 1999 season.

► Hill taking his Williams FW18 to a dominant victory in the 1996 Brazilian Grand Prix.

Damon Hill	
Nationality	British
Seasons	1992–99
Teams driven for	Brabham, Williams, Arrows, Jordan
Number of major victories	22

▲ (Top) Damon Hill making his Grand Prix debut in the outclassed Brabham BT60B at the 1992 British Grand Prix.

◄ Hill in 1998 when he drove for Jordan and gave them their first Grand Prix win.

Graham Hill

The World Champion of 1962 and 1968 became a folk hero of the sport for his gritty determination and winning public persona. He retired from the driving seat in 1975 to devote himself to running his own team, but was killed piloting his light aircraft in November of that year.

After talking himself into a mechanic's job with Lotus in the mid-1950s, Hill got himself into the driving seat of the team's Formula Two and sports cars. When Lotus graduated to Formula One in 1958, Hill was one of the drivers. It wasn't until he switched to BRM in 1960, though, that he began to show some form; he looked set to win a superb victory in that year's British Grand Prix, but spun it away. For 1962, BRM had produced a powerful new V8 engine, and with this he scored his first race successes, culminating in his first world title at the end of that season.

He stayed at BRM, a regular race winner, until transferring back to Lotus for 1967. In between, he won the 1966 Indianapolis 500. The new Cosworth DFV engine in the Lotus 49 gave Hill a highly competitive but unreliable

▲ Graham Hill in 1973.

▼ Graham Hill in the BRM P48 at the British Grand Prix, Silverstone, 1960. He stormed up the field after stalling on the grid, but retired from the lead late in the race after a spin caused by brake failure.

Graham Hill	
Nationality	British
Seasons	1958–75
Teams driven for	Lotus, BRM, Brabham, Hill
Number of major victories	14

1967 season. When his friend and team-mate Jim Clark was killed early in 1968, Hill pulled the team back together with some great performances, and he clinched his second title in the final round. He won his fifth Monaco Grand Prix in 1969, but badly injured his legs at Watkins Glen. He never regained his Formula One form subsequently, but battled on for a few more years, and won the 1972 Le Mans 24 Hours sports car race for Matra.

He was returning from a test session with his team when he crashed his plane in fog as he attempted to land at Elstree near London. Five team members, including his young driver Tony Brise, died with him.

Phil Hill

America's first World Champion, Hill took the title with Ferrari in 1961. The son of a California postmaster, Hill began racing sports cars in the early 1950s, working on and preparing them himself. Ever-improving form brought him to the attention of Ferrari importer Luigi Chinetti who got Hill a sports car chance with the Ferrari works team. He enjoyed considerable success here, but his constant badgering for a Formula One chance took a long time to be answered.

In his first Formula One drive for the team, at Monza in 1958, he took third place and fastest lap. At the next event in Morocco, he outpaced his team-mate and that year's World Champion, Mike Hawthorn. Such an impressive start ensured a permanent place in the Formula One team.

He took fourth place in the 1959 Championship, but suffered in 1960 through Ferrari's front-engined policy. The following year, the Ferrari 156 was by far the fastest car of the season, and Hill became locked in battle for the title with his team-mate Wolfgang von Trips. Into the penultimate round at Monza

▲ Race winner Phil Hill (Ferrari) at the Italian Grand Prix, Monza, 1961.

▼ Phil Hill in the Ferrari 156 leads team-mate Wolfgang von Trips at the Belgian Grand Prix, 1961. Hill won the race, and Trips came second in a Ferrari 1-2-3-4.

Phil Hill	
Nationality	American
Seasons	1958–66
Teams driven for	Ferrari, ATS, Cooper, Eagle
Number of major victories	3

there was little to split them, but von Trips crashed to his death. Hill won the race and the title in the most tragic of circumstances.

Hill never approached such heights again in Formula One. Ferrari was overwhelmed by the British teams in 1962, though Hill performed superbly. A move to the new ATS team for 1963 proved disastrous, and his last full season was with Cooper in 1964. He enjoyed further sports car success – having won Le Mans three times – before retirement at the end of 1966. He later devoted himself to his classic car restoration business in California.

Denny Hulme

▼ Denny Hulme took his only pole position at the South Africa Grand Prix in 1973, when he gave the McLaren M23 its debut drive.

New Zealand's first, and to date only, World Drivers' Champion, Denny Hulme took the title for the Brabham team in only his second full Formula One season.

After winning a "Driver To Europe" award in his home country, Hulme served his racing apprenticeship with Brabham, driving their Formula Two cars as well as being the truck driver. He got occasional runs in the Formula One car in 1965, and was promoted to the seat full-time the following year, after Dan Gurney left the team.

His role was one of back up to Jack Brabham in 1967. But frequently "improvements" made to the team leader's car proved unreliable, and Hulme was invariably there to pick up the pieces, and ultimately the title. He moved to fellow countryman Bruce McLaren's team for 1968, where he remained until the end of his Formula One career in 1974. He challenged for the Championship again in 1968, for McLaren, and was a regular race-winner until he left Formula One. He came out of retirement to race touring cars in Australia in the 1980s and early 1990s, and it was while competing in the Bathurst race in 1992 that he suffered a fatal heart attack. He was 55.

Denny Hulme	
Nationality	New Zealand
Seasons	1965–74
Teams driven for	Brabham, McLaren
Number of major victories	8

▼ Hulme driving the Brabham BT7 in his Grand Prix debut at the 1967 Monaco Grand Prix. He finished in eighth place.

▲ Third place in the 1967 Mexican Grand Prix secured Hulme's world title from his team-mate Jack Brabham.

James Hunt

World Champion of 1976 after a dramatic battle with Niki Lauda, Hunt was a controversial figure from the beginning of his Formula One career in 1973 to the end in 1979. In between he produced some brilliant drives for Hesketh and McLaren.

In the junior categories, he established a reputation as being quick but accident-prone, and was nicknamed "Hunt the Shunt". After being dropped by the March Formula Three team, he was picked up by Lord Hesketh's eccentric new team.

They initially planned to tackle Formula Two together in 1973, but after realizing they could compete

▲ James Hunt winning the 1976 British Grand Prix at Brands Hatch. He was later disqualified from the race.

in Formula One for a little more money by buying a car from March, they did just that. Hunt soon began to surprise the Formula One paddock with his speed, and within a few races was running near the front. In the American Grand Prix, he chased victor Ronnie Peterson hard all the way, and crossed the line just fractions of a second behind. The March was replaced by a Hesketh design in 1974, and Hunt won the non-championship International Trophy Formula One race at Silverstone. In 1975, he won the Dutch Grand Prix

in a brilliant drive, during which he held off the faster Ferrari of Niki Lauda.

It was the Austrian with whom Hunt was locked in combat after he moved to McLaren for 1976, with Hunt clinching the title by just one point in the final round at Japan. He won three more times in 1977, but the competitiveness of McLaren was on the wane. He switched to Wolf for 1979, but the car proved no more competitive than the McLaren, and he retired part way through the season. He died in 1993, aged 46, after suffering a heart attack.

◄ James Hunt: daring, dashing, all-British hero of the 1970s.

James Hunt	
Nationality	British
Seasons	1973–79
Teams driven for	Hesketh, McLaren, Wolf
Number of major victories	10

▼ When the 1979 Wolf WR7 – here, at Argentina – proved uncompetitive, Hunt decided to hang up his helmet.

Jacky Ickx

▼ Ickx at the German Grand Prix and his beloved Nürburgring circuit, on his way to his final Grand Prix victory.

Twice runner-up in the World Championship, the Belgian Ickx was one of the fastest drivers around in the late 1960s and early 1970s.

He graduated from motorcycle racing to Formula Three and touring cars with Ken Tyrrell. A move to Formula Two followed. At that time the German Grand Prix on the 22.5km (14-mile) Nürburgring circuit allowed for Formula Two cars to join Formula Ones. Ickx caused a sensation by qualifying third-quickest for the 1967 event, faster than Jackie Stewart, John Surtees and Jack Brabham, all of whom were in Formula One cars with engines 1.4 litres bigger than that in Ickx's Formula Two Matra.

This performance brought a Ferrari drive for 1968. He won that year's French Grand Prix in the rain, and his reputation as one of the greatest wet weather drivers took hold. A switch to Brabham for 1969 gave him second place in the World Championship, and then it was back to Ferrari for 1970, where he was the only man to threaten Jochen Rindt's posthumous title.

Ferrari were by then producing ever-less competitive cars, and this allowed Ickx to grab only the occasional victory before leaving the team in 1973. A disappointing spell with Lotus led to him leaving Formula One to concentrate on sports cars, where he continued to be highly successful. He retired in 1985, having won the Le Mans 24 Hours six times.

Jacky Ickx	
Nationality	Belgian
Seasons	1967–79
Teams driven for	Cooper, Ferrari, Brabham, Lotus, Wolf, Ensign, Ligier
Major victories	8

▲ Ickx in 1970, when he was in real contention for the world title.

◀ Ickx's Ferrari leads Peterson (March) and team-mate Clay Regazzoni at the German Grand Prix in 1972.

Alan Jones

T he first of many to win a World title with the Williams team, the Australian Jones drove Formula One cars from 1975 to 1981 before a brief retirement. He returned in 1985–86, but without the same level of success.

The son of Melbourne racing star Stan Jones, he moved to Britain in the early 1970s and became a front-runner in the British Formula Three and Formula 5000 categories. He drove for a series of small, underfunded Formula One teams in 1975 and 1976, but despite a race-leading drive for Surtees in the 1976 race of champions he entered 1977 without a drive. It looked as though his Formula One career was over, but after the tragedy of Tom Pryce's death in the South African Grand Prix, Jones was rescued by the Shadow team. He drove several very strong races, culminating in a surprise victory in Austria.

This led to his recruitment by Frank Williams to drive the first Patrick Head-designed Williams for 1978. This proved a highly competitive machine, and Jones was challenging for victory in the 1978 USA West Grand Prix. Head's ground-effect FW07 of 1979 was even better and, in the latter half of that year, Jones took four victories. This was the build-up to his title-winning campaign of 1980. He drove some superb, aggressive races in 1981, still in the FW07, and bowed out with victory in the final race at Las Vegas, having announced his retirement.

He was tempted back by Arrows into a brief comeback in 1983, and a more serious one, by the new Ford-backed Beatrice team, in 1985. Although the Ross Brawn-designed car was good, its Ford V6 lacked horsepower and Jones was never a serious contender. He called it a day – along with the Beatrice team – at the end of 1986.

▲ *(right)* Alan Jones took a surprise win for Shadow in the rain at Austria in 1977. It was this result that attracted him to Williams for 1978.

▶ Jones bowed out of Formula One for the first time in great style, winning the 1981 Las Vegas Grand Prix.

Alan Jones	
Nationality	Australian
Seasons	1975–86
Teams driven for	Hesketh, Hill, Surtees, Shadow, Williams, Arrows, Beatrice
Number of major victories	12

◀ Alan Jones on top of the podium for the first time at the Osterreichring in 1977.

Niki Lauda

The three-time World Champion Lauda became one of the all-time legends of the sport when, in 1976, he made a comeback from being given the last rites on his deathbed to fourth place in the Italian Grand Prix in just a matter of weeks.

Lauda was recruited by Ferrari in 1974 as a promising newcomer who had shown well in the outclassed BRM of 1973. His technical adeptness and capacity for testing made him the perfect partner for Ferrari designer Mauro Forghieri, as they spent hour upon hour testing at Ferrari's new Fiorano test track. The hard work paid off as Lauda reeled off a great sequence of nine pole positions and took his first two victories.

In 1975, his Ferrari 312T dominated the Championship, with five wins. After beginning 1976 in similar fashion, he crashed in the early laps of the German Grand Prix, incurring critical lung damage as he lay unconscious in his burning car. After a remarkable comeback, he pulled out of the title-deciding Japanese Grand Prix, unwilling to risk his life in the blinding spray. This lost him the title to James Hunt.

He won back the title in 1977, and then walked out on Ferrari with two races still to go – an act of revenge for the lack of support he felt the team gave him in his 1976 comeback.

▲ Niki Lauda in the BRM P160E of 1973. It was his pace in this car that brought him to the attention of Ferrari.

Niki Lauda	
Nationality	Austrian
Seasons	1971–85
Teams driven for	March, BRM, Ferrari, Brabham, McLaren
Number of major victories	25

▼ Lauda takes the lead from Andrea de Cesaris on his way to victory in the 1982 USA West Grand Prix at Long Beach.

He joined the Brabham team where he scored two victories in 1978, but at the penultimate race of 1979 he promptly retired, saying he was bored with driving round in circles.

After two years building up his airline business, he was tempted to return for 1982 by McLaren's Ron Dennis. He won on his third race back, and went on to victory in the 1984 World Championship. He retired permanently at the end of 1985.

▼ Lauda at Zolder, Belgium, in 1976, five races before his scarring accident, and the prelude to the bravest comeback of all time.

Vincenzo Lancia

T he son of a wealthy country squire who had a soup-manufacturing empire, Lancia was a trainee with the Ceirano car company – which hired its workshop space from Lancia's father – when the company was taken over by Fiat at the turn of the 20th century. He had already made his competition debut in a small-time race with Ceirano, and was used by Fiat for similar events as well as being employed by them as a test driver.

When Fiat progressed to international racing, Lancia went with them. He soon established a reputation as a furiously fast competitor, but often his mechanical sympathy seemed to desert him and he would invariably retire from leading positions – often leaving victory to his team-mate Felice Nazzaro.

Whilst still in the employ of Fiat, he founded his own company, Lancia, to produce sporting road cars. His driving career at Fiat continued until 1910, after which he concentrated on the running of his company. He would preside over this and engineer many innovations until his death in 1937, aged 56. His son Gianni took over the car company which bore the family name and later took it into Grand Prix racing. Just like Vincenzo, the 1954–55 Lancia proved to be very fast but, ultimately, unreliable.

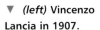 Lancia at the French Grand Prix of 1906.

▼ *(left)* Vincenzo Lancia in 1907.

Vincenzo Lancia

Nationality	Italian
Seasons	1900–10
Teams driven for	Fiat
Number of major victories	0

▼ Lancia winning the Florio Cup in a 75hp Fiat with an average speed of 115.70km/h (71.89mph) in 1904.

Emile Levassor

he winner of the first ever motorcar race, engineer Emile Levassor triumphed in the 1895 Paris–Bordeaux–Paris race in his Panhard-Levassor by over five hours.

As a partner in the former woodworking company, Panhard, he took it into car manufacture when a friend acquired the French commercial rights to the new Daimler engine. The engine was installed in a chassis more advanced than that of the Daimler, and this led to the car being the dominant force in the pioneer sport.

Levassor suffered an accident after hitting a dog during the 1896 Paris–Marseilles race. His car rolled, throwing him out, and although he was able to restart and finish the event in fourth place, the internal injuries he incurred proved fatal. He died the following year, aged 53. Motorsport's first hero had also become its first fatality.

▼ Emile Levassor.

◄ Emile Levassor, winner of the first true motor race, in 1895.

▼ Levassor is commemorated in stone at Porte Mallot near Paris.

Emile Levassor

Nationality	French
Seasons	1895–96
Teams driven for	Panhard
Number of major victories	1

LEVASSOR

Nigel Mansell

A dominant World Champion in 1992, Mansell's career was a Wurlitzer ride of high-drama and spine-tingling excitement.

He was a struggling Formula Three driver with a broken bone in his neck from a recent race accident when Lotus boss Colin Chapman invited him to test a Formula One car. Keeping his injury secret, Mansell did the test and performed well enough to be offered a test-driver role for the team in 1980. He made his race debut in Austria that year, sitting bathed in leaking petrol for many laps before the car eventually failed. He was signed as a full-time member of the race team in 1981, but his career received a setback with the death of Chapman in 1982.

Although Mansell was retained by the team, he no longer received the same treatment, and relations became strained with the new management. He was dominating the wet Monaco Grand Prix of 1984 when he made a mistake and crashed out. The following year he was replaced – Lotus signed Ayrton Senna – but Mansell's career was given a lifeline as he was recruited by Williams for 1985. Towards the end of the season, he made a breakthrough victory in front of his home crowd at Brands Hatch. He immediately followed it up with another, in South Africa.

His 1986 season was a fierce battle with new Williams team-mate Nelson Piquet, though both ultimately lost out

▲ **Nigel Mansell leading the 1984 Monaco Grand Prix in his Lotus 95T. He later crashed out of the race.**

Nigel Mansell

Nationality	British
Seasons	1980–95
Teams driven for	Lotus, Williams, Ferrari, McLaren
Number of major victories	31

▼ *(left)* **Mansell: determination always saw him through. He was one of the most exciting performers the sport has seen.**

▼ *(right)* **Mansell leading the 1990 British Grand Prix. He announced his retirement after the race but later changed his mind.**

to Alain Prost. Mansell was on course for the title, with 19 laps to go in the final race, when a rear tyre exploded dramatically. He was again in title contention in 1987, but injured his back in practice for the penultimate race.

He joined Ferrari in 1989, and won his first race for them. He won a total of three races for the team, but left at the end of 1990 to rejoin Williams. After narrowly losing the 1991 title to McLaren's Ayrton Senna, Mansell wiped up in 1992 with the devastatingly fast active-ride Williams FW14B. Unable to agree terms for 1993, he headed for America, where he became CART Champion. He returned to Williams in 1994 as a stand-in, and won the Australian Grand Prix. His full Formula One comeback with McLaren in 1995 was aborted after just a few races as the car proved uncompetitive.

Guy Moll

The Algerian driver Moll looked to have a brilliant career ahead of him after making an instant impact at the highest level of the sport, in the early 1930s.

A protégé of compatriot and Bugatti driver Marcel Lehoux, Moll finished second in the 1933 Pau Grand Prix, his first international competition. This brought him to the attention of Enzo Ferrari, who recruited him to drive Alfa Romeos alongside established stars, Achille Varzi and Louis Chiron.

Guy Moll	
Nationality	Algerian
Seasons	1933–34
Teams driven for	Alfa Romeo
Number of major victories	1

▼ Guy Moll, winner of the Monaco Grand Prix, in 1934. Enzo Ferrari is third from the top on the extreme left of the picture.

He instantly proved their match, and won the 1934 Monaco Grand Prix. For a virtial rookie, such performances bordered on miraculous.

He was fighting Mercedes driver Luigi Fagioli for victory at Pescara, in 1934, when he crashed trying to lap the Mercedes of Ernst Henne. He was thrown out of his car into a tree, suffering fatal injuries. Several decades later, Enzo Ferrari said he believed Moll would have proved himself to be one of the all-time great drivers had he lived.

Juan Pablo Montoya

▼ Montoya *(left)* and Michael Schumacher in one of several wheel-to-wheel battles: here, at Melbourne in 2002.

Since entering Formula One in 2001, the Colombian Montoya has established himself as one of the sport's most exciting performers.

After winning the 1998 European Formula 3000 Championship, Montoya transferred to American CART racing. He won the championship at his first attempt, astounding veterans of the series with his phenomenal car control and an ability to overtake in places never seen before. In 2000, he won the Indianapolis 500 at his first attempt.

The Williams team had put him on a long-term contract when he was still in Formula 3000, and in 2001 they brought him to Formula One. In Brazil, his third race, he created a sensation by overtaking Michael Schumacher, rubbing tyres, then pulling away to victory. Only the mistake of a lapped backmarker denied him. He won his first race later that year at Monza. In 2002 he scored seven pole positions, and in 2003 was in contention for the World Championship until the penultimate round. For 2005 he moved to McLaren.

Juan Pablo Montoya

Nationality	Colombian
Seasons	2001–present
Teams driven for	Williams, McLaren
Number of major victories	7

▼ Brazil 2001: Montoya makes his move inside Schumacher to take the lead, rubbing wheels along the way *(inset)*.

▶ Juan Pablo Montoya, a combative performer whose exciting driving style has captured imaginations.

Stirling Moss

▼ Moss drove one of his greatest races in the under-powered Rob Walker Lotus 18 to win the Monaco Grand Prix in 1961.

From the time of Juan Manuel Fangio's retirement in 1958 to his own injury-induced retirement in 1962, Stirling Moss was widely recognized as the world's greatest driver. That he never won the world title was seen as an indictment of the Championship rather than any slur on his skills.

After establishing a big reputation in the British junior classes, Moss competed in his first Formula One season in 1954 with a privately-owned Maserati 250F. His form in this was so impressive that he was later given a drive with the works team. Only mechanical failure lost him that year's Italian Grand Prix. This led to his recruitment by Mercedes for the 1955 season, when he drove alongside the acknowledged master of Formula One, Fangio. Moss won the British Grand Prix, but to this day he is unsure whether Fangio allowed him to do so.

Following Mercedes' withdrawal, Moss rejoined Maserati, but it was his switch to the British Vanwall team in 1957 that brought him bigger success. Between 1957 and 1958 he won six Grands Prix for the team. His tally of four wins in 1958 compared to one for the World Champion, Mike Hawthorn.

◄ Stirling Moss, photographed at Silverstone in 1955.

After Vanwall's withdrawal, Moss spent most of the remainder of his career driving for privateer Rob Walker, first in a Cooper and latterly a Lotus. In 1961, he produced two of his greatest drives to win the Monaco and German Grands Prix against the faster Ferraris. Early in 1962 he suffered a big accident at a non-championship race at Goodwood, and his life hung in the balance for a while. Though he made a full recovery, he felt his incomparable skills had been impaired, and reluctantly retired, still in his early 30s. He remains a household name in retirement.

▼ Stirling Moss beats Mercedes team-mate Juan Manuel Fangio to the chequered flag in the 1955 British Grand Prix.

Stirling Moss	
Nationality	British
Seasons	1951–62
Teams driven for	HWM, Connaught, Cooper, Maserati, Mercedes, Vanwall, Walker, BRP, Ferguson
Number of major victories	16

Felice Nazzaro

Nazzaro was one of the master drivers for a long period from the early-1900s to the early 1920s. His successes came almost exclusively with Fiat, for whom he later became competition director.

Like his compatriot Vincenzo Lancia, he was apprenticed to the Ceirano company at the turn of the century, but was retained when that company was bought out by Fiat. When Fiat moved into big-time international racing, Nazzaro immediately proved his class. His drives were a calculating blend of early race caution and searing speed when the occasion demanded it, and his finishing record was far superior to the more spectacular Lancia's. In 1907, he won all three major races of the season, and was still winning in 1922.

◀ A portrait of Felice Nazzaro in 1907 when he won all three major races of the season. He raced successfully until 1924.

▼ (left) Felice Nazzaro, in the 1913 French Grand Prix at Amiens. This was one of the few races in which he didn't drive for the Fiat marque.

Felice Nazzaro	
Nationality	Italian
Seasons	1900–24
Teams driven for	Fiat, Itala
Number of major victories	5

In that year he took victory in the French Grand Prix, the same race in which his nephew, Biagio Nazzaro, was killed in another Fiat. He retired from the driving seat at the end of 1924, but remained with the company until his death in 1940.

▼ Nazzaro's Fiat came second at the Italian Grand Prix of 1922, on the new Monza track, but here he leads a Bugatti and a Diatto.

Tazio Nuvolari

Still regarded by many as the greatest driver who has ever lived, Nuvolari's reign as a giant of the sport lasted from the late 1920s until the outbreak of World War II. Though his list of victories in Bugattis, Alfa Romeos, Maseratis and Auto Unions was long, it was his frequent giant-killing "impossible" victories against superior machinery that sealed his reputation.

Never interested in taking over the family farms, instead Tazio sold some of the land he had inherited to begin a career in motorcycle racing. He became a hero of that sport in the mid-1920s, his spectacular style in sharp contrast to the cool calculation of his arch rival, Achille Varzi.

The two drivers combined forces to form their own racing stable, in which to begin their car racing careers proper, though Nuvolari had already dabbled with four-wheel competition. Though they were both successful in their team of Bugattis, it was an uneasy relationship, and Varzi left after little more than a year.

▲ Tazio Nuvolari c. 1933.

▼ Nuvolari in action for Alfa Romeo at the Monaco Grand Prix of 1932.

Tazio Nuvolari	
Nationality	Italian
Seasons	1928–46
Teams driven for	Alfa Romeo, Bugatti, Maserati, Auto Union
Number of major victories	18

By the time Nuvolari received his first big break in a works Alfa Romeo, courtesy of Enzo Ferrari, he was already 37 years old. But it made no difference to his form, and he racked up one spectacular victory after another, often after stirring battles with Varzi.

The overwhelming superiority of the German cars from 1934 onwards left Nuvolari in uncompetitive machinery. Varzi, by contrast, had signed with Auto Union, and made it a stipulation that he would not drive alongside Nuvolari. In the 1935 German Grand Prix, Nuvolari drove the old-fashioned Alfa P3 to a staggering victory over a field of cutting-edge Mercedes and Auto-Unions, to the bewilderment of the officiating Nazis. He performed similar miracles with Alfa on several occasions in 1936.

Following the death of Auto Union's Bernd Rosemeyer, and the ill-health of Varzi, Nuvolari was recruited by Auto Union part-way through 1938. Despite never having raced mid-engined machines before, he showed that, at the age of 45, his genius was still intact. He took two victories, including a stirring comeback drive in that year's Donington Grand Prix and the 1939 Czechoslovakian Grand Prix.

Post-war, Nuvolari took up the sport once more but by now he was an ill man, and he frequently had to retire from races coughing up blood. Still he couldn't stop, and still the miraculous performances unfolded. In both the 1947 and 1948 Mille Miglia races, he was robbed of victory after truly staggering drives. He died in 1953.

◄ Nuvolari driving for Auto Union in 1938.

Riccardo Patrese

P atrese is the holder of the record for the greatest number of Grand Prix starts. Between 1977 and 1993 the Italian lined up to do battle on the Formula One grid no less than 256 times. He won on six occasions for the Brabham and Williams teams.

A graduate of karting, he rose to car racing prominence in Formula Three and Formula Two, and made his Formula One debut with the Shadow team at Monaco in 1977. A new team, Arrows, was formed for 1978 from Shadow, and Patrese became their lead driver. In only the team's second race, Patrese was dominating the South African Grand Prix when the car failed. He was the only driver in the team's history to have put an Arrows on pole position – a feat he achieved at Long Beach, in the United States in 1981.

Patrese's first victory didn't come until he transferred to Brabham, for whom he won the 1982 Monaco Grand Prix. After an interlude at Alfa Romeo he stayed with Brabham until Bernie Ecclestone sold it at the end of 1987. Patrese transferred to Williams in 1988, and went on to win four races for the team between 1990 and 1992. After a season with Benetton alongside Michael Schumacher in 1993, Patrese brought his distinguished career to an end.

Riccardo Patrese	
Nationality	Italian
Seasons	1977–93
Teams driven for	Shadow, Arrows, Brabham, Williams, Alfa Romeo, Benetton
Number of major victories	6

◀ Riccardo Patrese in 1988.

▼ (*below*) Patrese in his first Formula One season, finishing sixth for Shadow at the Japanese Grand Prix at Fuji in 1977.

▼ (*bottom*) Patrese in 1993, his final season in Formula One, driving for Benetton at the South African Grand Prix.

Ronnie Peterson

The Swede was known unofficially as "the world's fastest driver" during the peak of his career in the 1970s. Although he never managed to translate this tag into the World Championship title, he was twice runner-up and lit up many races with some electrifying performances and astonishing car control.

Winning the 1969 Monaco Formula Three race proved to be his catapult into Formula One the following year. In 1971, driving for March, he finished runner-up to Jackie Stewart in the World Championship. But it wasn't until his move to Lotus in 1973 that he began winning races. In 1973, he set what was then a record of nine pole positions during the season, and his raw speed comfortably eclipsed that of his reigning World Champion team-mate, Emerson Fittipaldi.

Lotus cars subsequently lost their competitiveness and Peterson left for a couple of barren seasons of his own, before returning in 1978, this time as a contracted number two driver to the incumbent Mario Andretti. Lotus were by now the dominant team once again,

▲ Ronnie Peterson in his Lotus 72E on his way to second place in the British Grand Prix at Silverstone in 1973, the year in which he set nine pole positions.

Ronnie Peterson

Nationality	Swedish
Seasons	1970–78
Teams driven for	Lotus, March, Tyrrell
Number of major victories	10

thanks to their 79 model. Although there were several races where Peterson was quicker than his team-mate, he dutifully fulfilled his contracted role. Two wins, including a superb wet weather performance in Austria, confirmed his speed was very much still there. At the Italian Grand Prix, he was involved in a startline collision, and his car was thrown into the barriers, breaking one of his legs. That night he died from a brain embolism triggered by the broken bone. His second place in the Championship to Andretti was thus taken posthumously.

▲ Ronnie Peterson in 1971. He died following an accident at the start of the Italian Grand Prix in 1978.

◄ Peterson finished a close second in the 1971 Italian Grand Prix after leading for much of the race.

Nelson Piquet

The great Brazilian driver won three World Championships in the 1980s, and brought his long Formula One career to a close at the end of 1991, a season during which he proved he was still capable of winning races.

The son of a diplomat, Piquet moved to Europe to pursue the career he had begun in his homeland, inspired by the success of Emerson Fittipaldi. He was recruited by the Brabham team at the end of 1978, after winning that year's British Formula Three Championship and making a few Formula One appearances with a privately-run McLaren. Teamed alongside Niki Lauda at Brabham in 1979 he proved every bit as quick, and following Lauda's retirement, Piquet entered 1980 as the clear team leader. After winning his first Grand Prix at Long Beach, he

▼ Piquet's Brabham BT49C took third place at Long Beach in 1981, the scene of his first victory 12 months earlier.

Nelson Piquet

Nationality	Brazilian
Seasons	1978–91
Teams driven for	Ensign, Brabham, Williams, Lotus, Benetton
Number of major victories	23

▼ Nelson Piquet, three times World Champion, seen here in 1986.

challenged Williams' Alan Jones hard for the title, but ultimately had to wait until 1981 for his first Championship.

He repeated the feat two years later, in the turbocharged Brabham-BMW, after a dramatic late-season comeback to overhaul a big points deficit to rival Alain Prost. The Brabham team's form dwindled subsequently, and Piquet switched to Williams for 1986, only narrowly losing out on the title. He won it in 1987 despite a big shunt at Imola that dulled his speed for some time afterwards. After poor seasons with

Lotus in 1988–89, many believed he was a spent force when Benetton recruited him in 1990. But he proved the doubters wrong with victories in the final two races of the year. He won again in Canada 1991 but retired from Formula One at the end of the season. He subsequently incurred serious leg injuries while practising for the 1992 Indianapolis 500.

▼ Piquet took a great victory in the 1987 Hungarian Grand Prix after passing the Lotus of Ayrton Senna.

Didier Pironi

F renchman Pironi looked to be on his way to the 1982 World Championship when he suffered a career-ending accident during the warm-up session for the German Grand Prix at Hockenheim.

The son of a wealthy construction company boss, he rose through the Elf-sponsored ranks of French junior racing in the 1970s, before graduating to Formula Two in 1977. There, he finished third in the Championship but earned wider recognition when he stepped back down to Formula Three for a one-off race supporting the 1977 Monaco Grand Prix, and won it. This was the springboard for his Formula One debut with Tyrrell in 1978.

It was not until he joined the more competitive Ligier team in 1980 that Pironi really began to show what he could do. He took his first Grand Prix victory in Belgium and produced some stunningly fast drives, not all of which were rewarded, through no fault of his own. His form in the Ligier led to his recruitment to Ferrari for the following year. Paired alongside Gilles Villeneuve, he struggled initially but with a much improved car for 1982 he began to look strong once more.

He took victory in the San Marino Grand Prix in controversial circumstances, Villeneuve feeling that Pironi had duped

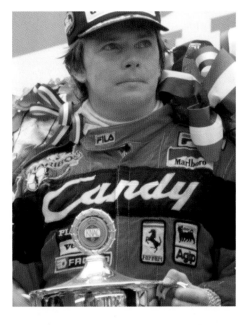

Didier Pironi	
Nationality	French
Seasons	1978–82
Teams driven for	Tyrrell, Ligier, Ferrari
Number of major victories	3

◀ **Didier Pironi celebrates his third victory at the Dutch Grand Prix in 1982. This result put him in the lead for that year's World Championship title.**

▼ **Pironi took his Ligier JS11/15 to his maiden victory at the Belgian Grand Prix at Spa in 1980.**

him and gone against team orders in passing him on the last lap. After Villeneuve's subsequent fatal accident, Pironi assumed leadership of the team. He won again in Holland, and by the time of the German Grand Prix had a comfortable Championship lead.

He crashed in conditions of blinding spray, hitting the back of Alain Prost's Renault at very high speed. The Ferrari reared high in the air before crashing down, and Pironi suffered serious leg injuries. Though he recovered, his right foot was no longer strong enough for the heavy braking required and he quietly retired. He took up power boating, and was killed competing in a race off the Isle of Wight in 1987.

◀ **Pironi in the Ferrari 126C2, the fastest car of 1982.**

Alain Prost

▼ Sparks flew when Prost joined Ferrari in 1990. Here, he takes the *Eau Rouge* corner at Spa, during the Belgian Grand Prix.

Winner of four World Championships and 51 Grands Prix, Frenchman Prost is statistically the second most successful driver in the sport's history, behind Michael Schumacher.

His Formula One career spanned 13 years, during which time he earned a reputation for searing speed disguised beneath silky smoothness. One of the most analytical of drivers, he was nicknamed The Professor.

He made his Formula One debut with McLaren in 1980 after winning the 1979 European Formula Three Championship. Promising form there led to his recruitment by Renault, for whom he won his first Grand Prix in 1981. Tension with team-mate René Arnoux in 1982 led to Prost's clear status as team leader in 1983. He established a big lead early in the Championship that year, but was ultimately thwarted by the late-season pace of Nelson Piquet's Brabham-BMW. He was sensationally sacked by Renault in the aftermath of losing the title, but this worked to his advantage in that he was able to sign for McLaren the following season, and McLaren produced the fastest car of 1984. Prost became locked in battle for the title with his team-mate Niki Lauda, but lost out by half a point in the last round.

But Prost couldn't be denied forever. He took a comfortable championship victory with McLaren in 1985, a feat he repeated in 1986, becoming the first back-to-back title winner since Jack Brabham in 1959–60. He was joined at McLaren in 1988 by Ayrton Senna, and so began one of the most dramatic and long-running feuds in Formula One. He lost out to his team-mate in the 1988 title battle, but won in 1989 after controversially blocking Senna's passing move in Japan. Transferring to Ferrari for 1990, he again battled with Senna's McLaren for the title, this time coming off second when Senna drove into him – again in Japan.

He was sacked from Ferrari after a disappointing 1991 season and sat out the following year. He returned in 1993

▲ Alain Prost, World Drivers' Champion in 1985, 1986, 1989 and 1993.

Alain Prost	
Nationality	French
Seasons	1980–93
Teams driven for	McLaren, Renault, Ferrari, Williams
Number of major victories	51

with Williams, and took his fourth title in the best car in the field. He retired – as the most successful driver in the sport's history – and turned team owner in 1997, after buying Ligier and renaming it Prost. The team went into receivership at the end of 2001.

▶ Prost won at Monaco in 1984, but was awarded only half points. It cost him the title.

Kimi Raikkonen

Raikkonen took over very big shoes when he stepped in to replace fellow Finn Mika Häkkinen at McLaren at the end of 2001.

Raikkonen was just 21 years old when, in 2001, he made his Grand Prix debut with Sauber. This marked only his second season of car racing. After a successful karting career he had graduated to cars in 2000, winning the British Formula Renault Championship. Inexperience proved to be little handicap in Formula One as he scored several World Championship points and was often quicker than his more experienced team-mate Nick Heidfeld.

Such performances brought Raikkonen to the attention of the McLaren team, where in 2002 he produced several stunning performances. He was within a few laps of winning the French Grand Prix that year when a backmarker's oil spillage cost him dearly. He won the 2003 Malaysian Grand Prix and followed it up with a campaign that took him to the final round with a chance of the World Championship. He narrowly lost out then, just as he did against Fernando Alonso in 2005, despite gaining a reputation as the sport's fastest driver.

Kimi Raikkonen	
Nationality	Finnish
Seasons	2001–present
Teams driven for	Sauber, McLaren
Number of major victories	9

◄ Kimi Raikkonen in 2002.

▼ *(below)* In the Sauber-Petronas C20 at the Australian Grand Prix, Melbourne, 2001.

▼ *(bottom)* In 2003, Raikkonen took victory in Malaysia and scored consistently high places throughout the season.

Marcel Renault

Marcel backed his elder brother Louis in establishing the Renault company at the turn of the 20th century, and together they raced the cars that Louis's factory built. Although both proved to be among the leading drivers of the day, it was Marcel who was particularly brilliant.

With Louis he had owned a repair shop in Billancourt for a steam yacht they both owned. His engineering skills then helped Louis develop an improved gearbox on Louis's de Dion car. When they went into business to produce cars, Marcel helped his brother fund it all. With a voiturette car that was far less powerful than the opposition, Marcel won the 1902 Paris–Vienna race outright. He was charging through the field in the 1903 Paris–Madrid when he tangled with Leon Théry. The Renault

Marcel Renault	
Nationality	French
Seasons	1900–03
Teams driven for	Renault
Number of major victories	1

speared off into a tree and Marcel received injuries from which he later died. His brother Louis – who finished the race second, not knowing of Marcel's accident – retired from race driving with immediate effect.

◀ Marcel Renault in 1903.

▼ Marcel Renault competing in the 1903 Paris–Madrid race in his Renault.

Carlos Reutemann

The Argentinian driver proved an often inspired performer in a Formula One career that lasted from 1972 to 1982, but losing the 1981 Championship to Nelson Piquet in the final round proved to be as close as he ever got to the world crown.

One of only three men to set pole position on their Grand Prix debuts, Reutemann achieved this feat at the 1972 Argentine Grand Prix, driving for Brabham. It was the beginning of a long love affair for the home fans, and Reutemann was a national hero for the rest of his career.

He took his first Grand Prix victories with the Brabham BT44 of 1974 and 1975 . His performances were occasionally in a class of their own, reducing everyone else to mere support roles, but finding such a level consistently proved to be elusive. Recruited to Ferrari at the end of 1976, he won races for them in 1977 and 1978, finishing third in the Championship in the latter year. A move to Lotus in 1979 proved ill-timed and he moved onto Williams for 1980, winning the Monaco Grand Prix and again finishing third in the title chase.

He began 1981 at the peak of his powers and after disobeying team orders to beat Alan Jones in Brazil,

Carlos Reutemann	
Nationality	Argentinian
Seasons	1972–82
Teams driven for	Brabham, Ferrari, Lotus, Williams
Number of major victories	12

◀ Carlos Reutemann, an enigmatic performer for 10 years. On his day he was unbeatable.

▼ Reutemann won from pole at the USA Grand Prix in 1974 in his Brabham BT44, the third victory of his season.

he went on to lead the Championship by a handsome margin by mid-season. The second half of his year was disappointing and, as Piquet caught up his points tally, they entered the final round in Las Vegas separated by just one point. Despite scoring a brilliant pole position, Reutemann had a disappointing race and finished eighth. With Piquet finishing fifth, Reutemann lost the Championship. He announced his retirement but changed his mind before the beginning of the 1982 season. He took second place in the South African Grand Prix, but after one more race decided that he did want to retire after all, and turned his back on the sport. He has since established himself as a leading politician in Argentina.

◀ Reutemann took a great second place in his non-turbo Williams at the 1982 South African Grand Prix, his penultimate race.

Jochen Rindt

ustrian Jochen Rindt became 1970
World Champion posthumously.
He was killed at Monza that season,
practising for the Italian Grand Prix.
But in the remaining four races no-one
was able to overhaul the points score
he had built up from five victories
earlier in the year.

He funded his early racing by selling
the business inherited from parents
who were killed in a wartime air-raid.
He broke onto the international scene
when, as a virtual unknown, he beat
Graham Hill to win a Formula Two race
at Crystal Palace in 1964. He made his
Formula One debut later that year, at
his home race with Rob Walker. For
the next three years, he drove Cooper's
outdated cars, finishing third in the
1966 Championship. A move to
Brabham in 1968 underlined his
stunning turn of speed, but the cars
were unreliable. This led to him taking
up an offer to join Lotus for 1969.
In Colin Chapman's 49 model, he was
devastatingly fast but didn't win until
the final race of the year, in the USA.

For 1970, Lotus produced the
ground-breaking 72 model. Initially it
proved uncompetitive and Rindt gave
the old 49 an unbelievable last-lap
victory at Monaco. Thereafter, he
transferred to the 72 and rattled off
four consecutive wins. He had confided
to friends that if he won the 1970 title,
he would consider retirement. It was an
option he was never granted.

▲ Jochen Rindt on his way to victory at the
Dutch Grand Prix of 1970. It was one of five
wins that season.

Jochen Rindt	
Nationality	Austrian
Seasons	1964–70
Teams driven for	Cooper, Brabham, Lotus
Number of major victories	6

◀ Rindt only hours before his death at the
Italian Grand Prix, Monza, September 1970.
He was said to be contemplating retirement.

▲ Rindt's Lotus 72 runs without wings.
It was perhaps a contributory factor in his
fatal accident at Monza, which occured
a short while after this picture was taken.

▶ Rindt's Brabham BT24 – here at South
Africa – was fast but unreliable in 1968.

Keke Rosberg

The World Champion of 1982, Rosberg was the first Finn to be successful in Formula One, blazing a path that others have since followed.

A tough, shrewd operator, he made his way up the racing ladder through enterprise, hard graft and a lot of talent. But even so, it was a struggle and by the time he made it to Formula One in 1978 he was already 29. In the non-championship International Trophy – his third ever Formula One race – he took the unfancied Theodore car to victory. But even this did not attract him to the top teams, and he served his time with ATS and Fittipaldi.

It was the late-notice retirement of Alan Jones at the end of 1981 that created Rosberg's opportunity with Williams. He responded by winning his first Grand Prix at Dijon 1982 and scoring highly throughout the season to clinch the Championship in the final round. He won a handful of races in his remaining three years with Williams, but he was never a Championship contender. He drove for McLaren in his final season of 1986 and was leading his final race, in Australia, when his car suddenly stopped.

His subsequent activities included racing in touring and sports car, managing the career of Mika Häkkinen and latterly that of son, Niko Rosberg.

Keke Rosberg	
Nationality	Finnish
Seasons	1978–86
Teams driven for	Theodore, ATS, Wolf, Fittipaldi, Williams, McLaren
Number of major victories	5

▲ Rosberg in his McLaren MP4/2C during his final Grand Prix, at Adelaide in 1986. He was leading the race when the car failed.

▼ (left) Rosberg cut a colourful figure in Formula One during the 1980s, and a cigarette was rarely far from his lips.

▼ (right) Rosberg took victory with Theodore in the International Trophy race at Silverstone in 1978.

Bernd Rosemeyer

osemeyer burst onto the Grand Prix scene of the mid-1930s like a meteorite, instantly causing a sensation with his speed for Auto Union, this despite never having raced a car of any description before, his only racing experience being with motorcycles.

The DKW team for which he raced motorcycles was part of the Auto Union group, and he got a trial in the awesome V16, mid-engined machine at the end of 1934, and subsequently made his debut part-way through 1935. He was heading for victory in his second-ever race before a misfire held him back to second. In his first full season of 1936, he became European Champion. His drives left onlookers spellbound, his talent seemingly limitless. He was widely considered to be the world's fastest driver during his brief career.

Bernd Rosemeyer	
Nationality	German
Seasons	1935–37
Teams driven for	Auto Union
Number of major victories	5

It all came to an end in January 1938. Attempting to set a world speed record for Auto Union on a German autobahn, a side wind blew his car out of control at over 400km/h (250mph). He was killed after hitting some trees.

◄ Bernd Rosemeyer.

▼ Rosemeyer in the Auto Union C type at the Donington Grand Prix in 1937.

Jody Scheckter

▼ Jody Scheckter's Wolf WR1 leads John Watson's Brabham at the Monaco Grand Prix of 1977. Scheckter won.

T he 1979 World Champion for Ferrari, South African Scheckter, entered Formula One in the early 1970s with a "wild boy" tag, and he left it as a respected elder statesman at the end of 1980.

After winning a "Driver to Europe" scheme in South Africa, Scheckter made his name in British Formula Ford and Formula Three racing. He was picked up by McLaren to drive its Formula Two car and by the end of that season, 1972, he was making his Grand Prix debut for the team.

He was comfortably leading the 1973 French Grand Prix, only his third Formula One race, until hit by Emerson Fittipaldi. In the following race at Silverstone, he created an impact for the wrong reasons, when his spin into the pit wall on the first lap took out much of the field. Despite this, he was chosen by Ken Tyrrell as the lead driver of his team in 1974, in the wake of Jackie Stewart's retirement and the

Jody Scheckter	
Nationality	South African
Seasons	1972–80
Teams driven for	McLaren, Tyrrell, Wolf, Ferrari
Number of major victories	10

death of François Cevert. He justified his selection with a strong third place in the World Championship, winning two Grands Prix along the way. In 1976, he became the only man to win a Grand Prix in a car with other than four wheels, when he took the six-wheel Tyrrell P34 to victory in Sweden. A move to the new Wolf team for 1977 saw Scheckter perform brilliantly, winning

on the team's debut in Argentina and leading the World Championship until mid-season. But it was his move to Ferrari for 1979 that consolidated his status. Three victories and some mature performances clinched him the title comfortably, with two rounds to go.

▼ Jody Scheckter led the 1973 French Grand Prix in this McLaren.

▲ Scheckter in 1980, the year of his retirement from Formula One.

Michael Schumacher

The most successful driver of all time, seven-time World Champion Schumacher continues to rack up wins after over a decade in Formula One.

With his early career subsidized by Mercedes-Benz, he graduated from German Formula Three into the World Sportscar Championship with the Mercedes team. His speed there created a sensation and marked him out as a likely Formula One star. His Grand Prix chance came with Jordan at the 1991 Belgian Grand Prix, where he was quicker than team-mate Andrea de Cesaris. By the next race he had been snapped up by Benetton, and he proceeded to outpace triple World Champion Nelson Piquet.

He won his first Grand Prix at Spa in 1992, the first anniversary of his debut. By 1994, he was ready to push for the Championship and was engaged in battle with his biggest rival, Ayrton Senna, when the Brazilian crashed to his death at Imola. In a controversial duel with the Williams of title rival Damon Hill at the final round in Australia, Schumacher drove his damaged car into Hill's, forcing them both to retire but ensuring the title was Michael's. He repeated the feat in 1995, this time without controversy.

◄ Schumacher caused a sensation by qualifying a Jordan in seventh place on his Formula One debut at Spa in 1991.

▼ (below left) Michael Schumacher, took his fifth world title in 2002.

Michael Schumacher	
Nationality	German
Seasons	1991–present
Teams driven for	Jordan, Benetton, Ferrari
Number of major victories	84

He then took up the challenge of turning the troubled Ferrari team back into world beaters. After a difficult first season in 1996, he was aided by the arrival of his design team from Benetton, Ross Brawn and Rory Byrne, and piloted an ever-faster succession of Ferraris. He lost the 1997 title to Jacques Villeneuve, when a similar move to the one he'd pulled on Hill went wrong, leaving him in the gravel trap. He again lost out in the last round in 1998, this time to Mika Häkkinen. In 1999 he broke his leg at Silverstone and was out for much of the season.

But in 2000 came the crowning glory of his career, when he won the title, the first Ferrari driver to do so for 21 years. He was a dominant champion in 2001, passing Alain Prost's record of 51 Grand Prix victories, and even more so in 2002, winning 11 races in that season alone. This brought him level with the record held since 1957 by Juan Manuel Fangio, and in 2003 he beat that by clinching his sixth championship. Title number seven came in 2004, when he also beat his own record for the number of race wins in one season.

◄ The Ferrari team celebrate Schumacher's Canadian Grand Prix victory in 2003.

Ralf Schumacher

▼ Ralf Schumacher guides his Williams-BMW FW23 to his first Formula One victory at Imola in 2001.

The younger brother of Michael is a talented Formula One racer in his own right, and took a succession of victories with the Williams-BMW team before moving on to Toyota for 2005.

After a karting career, Ralf took up junior car racing in Germany, progressing to German Formula Three in 1995, where he was runner-up. A move to the Japanese Formula Nippon series in 1996 secured him a major championship, and this proved his springboard to Formula One with the Jordan team in 1997.

He was quick from the start, but initially accident-prone. This continued until half-way through the 1998 season, after which his performances became

◀ (*far left*) Ralf Schumacher has driven for Williams since 1999.

◀ (*left*) Ralf was immediately quick in his debut season of 1997 with Jordan.

more mature. He was catching team-mate Damon Hill in the Belgian Grand Prix and looked ready to take the win before team orders were imposed, leaving him a frustrated second.

He moved to Williams in 1999, a team that initially couldn't offer him a potentially race-winning car but which promised a future partnership with

Ralf Schumacher

Nationality	German
Seasons	1997–present
Teams driven for	Jordan, Williams
Number of major victories	6

BMW. This came good in 2001, with Ralf taking his first victory at Imola and following it with two more. He continued his race-winning form into 2002 and 2003, but in 2004 he suffered spinal fractures in an accident at the American Grand Prix that kept him out for much of the season. During this time his move to Toyota for 2005 was announced.

▼ Ralf Schumacher took his Jordan-Peugeot to third place in the Argentinian Grand Prix in 1997.

Henry Segrave

egrave was the first British driver to win a Grand Prix when he took his Sunbeam to victory in France in 1923. In his short time in top flight racing, before he took up the challenge of the landspeed record, he established himself among the elite of drivers.

A British national, he was born in Baltimore in the United States, but raised in Ireland and educated at Eton, England. After serving in World War I, his imagination was captured by motorsport when he spectated at an American race. He took up the sport at Brooklands in Britain, and badgered Sunbeam racing boss Louis Coatalen to be included in Sunbeam's works team in 1921. In the 1922 French Grand Prix, he ran as high as third before retiring,

assuring himself a permanent place on the Sunbeam team. Following his victory of 1923, he was dominating the early stages of the 1924 race when the Sunbeam's electrics played up. He took some consolation with victory in the San Sebastian Grand Prix, in Spain, later in the year. After a further win at Miramas, France in 1926, he retired from racing altogether to concentrate on speed records.

In 1927, he became the first man to exceed 322km/h (200mph) and in 1929, he raised the record to 372.46km/h (231.44mph) in the Irving-Napier Golden Arrow. Later that year, he was killed attempting a water speed record, when his boat hit a log on Lake Windermere. He was 34.

▲ *(left)* Henry Segrave.

◀ Segrave in his Sunbeam at the French Grand Prix at Tours in 1923. He won the race.

▼ The 1921 Grand Prix at Le Mans. Segrave (10) finished ninth, and Jimmy Murphy in the Deusenberg (12) was the winner.

Henry Segrave	
Nationality	British
Seasons	1921–26
Teams driven for	Sunbeam
Number of major victories	3

Ayrton Senna

The World Champion of 1988, 1990 and 1991, Brazilian Senna proved himself one of the greatest exponents of the sport ever seen until his death at the 1994 San Marino Grand Prix.

He came to Britain to make his name after a successful karting career in Brazil that began when he was a child. He dominated in British Formula Ford, Formula 2000 and Formula Three, leading to Formula One tests with Williams, Brabham and McLaren in 1983. He opted, though, to make his debut with the smaller Toleman team for 1984. At a wet Monaco, in only his fifth Grand Prix, he was closing down fast on leader Alain Prost and looked set to pass when the race was stopped short of its allocated distance. Such form led to his recruitment by Lotus for 1985. He took his first victory at Estoril in Portugal, with an astonishing display of virtuosity in the wet conditions.

Further wins followed with Lotus, but it was no longer a World Championship calibre team, and for 1988 he joined McLaren – alongside the great Prost. It was arguably the strongest driver line up of all time and it was inevitable that their relationship became difficult. Amid some incredibly intense battles, Senna emerged on top in 1988, Prost in 1989. Senna's clinching of the 1990 title by aiming his car at Prost's Ferrari and not lifting as they reached the first corner added to the impression that utter ruthlessness backed up his talent. Although the 1992 and 1993 McLarens were outclassed by the cars of Williams, Senna still produced some stunning drives, none more so than at Donington, England, in 1993, when, in wet conditions, he put in one of his greatest ever performances to win.

He transferred to Williams for 1994, setting pole position for the first three races, taking his tally to 65, still an all-time record. He was leading at Imola from his new rival, Michael Schumacher, when he crashed to his death. Motorsport – and the nation of Brazil – went into deep mourning.

▶ Senna caused a sensation by taking a Toleman to second place at the rain-soaked Monaco Grand Prix in 1984.

▲ Ayrton Senna tragically lost his life in an accident on lap six of the San Marino Grand Prix at Imola, 1 May 1994.

◀ Senna at the Mexican Grand Prix, Mexico City, in 1992.

Ayrton Senna	
Nationality	Brazilian
Seasons	1984–94
Teams driven for	Toleman, Lotus, McLaren, Williams
Number of major victories	41

Raymond Sommer

his French driver was responsible for some of the greatest giant-killing acts seen in Grand Prix racing, from his early years in the 1930s up to the time of his death in 1950.

The son of a pioneer aviator, he was from a sufficiently wealthy background that he was able to indulge his passion for speed. He bought a succession of ex-works Grand Prix cars from Alfa Romeo and Maserati, and prepared and entered them himself. His form frequently embarrassed the works teams with the latest equipment, and he was repeatedly offered factory drives, but invariably turned them down. Fiercely independent, he preferred to race on his own terms.

In the 1932 Marseilles Grand Prix, Sommer sensationally defeated the factory Alfa and Maserati teams with his old Alfa Monza. It was a performance he looked on-course to repeat at Spa in 1950 when, at 43 years of age and with an outclassed Talbot, he pushed the far faster Alfa Romeos. Initially the Alfa pit crew believed he couldn't possibly be on the same lap, but he was. It was to Alfa's great relief

▲ **Raymond Sommer racing a Maserati in Jersey in 1947.**

that the Talbot broke down and took him out of the race, but those with long memories weren't surprised.

Sommer was killed competing in a minor French hillclimb event at the end of the year, when it is believed a wheelbearing on his Cooper seized.

Raymond Sommer	
Nationality	French
Seasons	1932–50
Teams driven for	Alfa Romeo, Ferrari
Number of major victories	3

▲ **Sommer at the Italian Grand Prix in 1950.**

◄ **Sommer's Alfa Romeo finished second at the 1946 Nice Grand Prix. Here he is leading Chaboud in the Delahaye.**

Jackie Stewart

Triple World Champion Jackie Stewart is remembered not only for his masterly performances behind the wheel, but also for initiating and progressing the sport's safety campaign in the late 1960s up to his retirement from racing in 1973.

The Scot began his single-seater career in British Formula Three, where he was a dominant champion in 1964, driving for Ken Tyrrell's team. He moved straight into Formula One in 1965 with BRM, scoring his first Grand Prix win that year and ending up third in the World Championship.

It was an incredible rookie year, but success was harder to come by in the two seasons that followed. In 1966 he suffered a frightening accident in the Belgian Grand Prix and it was this that initiated his safety campaign, something that continued throughout and beyond his driving career.

For 1968, he hooked up once more with Tyrrell who ran a Matra-Ford for him and the winning ways returned. He only narrowly missed out on that year's Championship, and in 1969 the partnership was dominant as Stewart took his first world title.

With the new "Tyrrell" car Stewart dominated in 1971, but a stomach ulcer compromised his 1972 season. He began 1973 having decided he would retire at the end of the year, though this was a secret shared by only his inner circle. He won five Grands Prix that year, and clinched his third title with a stunning recovery drive at Monza that showed he was every bit as fast as he'd ever been.

He subsequently continued his long relationship with Ford, and in 1996 became a Formula One team owner as he established Stewart Grand Prix, with Ford backing. The team won the 1999 European Grand Prix with Johnny Herbert, but Ford subsequently bought out Stewart and rebranded the team as Jaguar.

▲ Jackie Stewart was restricted to fifth place in the USA Grand Prix in 1971 because of chunking tyres on his Tyrrell 003.

◄ Stewart in 1971, the year of his second World Drivers' Championship title. This was his first season in the new Tyrrell car.

Jackie Stewart	
Nationality	British
Seasons	1965–73
Teams driven for	BRM, Tyrrell
Number of major victories	27

► Stewart outran BRM team-mate Graham Hill to win his first Grand Prix in his debut year, at Italy in 1965.

John Surtees

This Englishman is the only person to have won World Championships in both motorcycle racing and Formula One. He was one of the greatest drivers of the 1960s, and could conceivably have been even more successful had he made different career choices.

Between 1956 and 1960, Surtees won seven world titles in various motorcycle classes. He made his Grand Prix debut with Lotus in 1960, and his enormous potential on four wheels was made clear when he scored pole position at Portugal in only his third Grand Prix.

After two seasons in privateer teams, he was recruited by Ferrari for 1963. He won in Germany that year, and his analytical approach was fundamental in improving the team's competitiveness. This progressed into 1964 when, after a particularly strong second half of the season, he clinched the Championship at the final round. At the end of 1965, he suffered a serious accident in a Can-Am sports car, in which he was lucky to survive.

Impressively, he recovered in time for the start of the 1966 season. He and Ferrari were favourites for the title, and he took a superb victory in the wet

▲ Pole sitter John Surtees retired on lap 36 of the 1960 Portuguese Grand Prix.

John Surtees	
Nationality	British
Seasons	1960–72
Teams driven for	Lotus, Ferrari, Cooper, Honda, BRM, Surtees
Number of major victories	6

Belgian Grand Prix. Following a row with the Ferrari team manager, he left and drove the rest of the season for Cooper, winning the Mexican Grand Prix.

Thereafter, he was involved with the Honda Formula One project – giving the team victory in the 1967 Italian Grand Prix – and with BRM, before going off to form his own Formula One team. His last full season in the driving seat was 1971, after which he concentrated on running the team. In eight years of toil, Team Surtees was never able to succeed in the same way as Surtees the driver.

▲ John Surtees in 1968.

◄ Surtees in the Honda RA300 (car 14) leads Chris Amon's Ferrari 312 at the Italian Grand Prix, Monza, in 1967.

Leon Théry

Recognized as the greatest driver of his era, Théry won the Gordon Bennett Cup races – the equivalent of a World Championship today – in 1904 and 1905, driving Richard-Brasier cars.

Known as "The Chronometer" for his incredibly consistent speed, he won in machinery that was no better than that of his leading rivals, who would invariably make mistakes as they tried in vain to keep up. He was also noted for his very thorough preparation, and would spend weeks testing his cars before the races.

He left Richard-Brasier along with co-founder Georges Richard in 1906, to set up a new car company, though this was unsuccessful. He returned to Brasier for the 1908 French Grand Prix and ran third until the car failed. He died a year later from tuberculosis.

▲ A portrait of Leon Théry in 1904 after winning the Gordon Bennett cup.

▶ Théry in the 1905 Gordon Bennett trophy race in a Brasier. He won this race just as he had won the 1904 event.

Leon Théry	
Nationality	French
Seasons	1903–08
Teams driven for	Richard-Braiser
Number of major victories	4

Wolfgang von Trips

▼ Wolfgang von Trips during the 1960 Argentine Grand Prix in his Ferrari.

The German count was leading the World Championship for Ferrari, in 1961, when he crashed to his death during the Italian Grand Prix at Monza.

After beginning his career in sports car racing in the 1950s, von Trips was taken on by Ferrari, driving his first Grand Prix for the team at Monza in 1956. He was retained as an occasional driver by the team for the next three years, but got his chance as a full-time member in 1960 after the departures of Tony Brooks and Dan Gurney.

In between racing that season, he conducted much development work on the new mid-engined Ferrari, and this put him in good stead for the 1961

Wolfgang von Trips	
Nationality	German
Seasons	1956–61
Teams driven for	Ferrari
Number of major victories	2

season, when the 156 "sharknose" model was the fastest car in the field. He battled with his team-mate Phil Hill for the destiny of the crown, winning both the Dutch and British Grand Prix, and had a narrow points lead over the American as they began the penultimate round of the championship at Monza.

After a poor start, he was making his way towards the front. On lap three, he passed Jim Clark, but Clark's Lotus then slipstreamed him down the

following straight, and under braking for the Parabolica turn, moved to von Trips' inside to repass. Probably not realizing the Lotus was still there, von Trips moved the same way as Clark. Their wheels interlocked and the Ferrari was thrown up the banking and along the fence, killing 14 spectators along the way. Von Trips was thrown out on to the track, and killed upon impact. Germany would have to wait another 33 years for its first World Champion.

▲ Wolfgang von Trips after winning the 1961 British Grand Prix. It was a brave performance on a rain-soaked track.

◄ Von Trips (Ferrari 156) won the British Grand Prix at Aintree in 1961. He led the World Championship at this point.

Achille Varzi

One of the greatest drivers of the 1930s, Milanese Varzi won Grands Prix for Alfa Romeo, Maserati, Bugatti and Auto Union after a successful career as a motorcycle racer.

Known as "The Ice Man" for his unnatural calm and cool, his clinical but stunningly fast driving reflected his temperament. This formed an elemental contrast with the style of his great adversary, the flamboyant Tazio Nuvolari. The two were rivals in motorcycle racing and moved into car racing together, forming their own team to run a pair of Bugattis.

Although successful, Varzi was uneasy being in the same team as his biggest rival, and moved on to works drives with much success over the years. Many of his victories came after stirring battles with Nuvolari. For 1935, he was recruited by Auto Union and began well, but early in 1936, he became addicted to morphine and his form dropped off alarmingly. He was

▲ Achille Varzi at Monaco in 1933.

Achille Varzi	
Nationality	Italian
Seasons	1928–48
Teams driven for	Alfa Romeo, Maserati, Bugatti, Auto Union
Number of major victories	18

dismissed by the team and did not reappear in racing until after the war, by which time he had kicked the habit and was back in good health.

He immediately began winning races again for Alfa Romeo, but was killed in practice for the 1948 Swiss Grand Prix, when his car overturned as he was attempting to wrest pole position from his team-mate Jean-Pierre Wimille.

▼ Varzi in a Bugatti leads two similar models on the Monaco circuit in 1933.

Gilles Villeneuve

The French-Canadian was one of the fastest, most spectacular drivers the sport has ever seen. He looked set for a glittering future, but was killed after crashing his Ferrari, while qualifying for the Belgian Grand Prix at Zolder in 1982.

Villeneuve started out by racing snowmobiles in Canada, becoming World Champion in the discipline before moving into car racing. A dominant North American Formula Atlantic Champion in 1976, he gained big international recognition when World Champion-elect James Hunt took part in a round of the Atlantic series, as Villeneuve's team-mate, and was beaten by him. Hunt reported back to his Formula One team, McLaren, who entered a third car for Villeneuve in the 1977 British Grand Prix.

His debut in an obsolete model was sensational, and he was set to finish fourth when a faulty temperature gauge sent him to the pits. When Niki Lauda walked out on Ferrari before the season was over, the Italian team recruited Villeneuve as his replacement. At the end of 1978 he won his first Grand Prix – fittingly at his home track of Montreal. For 1979, he was

Gilles Villeneuve	
Nationality	Canadian
Seasons	1977–82
Teams driven for	McLaren, Ferrari
Number of major victories	6

◄ Gilles Villeneuve in 1978, his first full season in Formula One. He took victory in the final race of the season.

▼ Villeneuve made his Grand Prix debut at Silverstone in 1977. He was on course for fourth place. Until a faulty temperature gauge sent him to the pits.

contracted in a support role to the experienced Jody Scheckter, but initially was clearly quicker. He won three Grands Prix that year but stood by team instructions, following Scheckter home at Monza and finishing the season as runner-up in the Championship.

He took two remarkable victories in 1981, with an uncompetitive Ferrari, but began 1982 as title favourite with a much-improved car. He was duped by team-mate Didier Pironi into losing the San Marino Grand Prix and was afterwards furious. Still angry two weeks later in Belgium, he was attempting to beat Pironi's qualifying time when a slower car moved into his path. The Ferrari flew high in the air before crashing down nose-first. Villeneuve was fatally injured.

◄ Villeneuve suffered a very uncompetitive Ferrari in 1980. He finished in fifth place in the Monaco Grand Prix that season.

Jacques Villeneuve

▼ Villeneuve in characteristic hard-charging mode in his BAR 003 at Monza in 2000.

By winning the 1997 World Drivers' Championship, Jacques Villeneuve established himself as a Formula One star in his own right, rather than merely the son of Gilles.

He took up racing in the late 1980s, some years after the death of his father. With no karting experience, he initially struggled in the Italian Formula Three series, but subsequently made quick progress. With sponsorship from Players Tobacco, he moved to the United States, won the Formula Atlantic Championship and progressed to Indycars. In 1995, he won the Championship as well as the prestigious Indianapolis 500.

This was his springboard to Formula One with the mighty Williams team. In Australia in 1996, he became only the third man to set pole position on his Grand Prix debut. He took his first victory at the Nürburgring and finished runner-up to team-mate Damon Hill in the Championship battle.

Jacques Villeneuve	
Nationality	Canadian
Seasons	1996–present
Teams driven for	Williams, BAR, Renault, Sauber
Number of major victories	11

He clinched the 1997 title at the final round in Jerez, Spain, after his only rival, Ferrari's Michael Schumacher, attempted to drive him off the track. The outcome left Schumacher in the gravel trap and Villeneuve still running. The Williams team lost its form in 1998, and for 1999 Jacques joined BAR. In five years of struggle, Villeneuve never came close to winning another race. He left BAR at the end of 2003 and was forced to sit out for most of 2004. However, he made a comeback in the last three races with Renault, prior to a full season with Sauber from 2005.

▼ Villeneuve's BAR-Honda 002 comes to a fiery end at the Spanish Grand Prix in 2000.

▲ Jacques Villeneuve in 2002.

John Watson

The popular Ulsterman was a leading light of Formula One from the mid-1970s to the early 1980s, and only narrowly lost out on the 1982 World Championship.

After a promising but under-funded career in the junior categories, Watson was given his Formula One chance by Bernie Ecclestone's Brabham team in 1973. Unfortunately, he broke his leg on his debut as a result of a sticking throttle. He came back and, in 1974, showed good speed in a privately-entered Brabham. After a half-season in the uncompetitive Surtees for 1975, Watson was recruited by the Penske team at the end of 1975. He gave the team its only Formula One victory with a great drive at Austria in 1976, but even that wasn't enough to prevent the team withdrawing at the season's end.

Back at Brabham for 1977, Watson drove superbly and only appalling luck kept him from winning at least two

John Watson	
Nationality	British
Seasons	1973–84
Teams driven for	Brabham, Surtees, Lotus, Penske, McLaren
Number of major victories	5

◄ Watson with the beard he wore until he won his first Grand Prix in Austria in 1976.

Grands Prix. He left at the end of 1978 to join McLaren – unfortunately, just as the team was beginning a downward plunge. It took until 1981 to climb out of the rut, but Watson hung on and took an emotional victory in the British Grand Prix. In 1982, he won at Zolder and Detroit, and took the title battle with Keke Rosberg to the wire in Las

Vegas, but finished second. In his last season in 1983, he took a remarkable victory at Long Beach from 22nd on the grid. He was replaced at McLaren by Alain Prost in 1984.

▼ John Watson in the Penske PC4 at the Austrian Grand Prix in 1976. It was his first Grand Prix win.

Jean-Pierre Wimille

At the time of his death, while practising for a race in Argentina in 1949, Wimille was recognized as the world's number one driver.

After a series of remarkable drives in less than fully competitive cars in the 1930s, Wimille spent World War II as a member of the French Resistance. Returning to racing after the war, he finally got his hands on machinery worthy of his abilities in the early post-war years, when he was recruited by the dominant Alfa Romeo team.

In 1947 and 1948, he was clearly the quickest man in a squad that included the legendary Achille Varzi. He won the French and Italian Grand Prix in 1948 and, had there been a World Championship at that time, there is no doubt that Wimille would have taken the crown.

He crashed his Simca-Gordini into a tree on his third lap of practice for the 1949 Perón Grand Prix in Argentina,

Jean-Pierre Wimille	
Nationality	French
Seasons	1930–48
Teams driven for	Bugatti, Alfa Romeo
Number of major victories	4

with fatal consequences. It was believed that the early morning sun had blinded him. Bizarrely, it was the first time Wimille had ever worn a crash helmet.

◀ Jean-Pierre Wimille. The Frenchman was widely regarded as the world's greatest driver during the late 1940s.

▼ Wimille in the Alfa 158 at the Grand Prix of the Nations, Geneva, Switzerland, in 1946.

The Circuits

There are 19 battlegrounds in 16 countries and five continents on which the Formula One World Championship is fought. The demands of each track are very different, placing varying strains on both man and machine. But, like Formula One itself, the venues and tracks are constantly altering, evolving with the technology of the cars, circuit safety and the commercial packaging of the sport. It is this latter demand that is leading to a changing geography of the championship, as the sport spreads its tentacles to new countries. From 2004, the series no longer visited Austria but instead paid its first visit to Bahrain and China, with Turkey becoming a fixture in 2005. In the longer-term future, countries such as India and Dubai are expected to host Grands Prix, illustrating its global appeal.

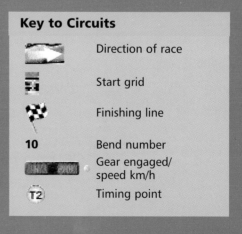

Key to Circuits

	Direction of race
	Start grid
	Finishing line
10	Bend number
	Gear engaged/ speed km/h
T2	Timing point

◀ **The Hockenheim track in 2000.**

Australia *Albert Park*

Australia hosted its first World Championship Grand Prix in 1985, around a street circuit in Adelaide. It was here in 1986 that Nigel Mansell suffered his famous 300km/h (190mph) tyre blow-out that lost him the World Championship. This circuit continued to host the event until 1995, but two years earlier Melbourne – which has traditionally been in competitive opposition with Adelaide – secured a deal with Formula One boss Bernie Ecclestone to host the Grand Prix from 1996. It is now the traditional season-opening race, where the form of the new cars and car/driver combinations is revealed for the first time, setting the tone of the season to come.

The track chosen for the Melbourne race was, like Adelaide, a street circuit, albeit one constructed around the roads of a public park in the seaside district of St Kilda. There had been motor racing at Albert Park in the 1950s, but only for national-level events.

There was some local opposition against the Grand Prix, but this has melted away since the event has proved such a prestigious commercial success for the city. Albert Park is now one of the most successful Grands Prix in terms of attendance and financial return for the city and its restaurants and hotels.

The circuit follows quite closely the outline of the park's boating lake. Its sequence of fast bends, punctuated by three tight corners demands a tricky aerodynamic compromise between straightline speed and downforce. Braking and traction are especially important here, though its smooth,

▲ *(top)* Second place finisher Juan Pablo Montoya fends off Michael Schumacher's winning Ferrari, having earlier passed his rival round the outside.

▲ *(above)* Montoya's Melbourne form in the Williams FW24 raised hopes of a strong season in 2002. It was not to be.

▲ Martin Brundle gets airbourne in his Jordan 196 after a first corner accident at the Australian Grand Prix, 1996.

◄ David Coulthard moves over to let Häkkinen through to win the Australian Grand Prix in 1998.

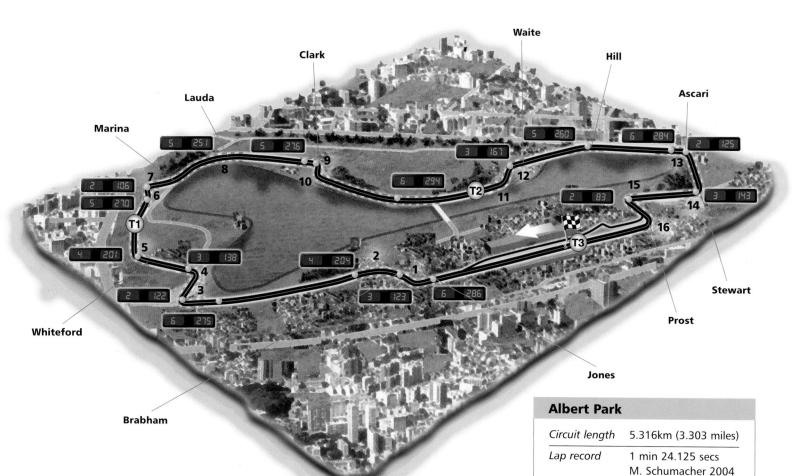

Marina
Lauda
Clark
Waite
Hill
Ascari

`5 251`
`5 276`
`5 260`
`6 284`
`2 125`

`3 167`

`2 106`
`6 294`

`5 270`

`4 201`

`2 83`

`3 143`

`3 138`

`4 204`

`6 286`

`2 122`

`3 123`

`6 275`

7 6 T1 5 4 3 8 9 10 T2 11 12 15 13 14 16 T3 1 2

Whiteford

Brabham

Stewart

Prost

Jones

Albert Park	
Circuit length	5.316km (3.303 miles)
Lap record	1 min 24.125 secs M. Schumacher 2004
Previous winners	2005 G. Fisichella 2004 M. Schumacher 2003 D. Coulthard

dusty surface means that tyre wear tends to be low. This has ramifications on strategy, as it usually proves quicker over a race distance to pit only once, as the tyres degrade slowly.

On the fast approach to the tight first corner in the opening seconds of Melbourne's first Grand Prix in 1996, Martin Brundle's Jordan got airborne after clipping a rival's car. He barrel-rolled through the air in spectacular fashion but, remarkably, stepped out completely unhurt. A day earlier Jacques Villeneuve had made a great Formula One debut by qualifying his Williams on pole position.

There was controversy in 1998 when, after mishearing an instruction on the radio, McLaren's Mika Häkkinen pitted from the lead when the team were not ready for him. His delay allowed team-mate David Coulthard to take over at the front, but Coulthard then acceded to a team request that he back off and allow Häkkinen back in front.

Tragically, a track marshal was killed in 2001 after being hit by a wheel from Jacques Villeneuve's crashing BAR. Improvements to the protective fencing were made in time for the 2002 event. Michael Schumacher won this race for Ferrari after a thrilling early battle with Juan Pablo Montoya. Australia's Mark Webber made a great Grand Prix debut by bringing his Minardi home in fifth place in front of a crowd of adoring countrymen.

▼ **Michael Schumacher's Ferrari F1-2001 races past the Albert Park Marina in practice for the 2002 Australian Grand Prix.**

Bahrain *Sakhir*

One of two new Grand Prix venues introduced to the calendar in 2004, Bahrain marks the Middle East region's first ever involvement with the Championship. A spectacular new circuit, Sakhir, was constructed on the edge of a desert area for the event, making for a striking sand-dune backdrop. The desert sand, in fact, meant that teams needed to increase the density of their air filters to keep sand from reaching engine internals.

Designed by Herman Tilke, the circuit features several gradient changes, one of them forming a thrilling downhill section of kinks that the cars can take almost – but not quite – at a flat-out pace, testing the nerve and skill of the drivers.

The inaugural event formed the third round of the 2004 Championship and saw an apparently convincing Ferrari 1–2, with Michael Schumacher leading home team-mate Rubens Barrichello.

◄ **Giancarlo Fisichella in the Sauber-Petronas C23 against the spectacular scenery of the desert.**

▼ **Cristiano da Matta in the Toyota TF104 on practice day for the 2004 Bahrain Grand Prix.**

▲ **Michael Schumacher takes his Ferrari F2004 round the new track at Sakhir while qualifying for the third round of the 2004 World Championship. The next day he became its first winner.**

However, beneath the still waters of their double victory, there was actually a serious concern about brake wear.

In the absence of any prior running on the new track, the teams had had to rely on computerized simulations to calculate such issues as brake wear, fuel

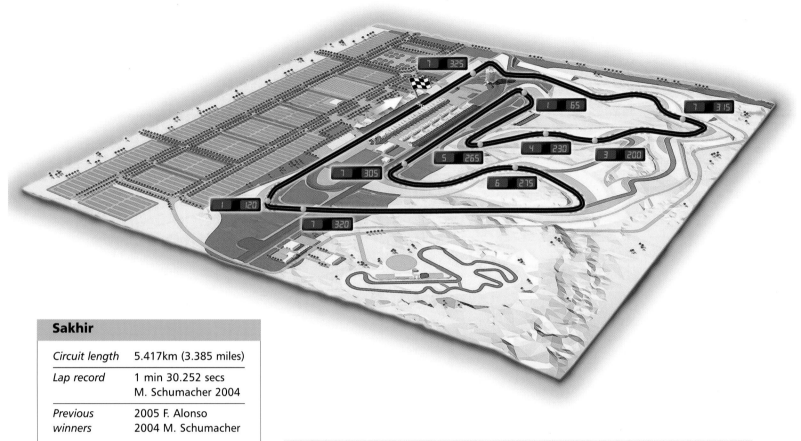

Sakhir	
Circuit length	5.417km (3.385 miles)
Lap record	1 min 30.252 secs M. Schumacher 2004
Previous *winners*	2005 F. Alonso 2004 M. Schumacher -

consumption and wing levels. However, several teams, notably Ferrari, had underestimated just how hard the track would prove to be on braking. The Italian team had to create new bigger brake cooling ducts overnight after the first day of practice. Even with these fitted, the duration of the brake discs was still going to be marginal over the race distance.

Such was the Ferrari F2004's level of competitiveness that Schumacher was able to drive relatively gently but still lead all of the way. Team-mate Barrichello stayed close in Schumacher's wheel tracks until a problem with a crossed wheel nut at a pit stop lost him critical time, though not enough to lose second place. Jenson Button took his second consecutive podium position with third place in the BAR-Honda.

It had been a successful introduction of the sport to the Middle East region, and another key step in the further globalization of Formula One.

▶ **Ralf Schumacher in the Williams-BMW FW26 at the 2004 Bahrain Grand Prix.**

Belgium *Spa-Francorchamps*

There have been two circuits within this spectacular wooded Ardennes valley, the first of which hosted Grands Prix between 1925 and 1970. Thereafter, it was deemed too dangerous for Formula One. A second, shorter track was built using part of the original public road circuit but then veering into a specially constructed downhill section. This first hosted a Grand Prix in 1983, and has been used ever since.

What both circuits had in common was their incredibly challenging nature. The original featured flat-out sweeps that followed the dramatically changing contours of the valley through villages, within inches of stone walls, trees and houses through its 12.8km (8 mile) length. In the final Grand Prix there, Chris Amon set the fastest lap at an average 244.74km/h (152.08mph). It was also dangerous, and had a horrific record of fatalities. Jackie Stewart's accident there in the 1966 Belgian Grand Prix initiated his long-running Formula One safety campaign.

The 1983 track used the same downhill section of public road to begin the lap, leading into the dramatic Eau Rouge bend, still considered the greatest challenge of all by most

▲ **Two competitors pass under a bridge as residents of a local hotel watch the action.**

▼ **The Jordan team took its first victory in fine style with a 1-2 in the wet 1998 Belgian Grand Prix, with Damon Hill leading team-mate Ralf Schumacher.**

Formula One drivers. In a good car with a brave driver, this left-right sweep, with a downhill approach and an uphill exit, can be taken foot-to-the-floor in top gear. A long, steep hill then leads to Les Combes, a tight second-gear right-hander, and the point where the new track parts with the old public road. A series of daunting, downhill bends takes the track to the valley's floor, where it rejoins the tail-end of the old circuit at Stavelot. A flat-out kink and short straight precede the "Bus Stop" chicane, so called because of its extreme tightness. The exit of this leads to La Source hairpin and the beginning of another lap.

The altitude variations and large area of forest lead to highly changeable weather conditions, and sudden heavy rain is always a possibility. Frequently, it can be raining on one side of the circuit and dry on the other.

One of the most dramatic Grands Prix of the modern era took place in 2000, with a wheel-to-wheel battle between title rivals Michael Schumacher and Mika Häkkinen. Schumacher had made a remarkable Formula One debut here in 1991 and, with four victories, had a special affinity with the place. For the 2000 race he had gambled on there being rain, and had set up his car with lots of downforce. But the rain held off,

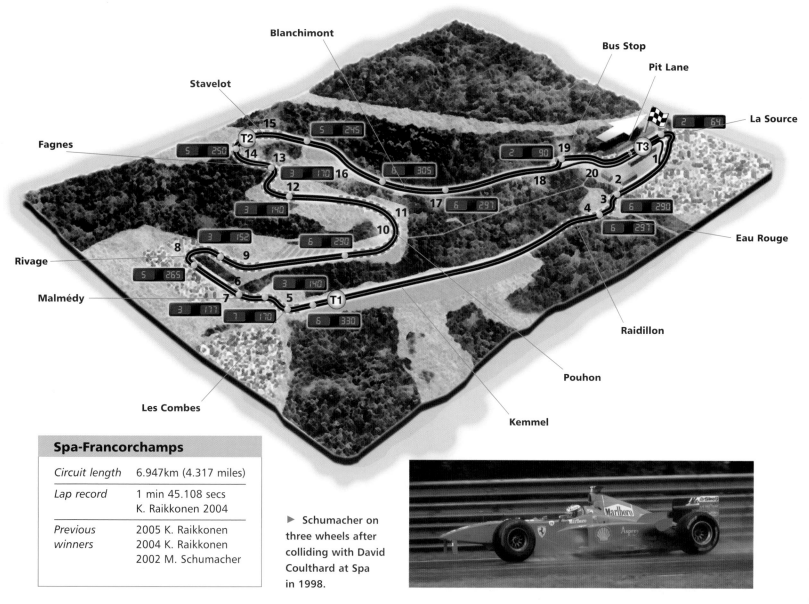

Blanchimont

Bus Stop

Pit Lane

Stavelot

La Source

15

| 5 | 245 |

T2

19

| 2 | 90 |

14

| 5 | 250 |

Fagnes

13

| 8 | 305 |

16

20

2

18

T3

1

| 2 | 64 |

| 3 | 170 |

12

3

| 3 | 140 |

17

| 6 | 297 |

4

| 6 | 290 |

11

| 6 | 297 |

Eau Rouge

10

| 3 | 152 |

8

| 6 | 290 |

Rivage

9

5

| 5 | 265 |

6

| 3 | 140 |

Malmédy

7

T1

| 3 | 177 |

| 7 | 170 |

Raidillon

| 6 | 330 |

Pouhon

Les Combes

Kemmel

Spa-Francorchamps

Circuit length	6.947km (4.317 miles)
Lap record	1 min 45.108 secs K. Raikkonen 2004
Previous winners	2005 K. Raikkonen 2004 K. Raikkonen 2002 M. Schumacher

► Schumacher on three wheels after colliding with David Coulthard at Spa in 1998.

allowing Häkkinen to close down Schumacher's lead. Much quicker up the hill to Les Combes, Häkkinen moved to the Ferrari's inside but, at almost 320km/h (200mph), Schumacher edged the McLaren towards the grass, forcing Häkkinen to back off. The Finn was now angry. On the next lap, at exactly the same place, Schumacher and Häkkinen came up to lap the BAR of Ricardo Zonta. Schumacher passed him on the left, Häkkinen on the right. A startled Zonta watched in amazement as Häkkinen took the lead, on his way to a great gladiatorial victory.

A row over tobacco advertising saw Spa-Francorchamps removed from the 2003 calendar, but its return for 2004 brought a collective sigh of relief from aficionados of the sport.

► Race winner Ayrton Senna leads McLaren team-mate Gerhard Berger in 1990.

Brazil *Interlagos*

Situated on shifting land between two underground lakes – hence its name – the Interlagos track first hosted local-level motor racing in the 1930s. Back then it was an open site within an unpopulated area south of the city of São Paulo. The subsequent population explosion of that city saw the site enveloped by shanty town *favellas*.

Nonetheless, with Emerson Fittipaldi giving Brazil her first World Champion in 1972, Interlagos hosted a round of the series the following year. In fairytale fashion, Fittipaldi won in his JPS Lotus, a feat he repeated the following year in a McLaren. In that race he could hear the screaming cheers of the crowd as he passed race leader, Ronnie Peterson. In 1975, another Brazilian, Carlos Pace, won the race for Brabham. It was to be his only Formula One victory before being killed in a plane crash two years later. The circuit was subsequently renamed in his memory.

The track used between 1973 and 1980 was wonderfully demanding, with a banked, almost flat-out first corner. Unusually, the track ran in an anti-clockwise direction. Concerns about lack of run-off areas for the ever-faster cars, and the intolerance of

ground-effect cars for the notoriously bumpy surface were the reasons given for moving the Brazilian Grand Prix to Rio de Janeiro in 1981, to a track that first hosted the race in 1978. Perhaps significantly, Brazil's new racing hero Nelson Piquet hailed from Rio.

But the later success of São Paulo's Ayrton Senna helped bring the impetus back to Interlagos. The mayor of the city struck a deal with Formula One supremo Bernie Ecclestone for the race to return there for 1990, on a new circuit within the same grounds.

Senna himself contributed to the design, which used some of the original

track but which by-passed the fast but dangerous former Turn One. The outer part of this track largely comprised part of the old circuit, and was very quick, with a fast uphill kink on to the pit straight. A downhill left-right S-bend (later named the Senna Esses) signalled the start of the new section, with an infield comprising mainly tight bends, though with one hugely challenging downhill fifth-gear left-hander, Turn 11.

Yet the bumps of the old track remained a problem, and no matter how much resurfacing work is done, new bumps always seem to appear. The shifting land beneath is the culprit,

▲ *(top)* Nigel Mansell got his Ferrari career off to a great start with a win at Brazil in 1989.

▲ *(above)* Alain Prost spun his Williams-Renault out of the lead in the 1993 event, handing victory to arch-rival Ayrton Senna.

◄ Race winner Ayrton Senna leads the field in the 1991 race; Mansell follows.

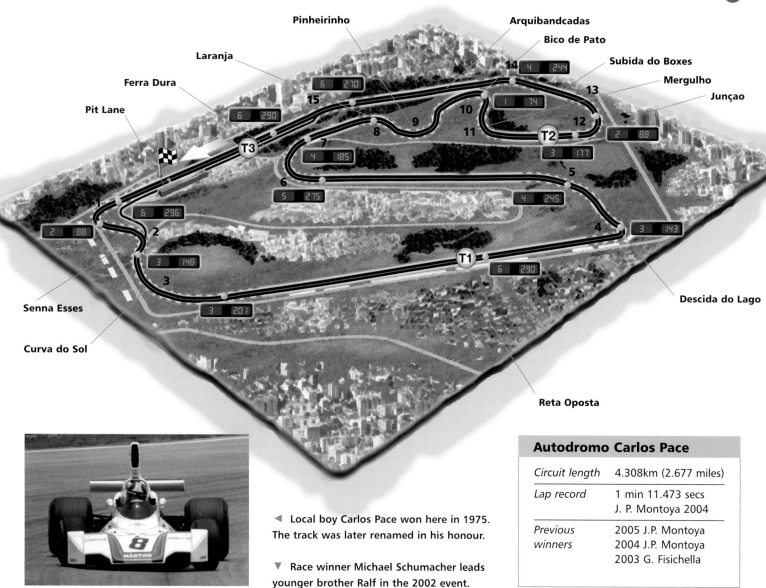

Pinheirinho

Arquibandcadas

Bico de Pato

Laranja

| 14 | 4 | 244 |

Subida do Boxes

Ferra Dura

| 6 | 270 |

Mergulho

15

13

Junçao

Pit Lane

| 6 | 290 |

| 1 | 74 |

10

| 2 | 88 |

8

9

11

12

T3

| 4 | 185 |

7

T2

| 3 | 177 |

5

1

6

| 5 | 275 |

| 4 | 245 |

| 6 | 296 |

2

4

| 3 | 143 |

| 2 | 88 |

| 3 | 148 |

T1

Descida do Lago

3

| 6 | 290 |

Senna Esses

| 3 | 201 |

Curva do Sol

Reta Oposta

◄ Local boy Carlos Pace won here in 1975. The track was later renamed in his honour.

▼ Race winner Michael Schumacher leads younger brother Ralf in the 2002 event.

Autodromo Carlos Pace

Circuit length	4.308km (2.677 miles)
Lap record	1 min 11.473 secs J. P. Montoya 2004
Previous winners	2005 J.P. Montoya 2004 J.P. Montoya 2003 G. Fisichella

and it brings an extra dimension to the problems faced by drivers and engineers as they try to set up the cars. Ride heights have to be bigger than at any other track on the calendar, reducing the aerodynamic efficiency and grip of the cars. Furthermore, the changeable weather can wreak havoc – as was seen in 2003 when a huge storm 30 minutes before the start created conditions that caused a chaotic, accident-infested race.

In 2001, Juan Pablo Montoya, in only his third Grand Prix, made himself a hero to millions, when he took the lead from Michael Schumacher with a daring wheel-rubbing move at the end of the straight into the Senna Esses. He pulled away quickly, and looked set for victory, but was later hit by the lapped car of Jos Verstappen. Despite his Colombian nationality, Montoya is a favourite with the wildly enthusiastic Interlagos fans. São Paulo native, Rubens Barrichello, closely follows him in their affections.

Canada *Montreal*

ituated on the Ile Notre Dame, a man-made island between the St Lawrence River and the St Lawrence Seaway, the Montreal track first hosted the Canadian Grand Prix in 1978, after the old Mosport circuit was deemed too dangerous.

The island had been built to house the world trade fair of 1967, and it hosted the Olympic Games of 1976, but more usually was parkland. The park roads were joined to form a circuit of long, fast straights and tight chicanes and hairpins. The fans went home very happy after the 1978 race, when local hero Gilles Villeneuve won for the first time in his Ferrari.

Villeneuve featured heavily in 1979 too, finishing second after a thrilling lead battle with the faster Williams of Alan Jones. In the wet 1981 race, he finished third despite running for much of the distance with no front wing.

◄ Gilles Villeneuve celebrates his first Formula One win with Quebec Premier Pierre Trudeau, on the Montreal podium in 1978.

▼ Mika Häkkinen's McLaren leading a lapped Arrows at the hairpin during the 2000 event.

But the month before he was due to take part in the 1982 event, he was killed during qualifying for the Belgian Grand Prix. The circuit was renamed in his memory.

The 1982 race saw further tragedy when Ricardo Paletti was killed in a startline accident, when his Osella rammed into the back of the stalled

pole position Ferrari of Villeneuve's former team-mate, Didier Pironi.

The circuit has changed little over the years, and it invariably produces an exciting race. The combination of high speeds on the long straights, followed by tight second-gear bends, means that it is the most punishing circuit of all for brakes. The carbon-fibre brake discs of

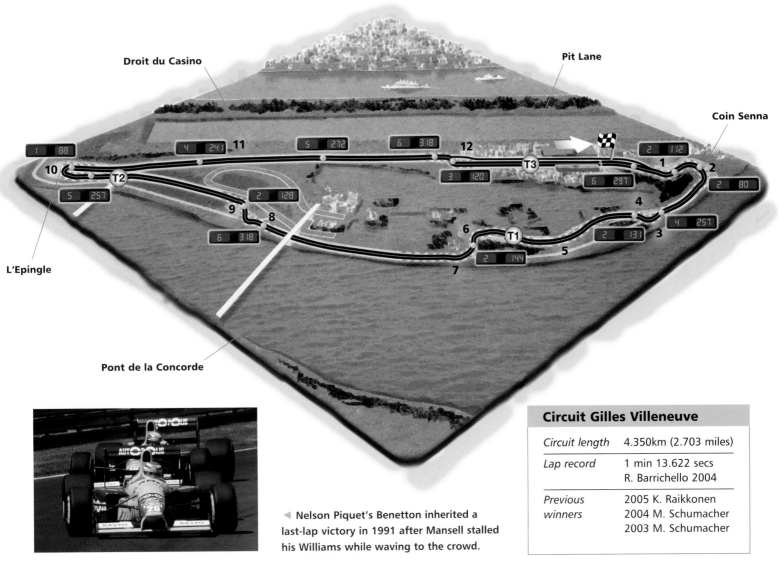

Droit du Casino

Pit Lane

Coin Senna

| 1 | 88 |
| 4 | 241 | 11
| 5 | 272 |
| 6 | 318 |
12
| 2 | 112 |
10
T3
1
2
T2
5	257
3	120
6	297
2	80
2	128
4
9 8
4	257
6	318
6
T1
2	131	3
5
L'Epingle
2	144
7

Pont de la Concorde

◄ Nelson Piquet's Benetton inherited a last-lap victory in 1991 after Mansell stalled his Williams while waving to the crowd.

Circuit Gilles Villeneuve

Circuit length	4.350km (2.703 miles)
Lap record	1 min 13.622 secs R. Barrichello 2004
Previous winners	2005 K. Raikkonen 2004 M. Schumacher 2003 M. Schumacher

modern Formula One cars begin to oxidize at temperatures over 600°C (1112°F). Here, they reach over 800°C (1472°F) repeatedly and are rarely allowed to drop below 500°C (932°F) before they are needed again. Brake wear is extreme, and lack of brakes is a frequent cause of retirement.

But it was the pressure of rival, Mika Häkkinen, rather than the lack of brakes that caused Michael Schumacher to crash out of the race in 1999. The two had engaged in a fierce duel that took them clear of the rest of the field. Finally, Michael took a little too much speed into the final corner and smashed hard into the unforgiving wall at its exit. Häkkinen duly took the win, a vital part of his successful campaign that year.

In 2001, the battle for victory was an all-Schumacher affair as Michael's Ferrari led early from brother Ralf's Williams-BMW. For lap after lap, Ralf would edge alongside in the final chicane, only to be discouraged as Michael veered toward him. The race's

turning point came when the Ferrari had to pit for fuel. Ralf's fuel tanks were bigger, and with little tyre wear from the dusty track, he was able to reel off four super-quick laps with clear air ahead of him. This enabled him to make his pitstop and rejoin the race in the lead for a comfortable victory.

Rows over tobacco advertising have threatened the future of this event (the 2004 event was initially cancelled) but its popularity with teams and fans has helped maintain its place on the calendar.

▼ Jean Alesi takes the flag for the only Formula One win of his career, in 1995.

China *Shanghai*

The idea of a Chinese Grand Prix was a dream Formula One had been chasing for a long time, and in 2004 it became a reality with a race around a stunning new venue outside the city of Shanghai.

The scale and opulence of the new track's facilities dwarfed any previously seen Formula One venue. The Herman Tilke-designed track earned high praise from the drivers for its variety of corners and the way in which they faciliated overtaking.

Ferrari's Rubens Barrichello was the inaugural winner of the Chinese Grand Prix after a tense race, with both Kimi Raikkonen's McLaren-Mercedes and Jenson Button's BAR-Honda staking claims to the win at various stages.

A full-to-capacity crowd of 150,000 also witnessed World Champion Michael Schumacher's toughest race of the season. He finished in twelfth place after an incident-filled weekend that began to go wrong for him in qualifying when he spun away his lap. In the race he had three separate incidents: a collision with Christian Klien's Jaguar, a spin and a puncture.

▲ **Ralf Schumacher in the Williams-BMW FW26 on practice day at the newly opened Shanghai track in 2004.**

◀ **Rubens Barrichello in the Ferrari F2004, winner of China's first ever Grand Prix.**

Up front, the race developed into a fascinating strategy struggle between three different drivers from three different teams. Barrichello and Raikkonen were on three-stop strategies, with Button stopping one time less. Barrichello led from the start, with Raikkonen soon trailing his every move. The Ferrari was slower early in each stint than the McLaren but Raikkonen couldn't take advantage by passing because his straightline speed was significantly slower than his rival's. In an attempt to overcome this McLaren brought their driver in early for his second stop and short-fuelled him. The tactic didn't work and, in fact, it caused Raikkonen to lose the second place to Button.

With one more stop to make than Button, Barrichello needed to pull out a lead over him of around 23 seconds before making his final stop. For a time Button managed to peg the gap to 21 seconds, putting him on course for victory. But Barrichello dug deep and began then to steadily extend the gap, and by the time he made his final stop he had enough comfortably in hand to emerge from his third stop still in the lead. Button took a great second, although he was put under severe pressure in the later laps by Raikkonen. Further down the field there had been lots of overtaking, notably between returning former champion Jacques Villeneuve and Williams driver Juan Pablo Montoya. In all, Formula One had given a good account of itself in front of its new audience.

With the importance of the lucrative Chinese market to sponsors set to escalate, the move of the sport into the country will almost certainly prove to be an historic one.

▼ *(below left)* **Ricardo Zonta in the Toyota TF104 on practice day in 2004.**

▼ *(below right)* **Felipe Massa in the Sauber C23 leads David Coulthard's McLaren M4/19B in the 2004 Chinese Grand Prix.**

Shanghai	
Circuit length	5.451km (3.387 miles)
Lap record	1 min 32.238 secs M. Schumacher 2004
Previous winners	2005 F. Alonso 2004 R. Barrichello -

Europe *Nürburgring*

T he European Grand Prix used to be a title bestowed in turn on a different European race each year, but fell into disuse in the mid-1970s. It was revived in 1983, when Brands Hatch hosted a Grand Prix just a few months after Silverstone's British Grand Prix. The title was subsequently used to cover any doubling-up of races in the same country: the new Nürburgring held the European Grand Prix in 1984 (Hockenheim held the German Grand Prix); in 1985, Brands Hatch featured the European race, while Silverstone's event bore the "British" tag. Then, in 1993, Donington Park was granted a Grand Prix of Europe, and Silverstone retained its regular British Grand Prix slot on the Formula One calendar.

More recently, the popularity of Formula One in Germany, following the success of Michael Schumacher, has made it viable for that country to host two Grands Prix per season. One of them, that held at the Nürburgring, now holds the full-time claim to the European Grand Prix title.

The "new" Nürburgring was first used in 1984. It was built as a modern venue to attract Formula One back to

▲ **An aerial view of the new Nürburgring. The new circuit was built because of serious safety concerns about the original track.**

▼ **Ralf Schumacher (*right*) fights out the first corner of the 2002 European Grand Prix with Williams-BMW team-mate Juan Pablo Montoya. Rubens Barrichello's Ferrari (*directly behind Montoya*) won the race.**

the region after the original track – a 22.5km (14 mile) section of road running through forested valleys – was deemed too dangerous, following Niki Lauda's near-fatal accident in 1976.

It is a relatively flat and featureless circuit, with constant radius bends and plenty of run-off area. Its surface is quite abrasive, demanding a fairly hard tyre compound. After a series of first corner incidents – where out-of-control cars going through the gravel trap had a tendency to come back on to the track on the exit as other cars filed past – the layout was changed for 2002. A double bend now takes the racing line out of reach of first corner spinners.

One of the most exciting races of modern Formula One took place at this track in 1995. It began in wet but drying conditions. Most chose to start on wet tyres, but not Jean Alesi in the Ferrari. As David Coulthard's Williams led from Michael Schumacher's Benetton and Damon Hill's Williams, Alesi was able to use his fantastic car control to hang on to them.

As the track began to dry, so the wet-tyred leaders had to pit – leaving Alesi with a 20-second lead and no

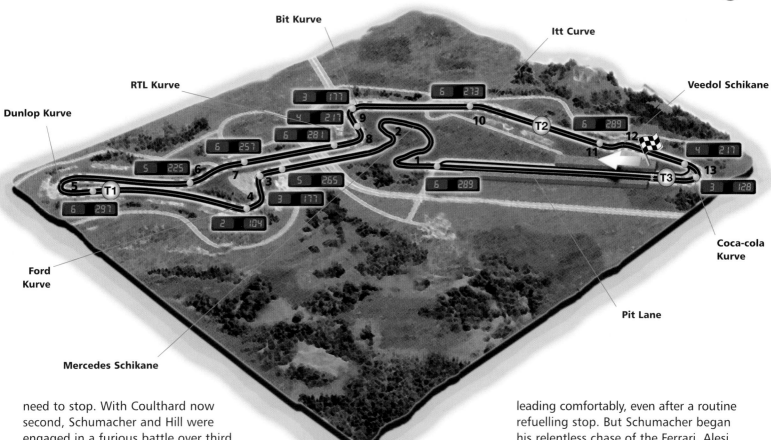

Bit Kurve

Itt Curve

RTL Kurve

Veedol Schikane

Dunlop Kurve

Ford
Kurve

Mercedes Schikane

Coca-cola
Kurve

Pit Lane

need to stop. With Coulthard now second, Schumacher and Hill were engaged in a furious battle over third place, and the German gave the Brit a chop on one occasion that almost took the Williams off the circuit. Eventually Hill succeeded in getting by, but then threw away the move by getting off line at the next corner, allowing Schumacher to retake the place. Michael then began to pull away.

Coulthard began to suffer handling difficulties, and was passed by both Schumacher and Hill, but still Alesi was

leading comfortably, even after a routine refuelling stop. But Schumacher began his relentless chase of the Ferrari. Alesi and his team took a long time to wake up to the threat of the closing Benetton. By the time Jean tried to respond, it was too late; Schumacher was now on his tail. With seven laps to go, Schumacher made an aggressive move down the inside into the chicane. It gave Alesi the option of making way or taking them both off. He chose the former, allowing Schumacher his seventh win of the season, on his way to the world title.

Nürburgring

Circuit length	5.144 km (3.196 miles)
Lap record	1 min 29.468 secs M. Schumacher 2004
Previous winners	2005 F. Alonso 2004 M. Schumacher 2003 R. Schumacher

▲ Johnny Herbert's Stewart took victory in the 1999 European Grand Prix.

▶ Jacques Villeneuve withstood pressure from Michael Schumacher to take his first Formula One win, at the Nürburgring, 1996.

▲ *(top)* Alain Prost's McLaren-Porsche won the first race held at the new Nürburgring for the 1984 European Grand Prix.

▲ *(above)* Niki Lauda's BRM in 1973: airborne action at the old Nürburgring.

France *Magny-Cours*

A race enthusiast farmer, Jean Bernigaud, built the original track on this site in 1960. Situated a few miles away from the town of Nevers, in the Loire Valley, it still nestles between green farmland and traditional French châteaux.

It was not until 1991 that the circuit played host to the French Grand Prix, by which time it was very different from the original. The current format was built in 1988, with the help of government grants. The Ligier team, later renamed Prost, was based here until Alain Prost moved it to Paris in 2000. Magny-Cours was also the base for the Winfield Racing School that established a whole generation of Elf-backed French racing drivers in the 1970s and 1980s. François Cevert, Patrick Depailler, Jacques Laffite and René Arnoux, among others, all started their careers here as raw novices. Laffite and Arnoux were consultants for the layout of the current track.

The most notable characteristic of this circuit is its incredibly smooth, bump-free surface. Teams can set the ride height of their cars lower here than at any other track, bringing big benefits in aerodynamic grip. Many of the corners are long and flowing, meaning the tyres are under lateral load for

◀ David Coulthard scythes down the inside of Michael Schumacher in 2000.

◀ Nigel Mansell (Williams) leads Alain Prost (Ferrari) in 1991.

▼ *(below left)* Ralf Schumacher's Williams-BMW leads brother Michael's Ferrari in 2001.

a long time. Combined with the soft compounds allowed by the surface, this makes tyre wear a critical factor.

The 1999 French Grand Prix at Magny-Cours was a fascinating struggle between several teams and drivers,

with changeable weather making the outcome uncertain right to the end.

The sky was threatening but the track dry as the race started, and Rubens Barrichello's Stewart led from pole position ahead of Jean Alesi's Sauber and David Coulthard's McLaren. At the end of the first lap, Heinz-Harald Frentzen's Jordan and Michael Schumacher's Ferrari followed in fourth and fifth place. Coulthard quickly passed both Alesi and Barrichello to take the lead. He pulled out a big gap over the rest before pulling to the side of the track with electrical failure on the 10th lap.

As Barrichello retook the lead, the rain began falling. But then stopped again after a couple of laps. Alesi was coming under pressure from Frentzen, and behind them was Mika Häkkinen, who had passed Schumacher. Häkkinen then passed Frentzen, Alesi and Barrichello in quick succession to take the lead in his McLaren.

On the 21st lap, the rain arrived properly, and everyone pitted for wet weather tyres. The Stewart team gave Barrichello a very quick stop, enabling

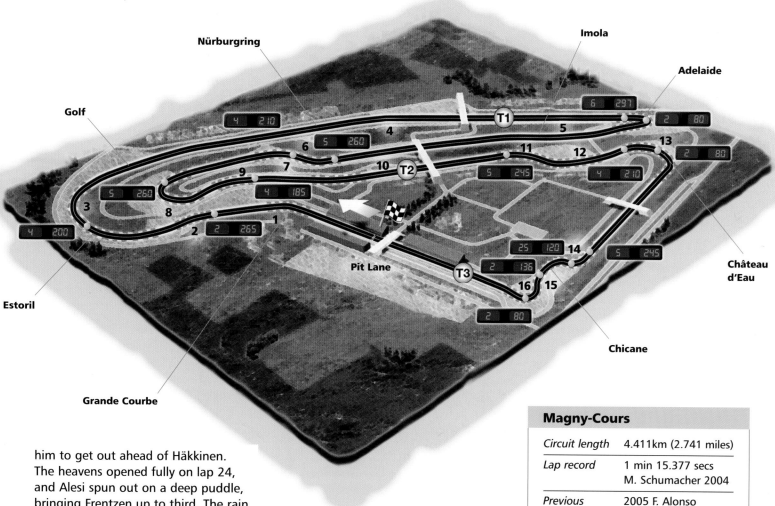

Nürburgring

Imola

Adelaide

Golf

| 4 | 210 |
| 2 | 80 |

| 6 | 297 |

5

T1

4

| 5 | 260 |

6

11

12

13

| 2 | 80 |

7

10

T2

9

| 5 | 245 |

| 4 | 210 |

| 5 | 260 |

| 4 | 185 |

3

8

| 4 | 200 |

2

| 2 | 265 |

1

Pit Lane

T3

| 25 | 120 |

14

| 5 | 245 |

| 2 | 136 |

Château
d'Eau

Estoril

16

15

| 2 | 80 |

Chicane

Grande Courbe

Magny-Cours

Circuit length	4.411km (2.741 miles)
Lap record	1 min 15.377 secs M. Schumacher 2004
Previous winners	2005 F. Alonso 2004 M. Schumacher 2003 R. Schumacher

him to get out ahead of Häkkinen. The heavens opened fully on lap 24, and Alesi spun out on a deep puddle, bringing Frentzen up to third. The rain was now so heavy that the safety car came out, neutralizing the race for the next 11 laps. With the race back on, Häkkinen attempted to wrest the lead back from Barrichello but spun, dropping to seventh. At around the same time, Schumacher – who had lost radio contact with his pit – had passed Frentzen and was in now second place.

After one failed attempt, Schumacher succeeded in passing Barrichello on lap 42. But soon after, he slowed due to electrical glitches in his car. He came in early for his second fuel stop to have the problem attended to. Barrichello thus led again but by now Häkkinen was carving back through the field and, after passing Frentzen, he took the lead from Barrichello for a second time. He began pulling away at the rate of three seconds per lap. Häkkinen and Barrichello made their second planned fuel stops, putting Frentzen in front.

Frentzen's Jordan had bigger fuel tanks than the other cars and, with the slower pace forced by the rain and the safety car, he now had enough fuel in reserve not to make his originally planned second stop. The McLaren and

Stewart teams waited for Frentzen to come in – and waited, and waited. At the end of 72 laps, Frentzen crossed the line to give Jordan an unexpected victory from Häkkinen and Barrichello.

▼ Schumacher leads into turn one at the start of the French Grand Prix, 2 July 2000.

Germany *Hockenheim*

H ockenheim has been the venue of the German Grand Prix since 1977 (with the exception of 1985, when the new Nürburgring hosted its second Grand Prix), though it hosted the event on one occasion before that, in 1970. For many years, it was the fastest Grand Prix track on the calendar, due to two very long straights. Even since being interrupted by chicanes in the 1980s, these stretches still allowed the Formula One cars of the 1990s to reach over 360km/h (224mph) in top gear. The straights – which ran through a wood – featured no spectating areas and were linked by a stadium section, where the crowds gather and where the pit lane is situated. This layout was used for the last time in 2001. For the 2002 race, a new section of track cut out much of the length of the straights, turning right through the former wood around half way down the first straight into a new infield section that then links back up with the truncated second straight just before the stadium. The new layout enables the cars to be seen by spectators for a greater proportion of the lap.

Situated around 112km (70 miles) south of Frankfurt, the original Hockenheim circuit was built as a test track by Mercedes in the late 1930s. When a new autobahn was built in the 1960s, it split the original track in two,

▲ *(top)* Jacky Ickx's Ferrari leads Jochen Rindt's Lotus in the first Grand Prix to be held at Hockenheim in 1970. Rindt won.

▲ *(above)* Niki Lauda on his way to an emotional Ferrari win in 1977.

▼ Jarno Trulli's Jordan leads Olivier Panis' BAR during a midfield battle in the last Grand Prix to be held on the unfettered Hockenheim track, in 2001.

but, using compensation money from the government, the circuit owners planned a new layout using only the far side of the former site. Racing began on this new track in 1966. Two years later, it gained notoriety when the great Jim Clark was killed here in a Formula Two race. His Lotus went out of control through a left-hand kink on the first straight, probably as the result of a slow puncture, and came to rest against a tree.

Safety standards were improved by the erection of barriers to protect cars from the trees. In 1970, under pressure from the Grand Prix Drivers' Association, the Nürburgring was being altered to improve safety, and so the German Grand Prix of that year was held at Hockenheim for the first time. The race was won by Jochen Rindt's Lotus. It would be another seven years before the event returned there, this time permanently, after the Nürburgring was finally dismissed as intrinsically too dangerous for Formula One. This had become clear through Niki Lauda's near-fatal accident there in 1976. It was therefore fitting that Lauda won the 1977 race at Hockenheim.

In 1980, Patrick Depailler was killed during a test session, when a suspected suspension failure put his Alfa Romeo head-on into the barriers at around 240km/h (150mph) at the Ost-Kurve. Another chicane was added to slow the cars through this section. Two years later, Didier Pironi's career came to an end after an accident caused by the

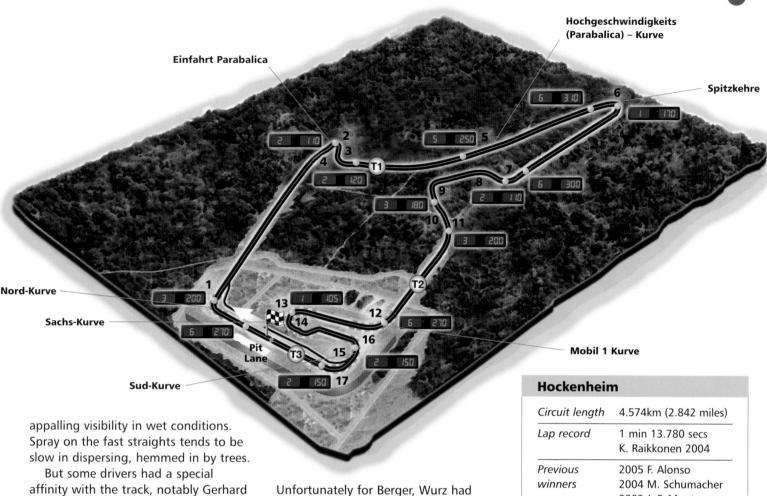

Einfahrt Parabalica

Hochgeschwindigkeits (Parabalica) – Kurve

Spitzkehre

Nord-Kurve

Sachs-Kurve

Mobil 1 Kurve

Sud-Kurve

Pit Lane

appalling visibility in wet conditions. Spray on the fast straights tends to be slow in dispersing, hemmed in by trees.

But some drivers had a special affinity with the track, notably Gerhard Berger. He won here for Ferrari in 1994, his only victory in his three-year second stint with the team. He was on-course to win the event in 1996 for Benetton until his engine blew on the last lap, handing victory to Damon Hill. But his greatest race here was his last one, in 1997. He had missed the previous three races because of a sinus problem, and been replaced by stand-in Alex Wurz.

Unfortunately for Berger, Wurz had performed superbly, and questions were being asked about whether Berger was needed. But worse, much worse, in the days leading up to his comeback, Berger learned that his father had been killed in a plane crash. It was somehow fitting that Berger should dominate the weekend. He started from pole position and led the race from beginning to end. At the end of the season he retired.

Hockenheim	
Circuit length	4.574km (2.842 miles)
Lap record	1 min 13.780 secs K. Raikkonen 2004
Previous winners	2005 F. Alonso 2004 M. Schumacher 2003 J. P. Montoya

▼ *(left)* Michael Schumacher in the Ferrari 310B on his way to second place in 1997.

▼ *(right)* A Toyota TF102 approaches the new hairpin at the heavily remodelled Hockenheim track during the German Grand Prix in 2002.

Great Britain *Silverstone*

In late-1940s Britain, the search was on for a major new race venue. Brooklands was no more, with half of its speed bowl destroyed to make room for aircraft production facilities. But as the war took away, so it created. In the heart of rural Northamptonshire, near the sleepy little village of Silverstone, there was a wartime airfield that was no longer needed. The perimeter roads of the runways made for a perfect high speed challenge. In 1948, it hosted the British Grand Prix. It has held it, on and off, ever since.

Initially, the country's governing body, the RAC, wished to spread its favours, and for a time the race alternated between Silverstone and Aintree near Liverpool. Subsequently – until 1986 – Brands Hatch in Kent took over the Aintree slot. But when Brands was deemed no longer suitable for Formula One, Silverstone monopolized the event.

It was a fast, flat and featureless track, very demanding and exacting, but for some drivers slightly disorienting. The early straw-bale markers soon gave way, first to oil drums, then concrete posts, and finally proper kerbs. But the farm remained in the track's infield – with the wheat usually high by the time

▲ *(top)* Jack Brabham took his Cooper to victory at Silverstone in 1960, on his way to a second World Championship.

▲ *(above)* Michael Schumacher (Ferrari) celebrates victory in the 2002 race at the same Silverstone venue at which he broke his leg in 1999.

of mid-July, the British Grand Prix slot – and the "Silverstone hare" still does invariably appear on-track during the weekend. Until the late 1980s, the layout remained much the same, once the original incorporation of the airfield runway was abandoned after 1948.

The corners were fast, and demanded a lot of commitment and precision on the way in. After Jody Scheckter crashed at the quick Woodcote corner, at the end of the first lap of the 1973 race, taking much of the field out with him, a chicane was incorporated there to slow things down. But it was still a fast track, and vied with the Osterreichring from the mid-1970s to mid-80s as the fastest on the calendar. In 1985, Keke Rosberg's turbocharged Williams-Honda set a qualifying lap speed of 258.97km/h (160.924mph), a Formula One record that stood until 2002.

This was rather too fast, in fact. The run-off areas demanded by these sort of speeds would have moved the spectators impossibly far back from the action. For the 1992 race, a complete redesign was in place. There was a new infield section before Woodcote, entered via the awesome Bridge Corner, a slightly banked top-gear right-hander. The right-left sweep of Becketts on to the Hangar Straight became more sharply defined, and there was a new section – Vale – between the Stowe and Club corners, which slowed things down further. Essentially, this remains the layout of the track today.

◀ Felippe Massa (Sauber) spinning at the first corner of the 2002 British Grand Prix.

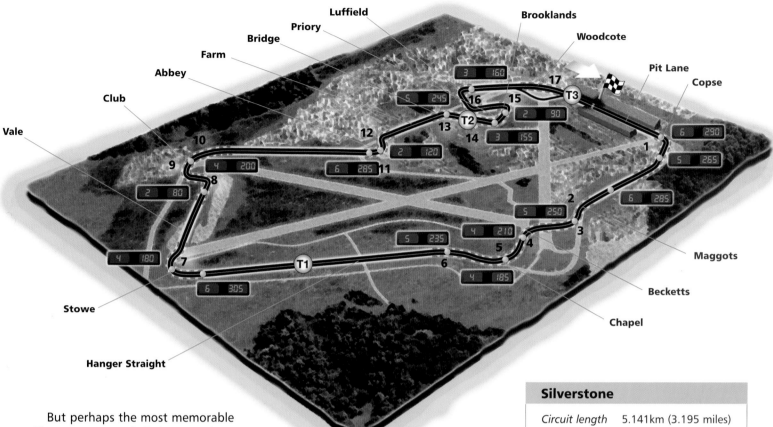

Luffield
Priory
Bridge
Farm
Abbey
Club
Vale
Brooklands
Woodcote
Pit Lane
Copse
Maggots
Becketts
Chapel
Stowe
Hanger Straight

But perhaps the most memorable Silverstone race of all time – and one of the greatest races in Formula One history – came on the old track, in 1987. The Williams-Hondas were the dominant machines of the time and no one other than their drivers, Nelson Piquet and Nigel Mansell, really had a chance. Piquet led the early going with Mansell chasing.

Then Mansell began to sense a vibration – a wheel weight had fallen off. It forced him to make an unplanned pit stop on lap 36 of the 65-lap race. With new tyres, he rejoined and with nothing to lose he turned up his turbo boost and set about catching his team-mate, now 28-seconds ahead.

He closed down at a rapid rate and the partisan crowd sensed something big was about to happen. With two laps to go, approaching Stowe corner at the end of the 305km/h (190mph) Hangar Straight, Mansell feigned for the outside. Piquet covered him and Mansell immediately darted to the inside and passed. Entering the last lap, Mansell's fuel read-out was telling him he had nothing left, but there was just enough to get him home. He ran out on the slowing down lap – and was mobbed.

Silverstone

Circuit length	5.141km (3.195 miles)
Lap record	1 min 18.739 secs M. Schumacher 2004
Previous winners	2005 J. P. Montoya 2004 M. Schumacher 2003 R. Barrichellor

▼ *(left)* Ayrton Senna's McLaren leads Gerhard Berger's Ferrari in the 1988 race. Senna won; team-mate Prost withdrew.

▼ *(right)* Mansell-mania: the crowd invade the track after homegrown hero Nigel Mansell dominated the 1992 race in his Williams-Renault FW14B. Mansell's successes attracted a new breed of race fan to Silverstone.

Hungary *Hungaroring*

It was Formula One supremo Bernie Ecclestone who pushed hardest for a Grand Prix behind the old Iron Curtain. For several years there was talk of a Moscow Grand Prix, but discussions always broke down at an early stage. It was then suggested to Ecclestone that he look at Hungary, where the regime might be more accommodating.

There was already a history of motor racing in the country as it had hosted a pre-war Grand Prix around the streets of Budapest, and even as late as the 1960 the city had been host to other European touring car events. The government was sold on the idea of a Grand Prix but, after looking at feasibility studies, decided that a new purpose-built track should be created. Work began in 1985, ready for the inaugural Grand Prix of 1986. The circuit was to be built in a rural valley some miles outside the city. Situated in a natural amphitheatre, it allowed for superb viewing for spectators.

However, as the allocated land area was fairly small, the track had to turn in on itself several times. Consequently it is very tight, offering no real chance for the cars to stretch their legs and there is only one possible overtaking spot. In terms of the set-up required of the

▲ *(top)* Nigel Mansell pulls off after a rear wheel came adrift while he was leading the late stages of the 1987 race.

▲ *(above)* Damon Hill's Arrows passes Michael Schumacher's Ferrari to lead the 1997 race. He later hit trouble.

cars, it needs maximum wing settings, just like at Monaco. For 2003, a new section of track was built in an effort to encourage more overtaking.

Nelson Piquet won the first race on the new Hungarian track, in August 1986, in his Williams-Honda. He had earlier taken the lead with a stunning round-the-outside pass of Ayrton Senna's Lotus at the first corner, the Williams on full opposite lock as it completed the manoeuvre. Piquet won again the following year, but only after his team-mate Nigel Mansell's wheel nut came off while leading.

The 1989 race was perhaps the most exciting Hungarian race. After early-leader Riccardo Patrese retired

◀ Fernando Alonso won at the Hungaroring in 2003. At 22 years and 26 days he became the youngest ever Grand Prix winner.

Pit Lane

Hungaroring

Circuit length	4.384km (2.724 miles)
Lap record	1 min 19.071 secs M. Schumacher 2004
Previous winners	2005 K. Raikkonen 2004 M. Schumacher 2003 F. Alonso

► Mika Häkkinen (McLaren-Mercedes) took a dominant win at Hungary in 1999 in the absence of injured rival Michael Schumacher.

his Williams with a punctured radiator, Ayrton Senna was leading in the McLaren and looked set for victory. But that was to reckon without Nigel Mansell, who had qualified his Ferrari in only 12th place. In the race his car was handling superbly, and he had quickly fought his way through the pack. He was on Senna's tail as they came up to lap the Onyx of Stefan Johansson, who kept well over to the left of the track, aware that the leaders were bearing down on him. Senna seemed caught momentarily off-guard and boxed himself in behind. Mansell, anticipating this superbly, swung across the back of Senna's gearbox with just millimetres to spare and passed both cars in one move, on his way to victory. It gave the lie to the track's no-passing reputation.

► The scenic Hungaroring in August 2000.

Italy *Monza*

Situated in a former royal park in suburbs around 24km (15 miles) north of Milan, Monza is the oldest track on which the World Championship is still fought. It held its first Grand Prix in September 1922, and has hosted it almost every year since.

Monza was not the first purpose-built racing circuit in Europe – that honour belonged to Brooklands in Britain – but it was the first to be used for a Grand Prix. The 1922 Italian race, in fact, marked the first time that spectators were charged an entrance fee to watch a Grand Prix.

Comprising two circuits in one, the "speed bowl" was in essence an American-style oval track, with two long straights joined by two heavily banked corners. Within this was a "road circuit" designed to replicate the demands of public road racing that had comprised Grands Prix up until this time. The two tracks criss-crossed one another via a bridge, and shared the same pit straight. The speed bowl was demolished in 1938, but part of the banking was incorporated into the road course. In 1955, a new banked circuit was built to replace the pre-war one, and the layout allowed for a combination of banked and road circuit to be used. This combined track hosted the Grands Prix of 1955 and 1956, but

▲ *(top)* The closest finish. Only 0.1seconds separated the first five finishers in the 1971 race. Peter Gethin got the verdict, from Peterson, Cevert, Hailwood and Ganley.

▲ *(above)* The first lap crash which claimed the life of Ronnie Peterson at the Italian Grand Prix on 10 September 1978.

there were concerns about the stresses tyres and suspensions were subject to by the banking, and from 1957 the road course was reverted to once more. Even this was an extremely fast track, with much flat-out running and high speed bends, such as the Lesmos and Parabolica, making the races fantastically gripping slip-streaming battles where, typically, the outcome would be in doubt right up to the finish line.

There was one last Grand Prix held on the banking in 1960, but subsequently that section fell into disuse – though it still remains, an impressive weed-infested monument to a bygone era.

The high speeds meant the Monza circuit bore witness to many tragedies, and, initially, poor spectator protection meant they, too, were often involved. In 1928, Emilio Materassi crashed into the spectator enclosure on the main straight, killing 27 people and himself. As late as 1961, the Ferrari of Wolfgang von Trips reared along the spectator

◄ The safety car leads the cars past the old banked circuit at the Italian Grand Prix in 2000.

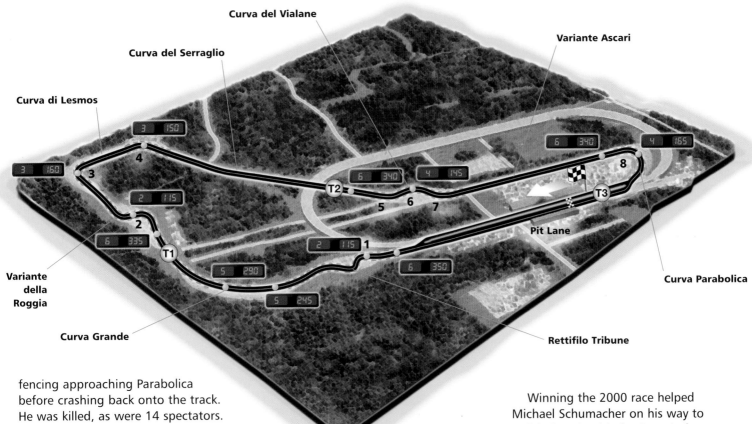

Curva del Vialane

Variante Ascari

Curva del Serraglio

Curva di Lesmos

| 3 | 150 |

| 3 | 160 |

4

3

| 2 | 115 |

2

| 6 | 335 |

T1

Variante
della
Roggia

| 6 | 340 |

| 4 | 145 |

T2

5   6   7

| 6 | 340 |

| 4 | 165 |

8

T3

Pit Lane

| 2 | 115 | 1

| 6 | 350 |

Curva Parabolica

| 5 | 290 |

| 5 | 245 |

Curva Grande

Rettifilo Tribune

fencing approaching Parabolica before crashing back onto the track. He was killed, as were 14 spectators. Jochen Rindt lost his life here during practice for the 1970 race, and Ronnie Peterson died as a result of a first-lap start-line crash in the 1978 event.

Amid the fanatical Ferrari fans, Peter Gethin won for BRM in 1971, and his average speed of 242.62km/h (150.76mph) still stands as the fastest Grand Prix race average of all time. Subsequently, chicanes were installed to slow the cars down, and whilst making it safer it also brought about the end of the classic slipstreaming battles.

Monza	
Circuit length	5.793km (3.600 miles)
Lap record	1 min 21.046 secs R. Barrichello 2004
Previous winners	2005 J. P. Montoya 2004 R. Barrichello 2003 M. Schumacher

Winning the 2000 race helped Michael Schumacher on his way to reclaiming the title for Ferrari after 21 years. It also marked Schumacher's 41st Grand Prix victory, which brought him level to the record of Ayrton Senna. Schumacher – who had been racing against Senna at Imola in 1994, when the Brazilian crashed to his death – broke down in tears in the press conference.

▼ (below) Schumacher wins in 2000.

▼ (bottom) Italian fans celebrate the World Championship title won by Ferrari in 2001.

◄ *Tifosi* shout for Scuderia Ferrari at the Italian Grand Prix in 2001.

Japan *Suzuka*

osting the Japanese Grand Prix since 1987, Suzuka is renowned as one of the greatest challenges an Formula One driver can face. Its sequence of super-fast bends demand ultimate commitment and many rank its 290km/h (180mph) corner, 130R, as the ultimate test of nerve and skill.

Owned by Japanese manufacturer Honda, the circuit was built as a test track by the company in the early 1960s. Subsequent races were held there, though the newly-inaugurated but short-lived Japanese Grand Prix of 1976 and 1977 ran at the rival Fuji track.

It was not until the time of Honda's prominence as a Formula One engine supplier, in the mid-1980s, that it was able to exert its influence and have a Japanese Grand Prix reinstated to the calendar, this time at Suzuka.

As the Japanese race has usually been either the penultimate or final race of the year, it has frequently been host to championship deciders. In 1989, title rivals Alain Prost and Ayrton Senna collided at the chicane. Prost retired but Senna rejoined from the escape road and went on to win the race. He was then disqualified for rejoining the track

▲ Gerhard Berger took his first Ferrari win at Suzuka, 1987, with the F1/87. It was Formula One's fastest car by the end of the year.

in a dangerous manner, leaving him unable to overhaul Prost's points advantage in the one race remaining. A year later, Senna took his revenge as he again fought out the destiny of the crown with Prost. Using his points advantage in his favour, as Prost had done the previous year, Senna simply drove his rival off the track at the first corner. Both retired into the gravel trap,

▼ Mika Häkkinen leads Michael Schumacher in the 2000 Japanese Grand Prix, as they fight for the World Championship title.

but Senna became World Champion. In 2000, Michael Schumacher clinched the first World Championship for a Ferrari driver in 21 years after a supremely tense battle with his only rival, McLaren's Mika Häkkinen. The Finn led the first part of the race, with Schumacher following in his tracks as both pulled well clear of the rest of the field. The McLaren was the first to make

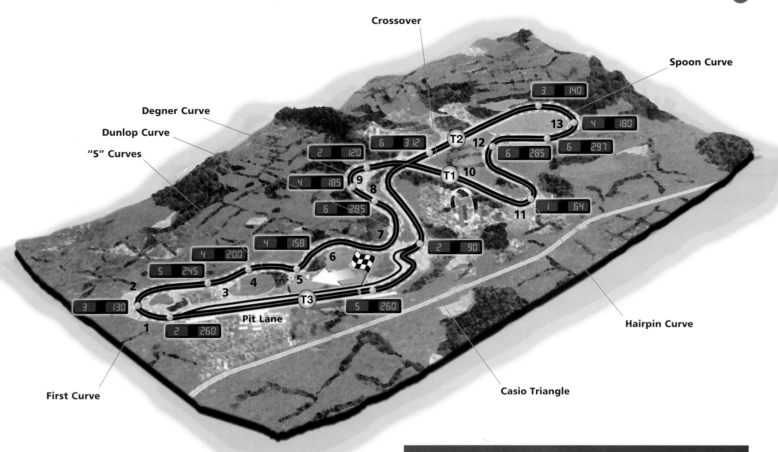

Crossover

Spoon Curve

Degner Curve

Dunlop Curve

"S" Curves

| 3 | 140 |

| 6 | 312 |

13

| 4 | 180 |

T2 12

| 2 | 120 |

| 6 | 285 |

| 6 | 297 |

| 4 | 185 |

9

T1 10

| 6 | 285 |

8

| 1 | 64 |

11

7

| 4 | 158 |

| 2 | 90 |

| 4 | 200 |

6

| 5 | 245 |

5

2

| 3 | 130 |

3   4

T3

Pit Lane

| 5 | 260 |

Hairpin Curve

1

| 2 | 260 |

First Curve

Casio Triangle

Suzuka

Circuit length	5.859km (3.641 miles)
Lap record	1 min 31.540 secs K. Raikkonen 2005
Previous winners	2005 K. Raikkonen 2004 M. Schumacher 2003 R. Barrichello

▶ **Damon Hill took a superb victory in the 1994 Japanese Grand Prix. Rival Michael Schumacher got stuck behind Mika Häkkinen, losing vital time.**

its routine fuel and tyre stop, but just as Häkkinen was rejoining, spots of rain began to fall. Critically, this meant Häkkinen was unable to generate sufficient heat into his new tyres and, for a couple of laps, he was slow. Schumacher, yet to stop and on tyres already up to temperature, was able to lap quickly enough to build sufficient gap to allow him to pit and rejoin without losing the lead. Häkkinen gave chase, but it was to no avail. In bringing the world title back to Italy, Schumacher had succeeded in doing what no one had managed since Jody Scheckter in 1979.

▶ **Michael Schumacher sealed a record-breaking sixth World Championship title in Japan at the final round of the 2003 world championship series.**

Malaysia *Sepang*

The Malaysian government sought to host a globally prestigious annual event as part of its programme of economic expansion, and Formula One fitted the bill perfectly. To this end, a brand new circuit was constructed on the outskirts of Kuala Lumpur, with facilities that rendered other Formula One venues previous-generation. It hosted its first Grand Prix in 1999.

The track is situated on a former stretch of derelict land adjacent to Kuala Lumpur airport. It was designed by German Hermann Tilke to incorporate a wide variation of corners. Two 0.9km (0.56-mile) straights are joined by a hairpin, but perhaps the most spectacular part of the track is an unusually wide and gradual chicane, where the Formula One cars sweep left-right at around 200km/h (125mph). Further around the lap, Turn 12 is a highly dramatic fourth gear downhill left-hander, leading into the loop that takes the cars down the first of the long straights.

Grand Prix spectators are housed in grandstands beneath spectacular sun-sensitive leaf-design roofing, with blinds that open and close according to the light. From there they can see much of the circuit, thanks to the land's contours and the site's relatively compact area.

▲ Eddie Irvine was helped to victory by second-placed team-mate Michael Schumacher in 1999.

◄ Schumacher drove his Ferrari F1-2000 to victory at Sepang in 2000.

The inaugural race, the penultimate round of the 1999 championship, got the event off to a great start. Michael Schumacher, after breaking his leg at Silverstone, had missed much of the season, leaving his Ferrari team-mate Eddie Irvine to battle McLaren's Mika Häkkinen for the championship. Schumacher was finally fit to race again for Malaysia, and his brief was to aid Irvine in the Championship fight.

After setting pole position by over a second, Schumacher took off into the lead ahead of Irvine, whom he allowed past after four laps. As Irvine pushed on, intent on building up his lead, Schumacher endeavoured to slow the

◄ Alex Yoong (Minardi PS02) in his home Grand Prix was meant to pack the Sepang grandstands in 2002.

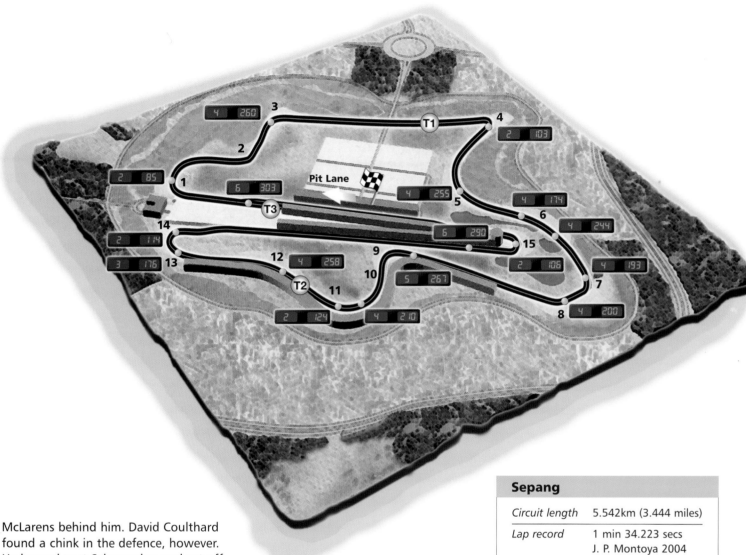

McLarens behind him. David Coulthard found a chink in the defence, however. He barged past Schumacher and set off after Irvine, but on lap 15, Coulthard's car lost its fuel pressure and retired.

As Schumacher repeatedly prevented Häkkinen from making progress, Irvine built up enough of a lead that he was comfortably back in front after all had made their first fuel stops. Irvine then did a short second stint, increasing his lead even further, before a second and final fuel stop. He rejoined just behind Häkkinen, who then made his second stop. This left Schumacher – who wasn't making a second stop – in the lead from Irvine. Schumacher allowed Irvine through for a second time, and the Ferraris finished 1-2, with Häkkinen a frustrated third, allowing the title fight to go to the final round in Japan. It was a superb demonstration of team work from the Italian team.

Post-race, it was announced that the aerodynamic barge boards on the side of the Ferraris were of a shape not permitted by the regulations. They were initially disqualified, but reinstated on appeal a few days later.

▼ The beautiful Malaysian paddock by night, illuminated by lasers.

Sepang	
Circuit length	5.542km (3.444 miles)
Lap record	1 min 34.223 secs J. P. Montoya 2004
Previous winners	2005 F. Alonso 2004 M. Schumacher 2003 K. Raikkonenr

Monaco *Monte Carlo*

T he race around the streets of the tiny principality, home of the jet-set crowd and super-rich, has become synonymous with the image of Grand Prix racing. Since 1929, cars have raced past the yachts in the Mediterranean harbour, around tortuous bends more usually clogged with traffic. The slowest Grand Prix track on the calendar, it is also the most exacting. Unlike other tracks, there are no run-off areas and no margin for error. One slip and the car is in the barriers, its race over.

The idea for the race came from Anthony Noghes, president of the Monegasque car club and close friend of the ruling Grimaldi family. The town was already host to the Monte Carlo rally, but Noghes conceived cars racing wheel-to-wheel through the streets. Even in the 1920s, the course was considered very narrow for such an event, but the inaugural race of 1929 – won by William Grover-Williams in a Bugatti – was considered a big success in attracting custom and prestige to

the area, and it has continued, on and off, to this day. It is the venue of choice for team sponsors to attend.

The course traces its way up a hill cut out of the cliff face and via the blind exit of Massenet corner into Casino Square. There, with the Casino on one side and the Hôtel de Paris on the other, the cars weave their way to the top of the hill that leads them down to Mirabeau, a very tight right-hander leading on to an even tighter left-hander, Loews. Taken in first gear at no more than 48km/h (30mph), this is the slowest corner in Grand Prix racing. Drivers have to be very careful to allow themselves enough room to get round, and cars frequently have extra steering lock made available to prevent the embarrassment of not being able to manage it. After a couple of successively quicker right-handers, the cars enter the famous tunnel, cut through solid rock beneath the Hôtel de Paris. After a flat-out kink in the middle, the cars exit the dim light at around 290km/h (180mph) before extreme braking for a first-gear chicane. The track then follows the harbour

◄ **The start of the race: eventual winner Michael Schumacher (Ferrari) leads the field towards Massenet in 2001.**

▼ **Chris Amon (Ferrari 312), in third, passes the fatal accident of Lorenzo Bandini at the 1967 Monaco Grand Prix.**

▲ **Ayrton Senna (McLaren) fends off Nigel Mansell's Williams during the closing stages to win at Monaco in 1992. Mansell had earlier been forced to pit while leading.**

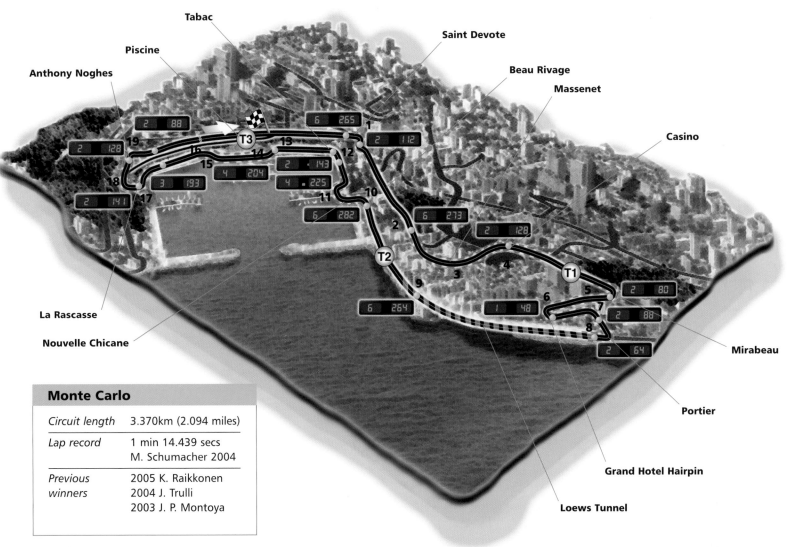

Tabac

Piscine

Anthony Noghes

Saint Devote

Beau Rivage

Massenet

Casino

| 2 | 88 |
| 2 | 128 |

19

T3

13

6 265

1

2 112

16

14

12

18

15

3 193

4 204

2 ·143

4 ·225

17

11

10

6 282

2

6 273

T2

2 128

9

3

4

T1

6 264

1 48

6

5

2 80

7

2 88

8

2 64

Mirabeau

La Rascasse

Portier

Nouvelle Chicane

Monte Carlo

Circuit length	3.370km (2.094 miles)
Lap record	1 min 14.439 secs M. Schumacher 2004
Previous winners	2005 K. Raikkonen 2004 J. Trulli 2003 J. P. Montoya

Grand Hotel Hairpin

Loews Tunnel

▲ Twenty-two cars are a tight squeeze through the streets of Monte Carlo on the first lap of the 2002 Monaco Grand Prix.

through Tabac, the swimming pool section and the slow Rascasse corner, before entering the pit straight on the way to Ste Devote, the right-hander that leads back up the hill to Casino.

Engineers will set the cars for Monaco with maximum wing settings, to give as much downforce as possible, as the low-speed nature of the track means there is very little penalty in drag. Suspensions will be set softer than usual, to allow for the bumps and to help traction out of the many slow, low-gear turns. The low-grip nature of the surface, and the lack of high-speed turns, means that tyre compounds are softer here than at any other track.

It is a circuit where drivers can make big gains by tuning into its rhythm, and there have been some notable Monaco specialists over the years, including five-time winners Graham Hill and Alain Prost. Ayrton Senna won the event six times between 1987 and 1993, while Michael Schumacher has met Prince Rainier on the top step of the podium five times since 1994.

▲ Michael Schumacher first took victory at Monaco in his Benetton B194 in 1994. He has since won it four times to date.

San Marino *Imola*

The principality of San Marino is used as a flag of convenience to give Italy two Grands Prix per season. The town of Imola is not in San Marino, but is around 145km (90 miles) south of Milan. The track is named in honour of Enzo Ferrari's son Dino, who worked for Ferrari but died from a illness in 1956, while still in his 20s.

The circuit was built in the 1960s, but it was not used for a Formula One Championship event until 1980, when it hosted the Italian Grand Prix, one of the few occasions that event was not held at Monza. Since 1981, the Italian Grand Prix has been back at Monza in its traditional September slot, while Imola takes an early-season space in the calendar.

One of only two anti-clockwise circuits in the schedule, it was originally a fast track, but has been constantly slowed by additional chicanes. This has made it one of the toughest circuits for brakes. The last round of changes came in the wake of the tragic events of 1994. Roland Ratzenberger was killed in qualifying when his Simtek left the track after damaging a front wing. The following day, Ayrton Senna died

◄ Nicola Larini, Michael Schumacher and Mika Häkkinen try not to show their emotions on the podium at Imola in 1994, following the tragic death of Ayrton Senna in the early laps of the race.

in the early laps of the race after his Williams left the track at the flat-out kink of Tamburello. After hitting the retaining wall at around 210km/h (130mph), a suspension component broke off and pierced his helmet.

Since then a chicane has been installed before Tamburello and a further one before "Villeneuve", the corner at which Ratzenberger lost his life. This corner was so named after Ferrari driver Gilles Villeneuve, who suffered a major accident here in 1980 as a result of a tyre blow-out.

It was at the 1989 San Marino Grand Prix that one of the biggest driver feuds in the sport's history was initiated.

Driving the dominant McLaren-Hondas, Ayrton Senna and Alain Prost had agreed between themselves that they would not fight out the first corner of the race, and that whichever of them got the better start would be given a clean passage by the other. For them, the race would effectively start after the first turn. It was Senna who made the better start and Prost duly tucked in behind for the first corner. They were in this order when, at the beginning of the fourth lap, Gerhard Berger suffered

▼ Finn Kimi Raikkonen's McLaren-Mercedes MP4/17 retired with exhaust problems after 44 laps at Imola in 2002.

Acque Minerale

Variante Alta

Piratella

Tosa

Villeneuve

Tamburello

Pit Lane

Rivazza

Variante Bassa

Traguardo

Circuit Dino Ferrari

Circuit length	4.933km (3.065 miles)
Lap record	1 min 20.411 secs M. Schumacher 2004
Previous winners	2005 F. Alonso 2004 M. Schumacher 2003 M. Schumacher

▶ **Juan Pablo Montoya (Williams-BMW FW24) takes off at the Variante Alta during the San Marino Grand Prix at Imola in 2002.**

an enormous accident in his Ferrari at Tamburello. The car hit the wall and burst into flames, and the race was stopped while he was released, amazingly with only light injuries.

The race was restarted, and this time Prost made the better start. He assumed Senna would not attack him into the first corner and did not drive defensively, but Senna chose to interpret their agreement as being valid only for the first start, and at the first corner he shot down the inside of his team-mate, and into the lead. He went on to win the race, with Prost a distant second. It was the sort of ruthlessness for which Senna was famous, but afterwards Prost was furious.

From that moment and until Prost's retirement at the end of 1993, the two greatest drivers of the era were at loggerheads with each other.

▶ **Winner Nelson Piquet (Brabham BT49) at the Italian Grand Prix in 1980.**

Spain *Barcelona*

he Barcelona circuit is known as
the "laboratory of Formula One",
owing to its extensive use as a test
track by the teams in between races.
It first hosted the Spanish Grand Prix
in 1991, and since 1998 has held
the event exclusively, though another
Spanish track, at Jerez, hosted the
European Grand Prix in 1997.

Built on industrial wasteland some
miles north of the city, the circuit makes
many conflicting demands of the cars.
It has a long, long pit straight but this
is immediately followed by a sequence
of fairly tight second- and third-gear
corners. Aerodynamic efficiency is
therefore paramount here. The cars
need fairly high wing settings to cope
with the tighter corners, but those cars
that can do this with the minimum
penalty on drag for the long
straight are the ones that do best.

◀ Graham Hill,
1969, and the high
wing that caused
his accident.

▼ David Coulthard
gives his McLaren
team-mate Mika
Häkkinen a lift back
after he had retired
on the last lap while
leading in 2001.

The advantage of an aerodynamically
efficient car will always be exaggerated
at this track. Long-duration turns and
a coarse surface also mean it is very
tough on tyres.

All these factors – and the season-
long favourable weather – have helped
give the circuit its testing popularity.
If the car works well at Barcelona, it
will tend to work well everywhere.

The 2001 race was a classic battle
between two foes Mika Häkkinen and
Michael Schumacher. The latter had
led the early going in his Ferrari, with
Häkkinen hanging on as best he could
in second with the McLaren. Opting for
longer stints between fuel stops than
the Ferrari, Mika was hoping he would
be able to gain the critical time needed
after Michael made his stop. Schumacher
made his first stop on lap 22, five short
of Häkkinen's planned stop. Now
leading, the Finn began pushing to the
very limit in an attempt to build up the
time needed to make his stop without
losing position.

It wasn't quite enough, and after his
stop Häkkinen rejoined just behind the
Ferrari. Again though, he was fuelled
for a longer stint, so giving him a
second chance at pulling out the vital
extra time after Schumacher made
his second stop on lap 43. This time
Häkkinen had seven laps on a low fuel
load in which to build up the necessary
cushion. Aided by Schumacher being
slowed slightly by a vibration, Häkkinen
this time was able to make his stop and
exit just in front of the Ferrari. All he

◀ The Barcelona start-finish straight and
pit lane, with the Pyrennees mountains
ever-present in the background.

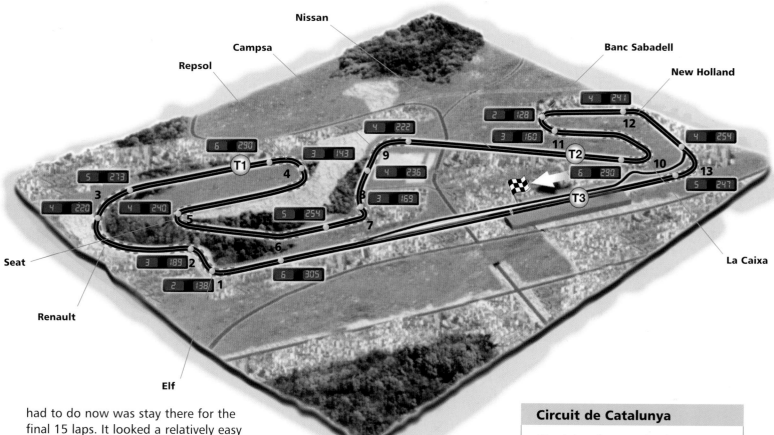

Nissan

Campsa

Repsol

Banc Sabadell

New Holland

| 4 | 241 |

| 2 | 128 |

| 6 | 290 |

| 4 | 222 |

| 3 | 160 |

| 12 |

| 4 | 254 |

T1

| 5 | 273 |

| 3 | 143 |

| 9 |

| 11 |

T2

| 10 |

| 13 |

| 4 | 236 |

| 6 | 290 |

| 3 | 220 |

| 4 | 240 |

| 4 |

| 8 |

T3

| 5 | 247 |

| 5 | 254 |

| 3 | 169 |

| 5 |

| 7 |

| 6 |

La Caixa

Seat

| 3 | 189 | | 2 |

| 2 | 138 | | 1 |

| 6 | 305 |

Renault

Elf

had to do now was stay there for the final 15 laps. It looked a relatively easy task for the Finn, who was notoriously cool under pressure.

The laps duly ticked away and, with Schumacher slowing even more, Häkkinen built up his lead to over half a minute. As he went past the pits for the last time, the McLaren's engine could be heard to be running rough. A few corners later, Mika pulled off to the side of the track. Michael couldn't believe his luck as he was handed victory on the last lap of the race.

On his slow-down lap, he stopped to give his disconsolate rival a lift back to the pits. Even Schumacher felt sorry for Häkkinen on that day.

▼ (left) Winner Mika Häkkinen (McLaren MP4-13) leads David Coulthard in the Spanish Grand Prix in 1998.

Circuit de Catalunya

Circuit length	4.730km (2.939 miles)
Lap record	1 min 15.641 secs G. Fisichella 2005
Previous winners	2005 K. Raikkonen 2004 M. Schumacher 2003 M. Schumacher

▼ Gerhard Berger leads McLaren team-mate Ayrton Senna into the first corner of the 1991 race. Winner Nigel Mansell is here in third, with Michael Schumacher fourth.

Turkey *Istanbul*

T he inaugural Turkish Grand Prix took place on 21 August 2005 around a stunning new purpose-built track on the Asian side of Istanbul.

Although the new venue was not quite as opulent as that in China – which held its first Formula One event the year before – the track was widely proclaimed by the drivers as an instant classic. Diving up and down through many elevation changes by way of blind brows and downhill braking areas, its centrepiece is a superbly challenging left hander – turn eight – that is effectively three fast corners joined together. The cars enter it in sixth gear and – if they have a seven-speed gearbox – exit in seventh. Additionally, there are a couple of mid-corner bumps that really test the quality of the car's chassis and the driver's reactions. Even flat out in a Formula One car this sequence lasts for over 7 seconds, during which time the driver is subjected to over 4g in lateral forces.

Circuit designer Herman Tilke has incorporated several classic features from other tracks in the layout of this one and the diving downhill S-bend forming turns 1-2 resembles that of the

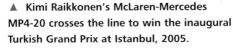
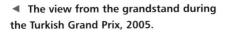
▲ **Kimi Raikkonen's McLaren-Mercedes MP4-20 crosses the line to win the inaugural Turkish Grand Prix at Istanbul, 2005.**

◄ **The view from the grandstand during the Turkish Grand Prix, 2005.**

Senna Esses at Interlagos. There are also recognizable elements of Spa and Imola on other parts of the lap. It all adds up to a beautiful whole and the long kinking back straight leading into two slow final corners makes for some of the best overtaking opportunities of any major circuit.

The first race here was dominated by the McLaren-Mercedes of Kimi Raikkonen as he sought to overcome a points deficit to the man with whom he was fighting for the world championship, Fernando Alonso. The Spanish Renault driver finished runner-up to Raikkonen here, gifted a bonus position on the last lap after Raikkonen's team-mate, the Columbian Juan Pablo Montoya, briefly left the track at turn eight.

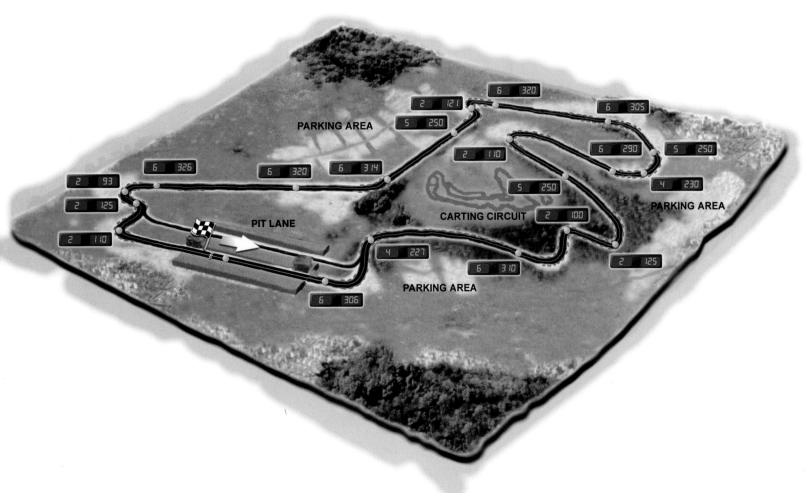

2	121
5	250
6	320
6	305
2	110
6	290
5	250
6	326
6	320
6	314
5	250
2	93
2	125
2	100
2	110
4	227
4	230
6	310
2	125
6	306

PARKING AREA

CARTING CIRCUIT

PARKING AREA

PIT LANE

PARKING AREA

Montoya's moment was triggered by a diffuser that had been damaged on the previous lap when he had an incident while lapping Tiago Monteiro's Jordan. At the end of the back straight on the approach to the braking area for turn 12 Montoya had chopped in front of the Jordan, leaving Monteiro with nowhere to go. The Jordan's brakes locked up and Monteiro hit the back of the McLaren. Both cars went spinning before rejoining. Despite the incident, Montoya retained his second place, but Alonso was now right with him. Entering the fast turn eight on the following lap, Montoya's damaged car did not have its previous level of grip and slid wildly, forcing Montoya to take to the tarmac run-off area. It lost him only a couple of seconds but was enough to allow Alonso past, thereby seriously damaging Raikkonen's championship chances.

An estimated 100,000 witnessed this fight and even though the road network struggled to cope on race day, the event was acclaimed as a major success.

▼ *(below left)* Mark Webber in the Williams-BMW FW27 on the first lap in 2005.

▼ *(below right)* Michael Schumacher's Ferrari F2005 during the 2005 race. He failed to finish due to steering problems.

Istanbul	
Circuit length	5.344km (3.340 miles)
Lap record	1 min 24.770 secs J.P. Montoya 2005
Previous winners	2005 K. Raikkonen - -

USA *Indianapolis*

Formula One's biggest challenge in the modern era has always been how to open up the American market. Hosting a race in the world's biggest economy would naturally make the sport more attractive to sponsors and television companies looking for advertising revenue. Yet America has always had its own domestic race series, namely NASCAR stock cars and ChampCar single-seaters. Formula One meant little, if anything, to the average American television viewer.

There had been American Grands Prix at Watkins Glen in New York State through the 1960s and 1970s, but in the end they became economically unviable. In the 1970s and 1980s, Formula One dallied with street circuits in Long Beach, Detroit, Phoenix and Las Vegas. But part of the problem was the slow average speeds to which the cars were limited. To race fans brought up on a diet of lap speeds in excess of 320km/h (200mph) from both NASCAR saloons and ChampCar single-seaters on their super-fast oval tracks, Formula One hardly captured the imagination.

Using Indianapolis as a venue for a new American Grand Prix from 2000 was an inspired idea. Virtually every

American knew about Indianapolis, home of "the world's greatest race", the Indy 500. This ChampCar race had run since 1911 and was part of the very fabric of American life, one of the great sporting classics. By holding a Formula One race here, Grand Prix racing would benefit from the fame of the venue.

However, the famous banked speed bowl was not a suitable circuit for a Formula One machine. Instead, a new circuit was constructed that used part of the traditional track, but which then veered off into an infield of more or

▲ Michael Schumacher spins his Ferrari F1-2000, but still goes on to win the USA Grand Prix at Indianapolis in 2000.

▼ *(left)* Juan Pablo Montoya's Williams-BMW FW23 leads the field around the famous Indy banking in 2001.

▼ *(right)* Mika Häkkinen celebrates what would turn out to be his final Grand Prix victory before retirement in 2001. He is flanked by Michael Schumacher *(left)* and McLaren team-mate David Coulthard.

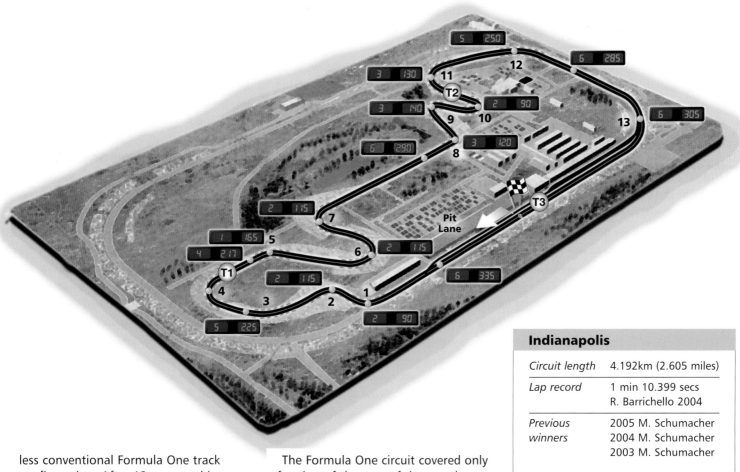

5	250	
6	285	
3	130	
3	140	
2	90	
6	305	
6	290	
3	120	
2	115	
1	165	
4	217	
2	115	
2	115	
6	335	
5	225	
2	90	

Pit Lane

Indianapolis

Circuit length	4.192km (2.605 miles)
Lap record	1 min 10.399 secs R. Barrichello 2004
Previous winners	2005 M. Schumacher 2004 M. Schumacher 2003 M. Schumacher

less conventional Formula One track configuration. After 12 corners this rejoined the existing track on the banking of what is "Turn One" in ChampCar parlance, but which became Turn 13 of the Formula One track, given that the cars were travelling clockwise, the opposite way to the Champcars.

The Formula One circuit covered only a fraction of the area of the speedway, leaving the huge grandstands of three-quarters of the oval deserted. Yet even this made for over 200,000 spectators, well up on most European venues. Since 2000, the event has begun the slow task of turning America on to Formula One.

▼ Jarno Trulli (*left*) and Jenson Button about to clash in the early laps of the USA Grand Prix at Indianapolis. This was their second tangle in three races. The pair later became team-mates at Renault.

Statistics

Who was the fastest, the greatest, the best qualifier, the top racer? Who made the best car? These are questions to which there are no definitive answers. Comparison between eras of motor racing is not strictly possible; in the pioneer days of the sport there was one major race per year, at the inauguration of the World Drivers' Championship in 1950 there were seven major Grands Prix. Today, the season comprises 19 races. Statistics therefore can be misleading, over-emphasizing modern achievements at the expense of earlier ones. But all have been recorded and heralded.

◄ Japanese Grand Prix, Suzuka, 2002.

World Champion Drivers

1950 Giuseppe Farina (Italy)
1951 Juan Manuel Fangio (Argentina)
1952 Alberto Ascari (Italy)
1953 Alberto Ascari (Italy)
1954 Juan Manuel Fangio (Argentina)
1955 Juan Manuel Fangio (Argentina)
1956 Juan Manuel Fangio (Argentina)
1957 Juan Manuel Fangio (Argentina)
1958 Mike Hawthorn (Britain)
1959 Jack Brabham (Australia)
1960 Jack Brabham (Australia)
1961 Phil Hill (USA)
1962 Graham Hill (Britain)
1963 Jim Clark (Britain)
1964 John Surtees (Britain)
1965 Jim Clark (Britain)
1966 Jack Brabham (Australia)
1967 Denny Hulme (New Zealand)
1968 Graham Hill (Britain)
1969 Jackie Stewart (Britain)
1970 Jochen Rindt (Austria)
1971 Jackie Stewart (Britain)
1972 Emerson Fittipaldi (Brazil)
1973 Jackie Stewart (Britain)
1974 Emerson Fittipaldi (Brazil)
1975 Niki Lauda (Austria)
1976 James Hunt (Britain)
1977 Niki Lauda (Austria)
1978 Mario Andretti (USA)
1979 Jody Scheckter (South Africa)
1980 Alan Jones (Australia)
1981 Nelson Piquet (Brazil)
1982 Keke Rosberg (Finland)
1983 Nelson Piquet (Brazil)
1984 Niki Lauda (Austria)
1985 Alain Prost (France)
1986 Alain Prost (France)
1987 Nelson Piquet (Brazil)
1988 Ayrton Senna (Brazil)
1989 Alain Prost (France)
1990 Ayrton Senna (Brazil)
1991 Ayrton Senna (Brazil)
1992 Nigel Mansell (Britain)
1993 Alain Prost (France)
1994 Michael Schumacher (Germany)
1995 Michael Schumacher (Germany)
1996 Damon Hill (Britain)
1997 Jacques Villeneuve (Canada)
1998 Mika Häkkinen (Finland)
1999 Mika Häkkinen (Finland)
2000 Michael Schumacher (Germany)
2001 Michael Schumacher (Germany)
2002 Michael Schumacher (Germany)
2003 Michael Schumacher (Germany)
2004 Michael Schumacher (Germany)
2005 Fernando Alonso (Spain)

▲ Chris Amon's Ferrari 312 takes second place at the British Grand Prix, Brands Hatch, in 1968.

World Champion Constructors

1958 Vanwall
1959 Cooper
1960 Cooper
1961 Ferrari
1962 BRM
1963 Lotus
1964 Ferrari
1965 Lotus
1966 Brabham
1967 Brabham
1968 Lotus
1969 Matra
1970 Lotus
1971 Tyrrell
1972 Lotus
1973 Lotus
1974 McLaren
1975 Ferrari
1976 Ferrari
1977 Ferrari
1978 Lotus
1979 Ferrari
1980 Williams
1981 Williams
1982 Ferrari
1983 Ferrari
1984 McLaren
1985 McLaren
1986 Williams
1987 Williams
1988 McLaren
1989 McLaren
1990 McLaren
1991 McLaren
1992 Williams
1993 Williams
1994 Williams
1995 Benetton
1996 Williams
1997 Williams
1998 McLaren
1999 Ferrari
2000 Ferrari
2001 Ferrari
2002 Ferrari
2003 Ferrari
2004 Ferrari
2005 Renault

Grands Prix Formulae

1906 Max weight 1000kg
1907 Max weight 1000kg
Fuel consumption: 30 litres/100km (9.4mpg)
1908 Max weight 1150kg
Max cylinder bore:
4-cylinder engines: 155mm
6-cylinder engines: 127mm
1912 Max width 175cm
1913 Min weight 800kg
Max weight 1100kg
Fuel consumption: 20 litres/100km (14.1mpg)
1914 4.5-litre max
Max weight 1100kg
1921 3-litre max
Min weight 800kg
1922–25 2-litre max
Min weight 650kg
1926–27 1.5-litre max
(1926) Min weight 600kg
(1927) Min weight 700kg
1928 Min weight 500kg
Max weight 750kg
1929–30 Min weight 900kg
Fuel consumption: 14 litres/100km (20.1mpg)
1931–33 No stipulation
1934–37 Max weight 750kg
1938–39 3-litre forced induction
4.5-litre normally aspirated
1947–51 1.5-litre forced induction 4.5-litre normally aspirated
1952–53 2-litre normally aspirated 0.5-litre forced induction
1954–60 2.5-litre normally aspirated 0.75-litre forced induction
1961–65 1.5-litre normally aspirated only. Min weight 450kg
1966–85 3-litre normally aspirated 1.5-litre forced induction
(1966–68) Min weight 500kg
(1969–81) Min weight 530kg
(1982) Min weight 580kg
(1983) Min weight 540kg
Forced induction fuel max 250 litres
(1984–85) Min weight 540kg
Forced induction fuel max 220 litres. No fuel stops
1986 1.5-litre forced induction. Min weight 540kg. Fuel max 195 litres. No fuel stops
1987 1.5-litre forced induction 3.5-litre

normally aspirated
Forced induction fuel max 195 litres. Forced induction boost 4-bar max. No fuel stops. Min weight 540kg
1988 1.5-litre forced induction 3.5-litre normally aspirated. Forced induction fuel max 150 litres. Forced induction boost 2.5-bar max. No fuel stops. Forced induction 540kg. Normally aspirated 500kg
1989–94 3.5-litre normally aspirated only. Min weight 500kg
(1994) Fuel stops allowed
(1995– 3-litre normally present) aspirated present) only. Fuel stops allowed. Min weight 600kg including driver
(1999– 10-cylinder engines present) only

Championship Race Wins (Drivers)

Driver	Wins
Michael Schumacher	84
Alain Prost	51
Ayrton Senna	41
Nigel Mansell	31
Jackie Stewart	27
Jim Clark	25
Niki Lauda	25
Juan Manuel Fangio	24
Nelson Piquet	23
Damon Hill	22
Mika Häkkinen	20
Stirling Moss	16
Jack Brabham	14
Emerson Fittipaldi	14
Graham Hill	14
Alberto Ascari	13
David Coulthard	13
Mario Andretti	12
Alan Jones	12
Carlos Reutemann	12
Jacques Villeneuve	11
Gerhard Berger	10
James Hunt	10
Ronnie Peterson	10
Jody Scheckter	10
Rubens Barrichello	9
Kimi Raikkonen	9
Fernando Alonso	8
Denny Hulme	8
Jacky Ickx	8
René Arnoux	7
Juan Pablo Montoya	7
Tony Brooks	6
Jacques Laffite	6
Riccardo Patrese	6
Jochen Rindt	6
Ralf Schumacher	6
John Surtees	6
Gilles Villeneuve	6

Michele Alboreto	5
Giuseppe Farina	5
Clay Regazzoni	5
Keke Rosberg	5
John Watson	5
Dan Gurney	4
Eddie Irvine	4
Bruce McLaren	4
Thierry Boutsen	3
Peter Collins	3
Heinz-Harald Frentzen	3
Mike Hawthorn	3
Johnny Herbert	3
Phil Hill	3
Didier Pironi	3
Elio de Angelis	2
Patrick Depailler	2
Giancarlo Fisichella	2
José Froilán González	2
Jean-Pierre Jabouille	2
Peter Revson	2
Pedro Rodriguez	2
Jo Siffert	2
Patrick Tambay	2
Maurice Trintignant	2
Wolfgang von Trips	2
Jean Alesi	1
Giancarlo Baghetti	1
Lorenzo Bandini	1
Jean-Pierre Beltoise	1
Jo Bonnier	1
Vittorio Brambilla	1
François Cevert	1
Luigi Fagioli	1
Peter Gethin	1
Richie Ginther	1
Innes Ireland	1
Jochen Mass	1
Luigi Musso	1
Alessandro Nannini	1
Gunnar Nilsson	1
Carlos Pace	1
Olivier Panis	1
Ludovico Scarfiotti	1
Piero Taruffi	1
Jarno Trulli	1

Championship Race Wins (Teams)

Ferrari	184
McLaren	148
Williams	113
Lotus	79
Brabham	35
Benetton	27
Renault	25
Tyrrell	23
BRM	17
Cooper	16
Alfa Romeo	10
Ligier	9
Maserati	9
Matra	9
Mercedes	9
Vanwall	9
Jordan	4
March	3
Wolf	3
Honda	2
Eagle	1
Hesketh	1
Penske	1
Porsche	1
Shadow	1
Stewart	1

Championship Pole Positions (Drivers)

Ayrton Senna	65
Michael Schumacher	62
Jim Clark	33
Alain Prost	33
Nigel Mansell	32
Juan Manuel Fangio	28
Mika Häkkinen	26
Niki Lauda	24
Nelson Piquet	24
Damon Hill	20
Mario Andretti	18
René Arnoux	18
Jackie Stewart	17
Stirling Moss	16
Alberto Ascari	14
James Hunt	14
Ronnie Peterson	14
Rubens Barrichello	13
Jack Brabham	13
Graham Hill	13
Jacky Ickx	13
Jacques Villeneuve	13
Gerhard Berger	12
David Coulthard	12
Juan Pablo Montoya	12
Jochen Rindt	10
Fernando Alonso	9
Kimi Raikkonen	9
Riccardo Patrese	8
John Surtees	8
Jacques Laffite	7
Emerson Fittipaldi	6
Phil Hill	6
Jean-Pierre Jabouille	6
Alan Jones	6
Carlos Reutemann	6
Ralf Schumacher	6
Chris Amon	5
Giuseppe Farina	5
Clay Regazzoni	5
Keke Rosberg	5
Patrick Tambay	5
Mike Hawthorn	4
Didier Pironi	4
Elio de Angelis	3
Tony Brooks	3
Teo Fabi	3
José Froilán González	3
Dan Gurney	3
Jean-Pierre Jarier	3
Jody Scheckter	3
Jarno Trulli	3
Michele Alboreto	2
Jean Alesi	2
Jenson Button	2
Giancarlo Fisichella	2
Heinz-Harald Frentzen	2
Stuart Lewis Evans	2
Jo Siffert	2
Gilles Villeneuve	2
John Watson	2
Lorenzo Bandini	1
Jo Bonnier	1
Thierry Boutsen	1
Vittorio Brambilla	1
Eugenio Castellotti	1
Peter Collins	1
Andrea de Cesaris	1
Bruno Giacomelli	1
Nick Heidfeld	1
Denny Hulme	1
Carlos Pace	1
Mike Parkes	1
Tom Pryce	1
Peter Revson	1
Wolfgang von Trips	1

Championship Pole Positions (Teams)

Ferrari	179
Williams	125
McLaren	122
Lotus	107
Renault	43
Brabham	39
Benetton	16
Tyrrell	14
Alfa Romeo	12
BRM	11
Cooper	11
Maserati	10
Ligier	9
Mercedes	8
Vanwall	7
March	5
Matra	4
Shadow	3
BAR	2
Jordan	2
Lancia	2
Toyota	2
Arrows	1
Honda	1
Lola	1
Porsche	1
Stewart	1
Toleman	1
Wolf	1

Engine Championship Race Wins

Ford Cosworth DFV	155 (1967–83)
Renault V10	84 (1989–05)
Ferrari Martinelli V10	61 (1996–05)
Mercedes Ilmor V10	43 (1997–05)
Honda turbo V6	40 (1984–88)
Ferrari Forghieri flat-12	37 (1970–79)
Porsche TAG turbo V6	25 (1984–87)
Coventry Climax V8	23 (1961–65)
Renault turbo V6	20 (1979–86)
Ford Cosworth HB	19 (1989–94)
Coventry Climax 4	17 (1958–61)
Ferrari Lampredi straight-4	16 (1952–55)
Honda Goto V10	16 (1989–90)
Ferrari Forghieri turbo V6	15 (1981–88)
Honda Goto V12	13 (1991–92)
Alfa Romeo straight-8	12 (1950–51)
BRM V8	12 (1962–66)
Ferrari Lombardi V12	11 (1989–95)
Maserati straight-6	9 (1953–57)
BMW turbo 4	9 (1982–86)
BMW V10	10 (2001–05)
Mercedes straight-8	9 (1954–55)
Vanwall straight-4	9 (1957–58)
Repco V8	8 (1966–67)
Ferrari Chiti V6	6 (1961–63)
Ferrari Jano V6	5 (1958–60)
Lancia V8	5 (1956)
BRM V12	4 (1970–72)
Mugen Honda V10	4 (1996–99)
Ferrari Lampredi V12	3 (1951)
Ferrari Bellai V8	3 (1964)
Ferrari Colombo V12	3 (1966–68)
Matra V12	3 (1977–81)
Ford Cosworth CR V10	2 (1995–03)
Maserati V12	2 (1966–67)
BRM straight 4	1 (1959)
BRM H16	1 (1966)
Honda Nakamura V12	1 (1965)
Honda Irimagiri V12	1 (1967)
Porsche flat-8	1 (1962)
Weslake V12	1 (1967)
Renault 111-deg V10	1 (2003)

Engine Championship Race Wins by Manufacturer

Ford	176
Ferrari	174
Renault	105
Honda	75
Mercedes	53
Coventry Climax	40
Porsche	26
BMW	19
BRM	18
Alfa Romeo	12
Maserati	11
Vanwall	9
Repco	8
Lancia	5
Matra	3
Weslake	1

Fastest Race Laps in Championship Grands Prix (Drivers)

Michael Schumacher	70
Alain Prost	41
Nigel Mansell	30
Jim Clark	28
Mika Häkkinen	25
Niki Lauda	25
Juan Manuel Fangio	23
Nelson Piquet	23
Gerhard Berger	21
Stirling Moss	20
Damon Hill	19
Ayrton Senna	19
David Coulthard	18
Kimi Raikkonen	16
Clay Regazzoni	15
Jackie Stewart	15
Rubens Barrichello	14
Jacky Ickx	14
Alan Jones	13
Riccardo Patrese	13
René Arnoux	12
Juan Pablo Montoya	12
Alberto Ascari	11
John Surtees	11
Mario Andretti	10
Jack Brabham	10
Graham Hill	10
Denny Hulme	9
Ronnie Peterson	9
Jacques Villeneuve	9
James Hunt	8
Ralf Schumacher	8
Jacques Laffite	7
Gilles Villeneuve	7
Giuseppe Farina	6
Emerson Fittipaldi	6
Heinz-Harald Frentzen	6
José Froilán González	6
Dan Gurney	6
Mike Hawthorn	6
Phil Hill	6
Didier Pironi	6
Jody Scheckter	6
Carlos Pace	5
John Watson	5
Michele Alboreto	4
Jean Alesi	4
Jean-Pierre Beltoise	4
Patrick Depailler	4
Carlos Reutemann	4
Jo Siffert	4
Chris Amon	3
Tony Brooks	3
Richie Ginther	3
Jean-Pierre Jarier	3
Bruce McLaren	3
Jochen Rindt	3
Keke Rosberg	3
Fernando Alonso	2
Lorenzo Bandini	2
Vittorio Brambilla	2
François Cevert	2
Teo Fabi	2
Giancarlo Fisichella	2
Jochen Mass	2
Alessandro Nannini	2
Patrick Tambay	2
Derek Warwick	2
Richard Attwood	1
Giancarlo Baghetti	1
Jean Behra	1
Thierry Boutsen	1
Andrea de Cesaris	1
Bertrand Gachot	1
Mauricio Gugelmin	1
Mike Hailwood	1
Brian Henton	1
Hans Herrmann	1
Innes Ireland	1
Eddie Irvine	1
Karl Kling	1
Onofré Marimon	1
Roberto Mieres	1
Roberto Moreno	1
Luigi Musso	1
Sataru Nakajima	1
Jackie Oliver	1
Jonathan Palmer	1
Henri Pescarolo	1
Pedro Rodriguez	1
Lodovico Scarfiotti	1
Marc Surer	1
Piero Taruffi	1
Maurice Trintignant	1
Luigi Villoresi	1
Alex Wurz	1

Fastest Race Laps in Championship Grands Prix (Teams)

Ferrari	185
Williams	127
McLaren	126
Lotus	70
Brabham	41
Benetton	36
Renault	22
Tyrrell	20
BRM	15
Maserati	15
Alfa Romeo	14
Cooper	13
Matra	12
Ligier	11
Mercedes	11
March	7
Vanwall	6
Surtees	4
Eagle	2
Honda	2
Jordan	2
Shadow	2
Wolf	2
Ensign	1
Gordini	1
Hesketh	1
Lancia	1
Parnelli	1
Toyota	1

Age of World Champions (years)

1950	Farina	44
1951	Fangio	40
1952	Ascari	34
1953	Ascari	35
1954	Fangio	43
1955	Fangio	44
1956	Fangio	45
1957	Fangio	46
1958	Hawthorn	29
1959	Brabham	33
1960	Brabham	34
1961	P. Hill	34
1962	G. Hill	33
1963	Clark	27
1964	Surtees	30
1965	Clark	29
1966	Brabham	40
1967	Hulme	31
1968	G. Hill	39
1969	Stewart	30
1970	Rindt	28
1971	Stewart	32
1972	Fittipaldi	25
1973	Stewart	33
1974	Fittipaldi	27
1975	Lauda	26
1976	Hunt	29
1977	Lauda	28
1978	Andretti	38
1979	Scheckter	29
1980	Jones	34
1981	Piquet	29
1982	Rosberg	34
1983	Piquet	31
1984	Lauda	35
1985	Prost	30
1986	Prost	31
1987	Piquet	35
1988	Senna	28
1989	Prost	34
1990	Senna	30
1991	Senna	31
1992	Mansell	39
1993	Prost	38
1994	M. Schumacher	25
1995	M. Schumacher	26
1996	D. Hill	36
1997	Villeneuve	26
1998	Häkkinen	30
1999	Häkkinen	31
2000	M. Schumacher	31
2001	M. Schumacher	32
2002	M. Schumacher	33
2003	M. Schumacher	34
2004	M. Schumacher	35
2005	F. Alonso	24

Average age of World Champion: 34 years

Youngest World Champion when title sealed: Fernando Alonso (2005) 24 years, 58 days

Oldest World Champion when title sealed: Juan Manuel Fangio (1957) 46 years, 41 days

Top 10 Youngest Championship Grand Prix winners

Fernando Alonso (2003)
22 years 26 days
Bruce McLaren (1958)
22 years, 80 days
Jacky Ickx (1968)
22 years, 104 days
Michael Schumacher (1992)
23 years, 188 days
Emerson Fittipaldi (1970)
23 years, 296 days
Mike Hawthorn (1953)
24 years, 86 days
Jody Scheckter (1974)
24 years, 131 days
Elio de Angelis (1982)
24 years, 148 days
David Coulthard (1995)
24 years, 181 days
Peter Collins (1956)
24 years, 208 days

Top 10 Oldest Championship Grand Prix Winners

Luigi Fagioli (1951)
53 years, 22 days
Giuseppe Farina (1955)
46 years, 276 days
Juan Manuel Fangio (1957)
46 years, 41 days
Piero Taruffi (1952)
45 years, 219 days
Jack Brabham (1970)
43 years, 339 days
Nigel Mansell (1994)
41 years, 97 days
Maurice Trintignant (1958)
40 years, 200 days
Graham Hill (1969)
40 years, 90 days
Clay Regazzoni (1979)
39 years, 312 days
Carlos Reutemann (1981)
39 years, 35 days

Top 10 Youngest Championship Grand Prix Participants

Mike Thackwell (1980)
19 years, 82 days
Ricardo Rodriguez (1961)
19 years, 209 days
Fernando Alonso (2001)
19 years, 261 days
Esteban Tuero (1998)
19 years, 320 days
Chris Amon (1963)
19 years, 326 days
Jenson Button (2000)
20 years, 52 days
Eddie Cheever (1978)
20 years, 54 days
Tarso Marques (1996)
20 years, 71 days

Peter Collins (1952)
20 years, 94 days
Rubens Barrichello (1993)
20 years, 295 days

Laps in the Lead of Championship Grands Prix

Michael Schumacher	4,837
Ayrton Senna	2,982
Alain Prost	2,705
Nigel Mansell	2,099
Jim Clark	2,039
Jackie Stewart	1,893
Niki Lauda	1,620
Nelson Piquet	1,572
Mika Häkkinen	1,490
Damon Hill	1,352
Graham Hill	1,073
David Coulthard	891
Jack Brabham	827
Mario Andretti	799
Ronnie Peterson	706
Gerhard Berger	695
Jody Scheckter	671
Carlos Reutemann	648
Rubens Barrichello	640
James Hunt	634
Jacques Villeneuve	628
Alan Jones	594
Riccardo Patrese	570
Gilles Villeneuve	533
Jacky Ickx	529
René Arnoux	506
Keke Rosberg	506
Emerson Fittipaldi	478
Denny Hulme	436
Jochen Rindt	387

Number of Championship Grands Prix Contested (Drivers)

Riccardo Patrese	256 (1977–93)
Michael Schumacher	220 (1991–2005)
Rubens Barrichello	212 (1993–2005)
Gerhard Berger	210 (1984–97)
Andrea de Cesaris	208 (1980–93)
Nelson Piquet	204 (1978–91)
Jean Alesi	201 (1989–2001)
Alain Prost	199 (1980–93)
Michele Alboreto	194 (1981–94)
David Coulthard	191 (1994–2005)
Nigel Mansell	187 (1980–95)
Graham Hill	176 (1958–75)
Jacques Laffite	176 (1974–86)
Niki Lauda	171 (1971–85)
Thierry Boutsen	163 (1983–93)
Mika Häkkinen	162 (1991–2001)
Ayrton Senna	161 (1984–94)
Martin Brundle	158 (1984–96)
Heinz-Harald Frentzen	157 (1994–2003)
Giancarlo Fisichella	156 (1997–2005)
Olivier Panis	156 (1994–2004)

John Watson	152 (1973–85)
René Arnoux	149 (1978–89)
Derek Warwick	147 (1981–93)
Carlos Reutemann	146 (1972–82)
Eddie Irvine	146 (1993–2002)
Emerson Fittipaldi	144 (1970–80)
Johnny Herbert	144 (1989–2000)
Jean-Pierre Jarier	135 (1971–83)

Number of Championship Grands Prix Contested (Teams)

Ferrari	720 (1950–2005)
McLaren	593 (1966–2005)
Williams	512 (1975–2005)
Lotus	490 (1958–94)
Tyrrell	418 (1970–98)
Brabham	399 (1963–92)
Arrows	382 (1978–2002)
Minardi	337 (1985–2005)
Ligier	326 (1976–96)
Benetton	317 (1986–2001)
Jordan	247 (1991–2005)
March	230 (1970–92)
Sauber	213 (1993–2005)
BRM	197 (1951–77)
Renault	190 (1977–2005)
Lola	139 (1962–93)
Osella	132 (1980–90)
Cooper	129 (1955–68)
Surtees	118 (1970–78)
Alfa Romeo	112 (1950–85)
BAR	115 (1999–2005)
Fittipaldi	104 (1976–82)
Shadow	104 (1973–80)
ATS	99 (1977–84)
Ensign	99 (1973–82)
Jaguar	82 (2000–2004)
Dallara	78 (1988–92)
Maserati	69 (1950–58)
Matra	60 (1968–72)
Zakspeed	54 (1985–89)

Greatest Number of Championship Points Scored (Drivers)

Michael Schumacher	1,236
Alain Prost	798.5
Ayrton Senna	614
David Coulthard	499
Nelson Piquet	485.5
Nigel Mansell	482
Rubens Barrichello	473
Niki Lauda	420.5
Mika Häkkinen	420
Gerhard Berger	386
Damon Hill	360
Jackie Stewart	360
Carlos Reuteman	310
Ralf Schumacher	293
Graham Hill	289
Emerson Fittipaldi	281
Riccardo Patrese	281
Kimi Raikkonen	281
Juan Manuel Fangio	277.5
Jim Clark	274
Juan Pablo Montoya	265

Jack Brabham	261
Jody Scheckter	255
Denny Hulme	248
Fernando Alonso	247
Jean Alesi	240
Jacques Laffite	228
Jacques Villeneuve	228
Clay Regazzoni	212
Alan Jones	206
Ronnie Peterson	206
Bruce McLaren	196.5

Greatest Number of Championship Points Scored (Teams)

Ferrari	3,416.5
McLaren	3,024.5
Williams	2,467.5
Lotus	1,370
Brabham	865
Benetton	851.5
Renault	705
Tyrrell	621
BRM	433
Ligier	390
Cooper	333
Jordan	291
BAR	197
Sauber	189
March	180.5
Arrows	167
Matra	155
Toyota	115
Wolf	79
Shadow	67.5

World Championship Points Systems

1950–59: 8-6-4-3-2 for first five places in race; 1 point for fastest lap.

1959–90: 9-6-4-3-2-1 for first six places.

1991–2002: 10-6-4-3-2-1 for first six places.

2003–on: 10-8-6-5-4-3-2-1 for first eight places. (shortened races awarded half-points)

Closest Grand Prix finishes

Italy 1971 0.010 secs
    Peter Gethin/
    Ronnie Peterson)
USA 2002 0.011 secs
    (Rubens Barrichello/
    Michael Schumacher)
Spain 1986 0.050 secs
    (Ayrton Senna/
    Nigel Mansell)
Austria 1982 0.080 secs
    (Elio de Angelis/
    Keke Rosberg)
France 1954 0.100 secs
    (Juan Manuel Fangio/
    Karl Kling)
France 1961 0.100 secs

    (Giancarlo Baghetti/
    Dan Gurney)
Austria 2002 0.182 secs
    (Michael
    Schumacher/
    Rubens Barrichello)
Britain 1955 0.200 secs
    (Stirling Moss/
    Juan Manuel Fangio)
Holland 1955 0.200 secs
    (Juan Manuel Fangio/
    Stirling Moss)
Italy 1967 0.200 secs
    (John Surtees/
    Jack Brabham)
Spain 1981 0.210 secs
    (Gilles Villeneuve/
    Jacques Laffite)
Monaco 1992 0.215 secs
    (Ayrton Senna/
    Nigel Mansell)
Holland 1985 0.232 secs
    (Niki Lauda/
    Alain Prost)
Hungary 1990 0.288 secs
    (Thierry Boutsen/
    Ayrton Senna)
Switzerland 1950 0.300 secs
    (Giuseppe Farina/
    Luigi Fagioli)
France 1956 0.300 secs
    (Peter Collins/
    Eugenio Castellotti)
Austria 1999 0.313 secs
    (Eddie Irvine/
    David Coulthard)
Holland 1978 0.320 secs
    (Mario Andretti/
    Ronnie Peterson)
France 1993 0.342 secs
    (Alain Prost/
    Damon Hill)
Japan 1991 0.344 secs
    (Gerhard Berger/
    Ayrton Senna)

▲ Giancarlo Fisichella (Jordan) leads team-mate Takuma Sato, Enrique Bernoldi (Arrows) and Jacques Villeneuve (BAR) in the Spanish Grand Prix, 2002.

Index

▲ Race winner Michael Schumacher in the Ferrari F2002 at the German Grand Prix, Hockenheim, in 2002.

▲ **Nelson Piquet (Brabham BMW BT52)
retired but was classified 13th at the 1983
German Grand Prix at Hockenheim.**

▲ **Stuart Lewis-Evans (Vanwall), 1957.**

PICTURE CREDITS
All photographs supplied by
Sutton Motorsport Images
except for the following.
t = top; b = bottom; l = left;
r = right; c = centre
Malcolm Jeal 146br; 175t, tr, b.
Ludvigsen Library 24bl, br; 25t, b; 96t; 105t;
106t, c, b; 114t; 117t, b; 119br; 122b; 147cl,
b; 149tl, tr; 154t, c; 165t, c, br; 174t, b; 177;
180b; 192b; 196c; 198t, bl, br; 207b.
National Motor Museum 17t; 22t; 23b; 26b;
29tl, b; 30b; 31t; 95t; 101t, b; 104b; 106t, b;
109t, c; 140t, bl, br; 143t; 151b; 170c; 177t,
c, b; 192t, b; 199t, b.